WRITING, TEACHING, AND RESEARCHING HISTORY

in the

ELECTRONIC AGE

WRITING, TEACHING, AND RESEARCHING HISTORY

in the

ELECTRONIC AGE

Historians and Computers

Dennis A. Trinkle, Editor

M. E. Sharpe
Armonk, New York
London, England

Library of Congress Cataloging-in-Publication Data

Writing, teaching, and researching history in the electronic age : historians and computers
/ Dennis A. Trinkle, editor.
p. cm.
Includes bibliographical references and index.
ISBN 0–7656–0178–8 (alk. paper)   ISBN 0–7656–0179–6 (pbk. : alk. paper)
1. History—Research. 2. History—Methodology. 3. History—Study and teaching.
4. Historiography. 5. History—Computer network resources.
6. History—Computer-assisted instruction. I. Trinkle, Dennis A., 1968–
D16.W95 1997
907—dc21
97–29298
CIP

Printed in the United States of America

The paper used in this publication meets the minimum requirements of the
American National Standard for Information Sciences—
Permanence of Paper for Printed Library Materials,
ANSI Z 39.48-1984.

∞

MV (c)   10   9   8   7   6   5   4   3   2
MV (p)   10   9   8   7   6   5   4   3   2

In Honor of Frank A. Kafker

Contents

Preface

According to popular mythology, historians are a neo-Luddite bunch. In reality, historians are not strangers to computer technology. They have long been at the forefront of the humanities in adapting electronic innovations to their discipline. The birth of social history during the decades following World War II was directly tied to the invention of programmable computers that could manipulate large, complex groups of data. When personal computers began to enter schools and households during the mid-1970s, historians again quickly responded to the possibilities for easing and improving their teaching, research, and communication. With the advent of the Internet, the World Wide Web, and faster, more sophisticated personal computers, historians are again moving rapidly to embrace the possibilities and benefits afforded by computer technology.

Consequently, history is a field of vibrant discussion about the future these days. The Internet, the World Wide Web, and hosts of new software packages have opened up seemingly limitless possibilities for historians. From multimedia presentations that combine sights, sound, and text to virtual universities that conduct classes on-line, from immense collections of primary sources that can be accessed from anywhere in the world at any time of day to discussion groups where scholars share insights and questions with colleagues from across the globe, the new technologies are presenting invigorating new modes and mediums for practicing history. These new technologies are not all milk and honey, however; they do not come without economic and human costs or limitations.

Fortunately, history at its best is a discipline that inspires a grounded and reasoned approach to the present and to the future. The 200 scholars from forty-two states and eight foreign countries who gathered together in Cincinnati in May 1997 to discuss the future of history in the computer age provide proof that a continuing and productive debate about the marriage of history and computers has begun. This volume, which grew out of that conference, is intended to help present a panorama of the new prospects introduced by computer technology and to foster a dialogue about their consequences and pratfalls.

The essays are divided into four areas: "Redefining History in the Electronic Age," "Scholarly Communication and Publication in the Electronic Age," "Multimedia Approaches to Teaching History," and "Computers and Historical Research." In Part I, David Staley and Daniel Price explore the ways in which the World Wide Web and Internet have the potential to reshape our understanding of history as a discipline. In Part II, Timothy Messer-Kruse, Ellen Meserow Sauer, and Scott Merriman look at the new forms of scholarly interaction and publication being fostered by the Internet. The essays by Larry Easley, David Sicilia, James Jones, John Thomas, Leslie Hunter, Barbara Winslow, Kacy Wiggins, Marisol Carpio, and Frank Johnson presented in Part III explore the various ways that computers can be employed to improve and extend the teaching of history. Finally, in Part IV, Ryan Johnson, Jeffrey Barlow, Etan Diamond, Cynthia Cunningham, and Arthur Farnsley II provide concrete examples of how electronic technology can be profitably used in historical research, and they offer balanced assessments of the prospects and perils presented by new technologies.

For historians grappling with the place of computer technology in their lives, these essays present an excellent starting point, and a good starting point is all that anyone possesses at this stage. Where computer technologies will lead and how they will be employed is very much an open question. As these essays illustrate, technology does not impose its own determinism. The path that history takes in the electronic age will be the result of choices made by individual historians and by professional groups. If these essays offer historians constructive suggestions for taking advantage of existing technologies and help spur a discipline-wide discussion about the union of technology and history, they will have served their purpose.

Acknowledgments

The essays that appear in this volume were first presented as papers at a conference on "The Future of History in the Electronic Age" held at the University of Cincinnati in May 1997. The conference was funded by the Charles Phelps Taft Memorial Fund and the Department of History. Additional funding was provided by *History Reviews On-Line* and the History Graduate Student Association. Margaret Hill, Christina Hartlieb-Reichardt, and Julie Turner provided invaluable assistance in organizing and overseeing the conference. Anna Sobol provided invaluable assistance with the index. Finally, the conference and the essays in this volume benefited immeasurably from the comments and suggestions offered by the conference participants. We are grateful to all those who took part.

This work is dedicated to Frank A. Kafker, who is retiring from the University of Cincinnati after a long and distinguished career in history. For many years, he has shared his knowledge, insights, and human warmth with his colleagues and students at the University of Cincinnati. He has provided, directly and indirectly, a constant source of inspiration to the organizers of the conference that resulted in these papers and to the editor of this volume. We thank him with deepest gratitude.

Part I
Redefining History in the Electronic Age

1

From Writing to Associative Assemblages
"History" in an Electronic Culture

David J. Staley

The cartoon used on the call for papers for the Cincinnati Symposium on Computers and History depicts a monk in his scriptorium, illuminating a manuscript with the "old tools" and also with the "new tool," namely, a computer. This image leaves the viewer with the impression that "monks" (historians) will continue to do the same activities, only aided by a new gadget, which will render their work more efficient but fundamentally unchanged. All that changes in this image is the tool, not the user or his task. This is, I believe, a misleading visual metaphor. In this essay, I will be considering changes in the attributes and requirements of the *user* of the tool. In embracing electronic communications, Western culture has severed its dependence upon the written word, a condition which has immediate implications for historians. Electronic tools alone, however, have not provided historians with the cognitive skills necessary for elegant communication with these tools. Developing these skills should be a priority for all practitioners.

In order to make this claim, I must clarify my views about the nature of technology. The root of the word "technology"—the Greek *techne*—refers to the skill or craft of making tools. In Chinese the word is *ji shu,* meaning the knowledge of a skill or craft. Before using the word *technologie,* Germans used *gewerbekunde*—knowledge of a trade or occupation. In each language, "technology" refers to the skills associated with the making of a tool, not the object produced by that skill. In contemporary American usage, in contrast, the word has come to refer only to the object itself. As a result, when considering the impact of technology on our culture, many observers have become far too fixated on the attributes of the object and not those of the user. To my way of thinking, tools are but by-products, artifacts of changes in who *we* are as users.

The technological environment created by the electronic revolution, therefore, is distinguished not only by the new tools present, but more significantly by the new users required. Every technological environment is marked by certain cognitive skills necessary for an individual to be considered acculturated; the electronic environment emphasizes and places value upon visual skill and associative thought, as opposed to written skill and linear thought. Therefore, this emerging technological and cognitive environment has ramifications for "history"; the practice of representing the past will appear as different to us as do oral epics, although in ways that will also appear quite familiar.

To further clarify the relationship between the user and the tool, I wish to distinguish between "cognitive" skills and "procedural" skills. "Procedural" skills refer to the steps needed to operate the tool; as such, these are the skills that draw attention to the requirements of the machine. By "cognitive," I refer to higher order thinking skills; these skills draw attention to the attributes of the user of the tool. Thus, fingering a keyboard, strumming a lute, or striking a drum are procedural abilities; "musical intelligence" reflects a higher-order ability needed by a user to perform each of these procedures.[1] It is difficult to foresee the unlimited variety of tools technologists will invent in this electronic culture or the procedural skills needed to operate them. Therefore, historians should not enter the business of teaching apprentices evanescent procedural applications. Instead, our pedagogy might be stated in the form of a categorical imperative: tools and their procedures must enhance cognitive skill.

Cognitive skills, such as musical or linguistic or spatial intelligence, have exhibited little change throughout the human past; we might even consider these higher-order abilities "archetypical."[2] These archetypical abilities—artifacts of which exhibit variation across space and time—relate to each other as on a circular continuum, shaped by four cardinal points: written, oral, visual, and kinesic ability. "Cognitive artifacts"—a cave painting or a hypertext—may draw upon varying combinations of these skills, determining their place within the resulting circle. I believe that the cognitive artifacts of the electronic age—many of which have yet to be created—will similarly be located somewhere within this circle.[3]

My purpose here is not to hasten the end of the written word. I am, instead, attempting to describe the cognitive landscape of the electronic culture, which appears more "visual" than "linguistic." At this moment in time, the written word is being "crowded out" by electronically reproduced sound and image and movement. I am proposing "cognitive balance and flexibility": teaching apprentice historians the skillful use of words *as well as* the skillful use of pictures, sounds, and movement as ways to display "the past." Such a strategy, I am convinced, will help us to find our way through this uncertain technological landscape.

What follows, therefore, is not a prediction of future possibilities. My training as an historian warns me about the hubris of making predictions. That same training has taught me, however, the value of cautious speculation and anticipation of the shape of the future in order to create a guide or a map of the plausibilities to come. Thus, this essay is the beginning of a discussion, the purpose of which is to help us navigate and orient this *terra incognito.*

It is almost axiomatic to argue that writing is the foundation of the discipline of history. To my way of thinking, "history" is a disciplined inquiry into the past, conveyed via the written word. I may sing songs about the past, weave tapestries, paint a portrait, or compose a symphony commemorating a great event, but these are not examples of "history" as I would define the term. This distinction is important, for I believe that since the dominant mode of representation in this electronic environment is visual, not written, the very activity of representing the past will be altered by new technologies.

Visual displays of information are not inferior to (or superior to) linguistic displays; however, each display conveys information differently. The psychologist of art, Rudolf Arnheim, argued that humans visualize reality as a "four-dimensional world of sequence and spatial simultaneity." Language, in contrast, is a one-dimensional medium; when employing language, the mind "cuts one-dimensional paths through the spatial landscape . . . [dismantling] the simultaneity of spatial structure." Citing eighteenth-century botanist Albrecht von Haller, Arnheim notes that "nature connects its genera in a network, not in a chain; whereas men can only follow chains, as they cannot present several things at once in their speech."[4] Pictures, in contrast, allow us to present "several things at once." Compare how the relative sizes of three figures in an illustration are depicted simultaneously, versus a linear written account of the same information: "a is taller than b, b is taller than c, meaning a is taller than c." Both types of representation rely on seeking the relationships between meaningful signs. In the first case, these relationships are non-linear and spatial (i.e., associative), in the second, the relations are linear and sequential (i.e., logical). Language by its very nature linearizes the communicative process, much as calculus linearizes non-linear equations. Visual media, according to Arnheim's argument, are by nature able to capture these ubiquitous spatial relations.

Although we perceive the world in three-dimensional spatial terms, those of us schooled in a written culture seek to represent this multi-dimensional reality by cutting one-dimensional written paths across it. This description perfectly describes the activities of historians. Gerda Lerner, in *The Creation of Patriarchy,* clearly perceived the spatial simultaneity of reality. In seeking a metaphor to use in thinking about the history of women, Lerner looked to the visual capabilities of the computer, which allow us to perceive objects in four dimensions. "Seeing as we have seen," she argued, "in patriarchal terms is two-dimensional. 'Adding women' to the patriarchal framework makes it three-dimensional. But only when the third dimension is fully integrated and moves with the whole, only when women's vision is equal with men's vision, do we perceive the true relations of the whole and the inner connectedness of the parts."[5] Lerner clearly understands the spatial nature of reality, yet is still compelled to *write* this history of women. Lerner is hardly exceptional; almost all historians are similarly moved to communicate their understanding of the past by writing about it, including myself, obviously, since this essay is chiefly a written expression. (There are notable exceptions, of course. Many of us make reference to maps in our work. Consider trying to convey the same spatial information in written form. It is possible, but cumbersome and unnecessarily linearizing. Despite their value to us, however, maps and diagrams are supplements to our written thinking.)

Historians generally write about the past in linear terms, since they tend to view that past in linear terms.[6] And they also believe in cause and effect, that one action leads to one or more consequences. They also believe in the importance of chronology, that the temporal sequence and ordering of events is a necessary first step toward historical understanding. Whigs, Marxists, and Hegelians assume that this linear sequence is also teleological, that these events lead ultimately toward a higher, transcendent goal, and that when this line of development is completed, history "ends." Historians build such arguments upon a written cognitive foundation that remains largely unexamined.

Writing, however, has not been the sole means humans have devised to represent the spatial simultaneity of reality and, by extension, record past events. Consider these examples: Homeric bards sang of the heroic age in *The Iliad;* to commemorate the Battle of Hastings, weavers constructed the Bayeux Tapestry, which is a visual (and written) depiction of that event; Thucydides inquired into the causes and consequences of the Peloponnesian War and wrote one of Western culture's first "histories"; the Sioux created the Ghost Dance to evoke ancient glories and to hasten their return. Each is an effort to represent the "past," although in each case the "past" has very different meanings.[7] In addition, each form of representation relies on specific cognitive abilities—oral, visual, written, or kinesic—esteemed by those living in the technological environment.

Our culture esteems the visual. As the art historian Horst Bredekamp observes, "Highly technological societies are experiencing a phase of Copernican change from the dominance of language to the hegemony of images."[8] The acculturated of this electronic age favor the visual image rather than the linguistic word and emphasize associative rather than linear thought. Since the tools created in this environment emphasize different intellective skills, historians will need to consider new ways—which are actually quite old—to think about and display the past.

Electronic technology has incubated this cognitive change. The telegraph was the harbinger; the tool "broke up" written words into a binary code of dashes and dots, reassembling them at the end of the transmission. The die had been cast. In the electronic culture, written words were to be disintegrated. The radio—an oral medium—transmitted the sound of words by similarly deconstructing them into electronic impulses, the effect of which being the emphasis on the spoken over the written. Film and television proved incapable of displaying meaningful amounts of text and thus place the spoken before the written word, adding the visual image to the semantic landscape. In short, long before the appearance of the networked computer, the story of electronic communications featured the dismemberment of the written word. The digital computer is the next step in this process.

Enthusiasts like to describe the digital computer as "multimedia": a "cognitive democracy" of sound, image, and word. Words and writing will continue to be valued, according to this argument. In contrast, I prefer to see the conceptual space of the computer as a "cognitive survival of the fittest." Writing—and the cognitive features therein—will begin to appear slow and cumbersome when placed next to sound, image, and movement. Having been placed in this digitally mediated environment, and given its status in the larger story of electronic communications, the written word is beginning to take on the characteristics of a visual image.

It would be misleading, therefore, to conclude that because the written word continues to be featured in the digital environment, writing will retain all of its recognizable cognitive features, features central to the discipline of history—as anyone who has read a hypertext has observed. Like the "nature" described by Haller,* hypertext is an associative web of linguistic elements through which the reader must navigate. Hypertext theorists, especially, have understood the implications of this associative web of text: that the linear thought process imposed and enhanced by printed writing is being replaced with a non-linear, associational reading mode that appears more "image-like" and "visual." "The computer," writes J. David Bolter, "can not only represent [textual] associations on the screen; it can also grant these associations the same status as the linear-hierarchical order." This fact has clear ramifications for the writing of history. "A hypertext on the fall of the Roman Empire," Bolter continues, "might include several explanations without seeking either to combine or to reconcile them [as in a linear argument]."[9] Since hypertext challenges our notions of linearity, notes the theorist George Landow, "Aristotelian definitions and descriptions of [linear] plot do not apply to stories read and written in a hypertext environment."[10] Bolter contends that if one were to write about the fall of the Roman Empire in a hypertext environment, such a resulting display would not be "history," that is, a printed, linear account.[11] Hypertexts written about the past—which may in fact be a reality very soon—are *not* examples of historical writing, but are examples of cognitive artifacts I call "associative assemblages."

Given the visual and non-linear characteristics of the new technological environment, "history" will be minimized as our representations of the past are conveyed through associative channels. "History" will be supplanted by some other activity (for which I have no name yet), which will feature "associative assemblages." Examples of these assemblages already exist; the historical profession, however, considers these forms of representation "poor relations" to the "real" history codified in scholarly journals, manuscripts, and dissertations. We historians as a profession might wish to pay greater attention to these "poor relations"; indeed, we might draw inspiration from them, for I believe they represent the

---

*Haller as quoted in Rudolf Arnheim, *Visual Thinking* (Chicago: University of California Press).

types of activities and artifacts that will be central to whatever the new display of the past will be called.

As I noted earlier, historians already rely on spatial information, such as that provided in maps. Rather than viewing maps as supplements to our thinking, we could draw important lessons about the skills needed to arrange visual symbols in space. As a first step, "historians" (for I can think of no other term to describe our intellectual descendants) could be trained to produce their own maps. This is much more involved than a procedural problem of learning cartography software: historians would be trained in the elements of map construction and design. Ideally, as Mark Monmonier notes, "writing with maps and with words should be a holistic process in which the author uses words and graphic symbols in concert."[12] I view Monmonier's suggestion as a model for how we might begin to think about spatial and associative thought in our own work: to think about maps not as a supplement to our words but as a complementary—although cognitively distinct—channel for our thoughts.

The use of visual symbols and words in concert is not without precedent in historical scholarship. In *The Rise of the West,* William McNeill included maps, photographs, and, most noteworthy, illustrations. These line drawings took major themes—agriculture, absolutism, global society—and rendered them in visual forms. This assemblage was "designed to be like a three-legged stool, for the text, the photographs and . . . maps and charts [were] intended to support and mutually reinforce one another."[13] In *The Rise of the West,* the diagrams and visual sources are included not simply to "break up the text," but to serve as a didactic function—that is, to convey information about the past via visual associative form. A digital associative assemblage would need to be as well thought out as McNeill's "low tech" assemblage.

The illustrations in H.G. Wells's *Outline of History* similarly reflect visual skill. Wells places the leading events from 400 B.C. to 300 A.D. on a Cartesian spatial and temporal chart, combining features of a map and a timeline. In this example, the Roman Empire "grows" on the chart in size, geographic extent, and duration. As a result, the Roman Empire becomes a shaded "area" within this spatial and temporal framework. The Huns move westward across the chart after being "deflected" by a miniature Great Wall piercing the Roman area, thus reducing its size and extent.

One can easily envision how such a display would appear in a computer environment. The Roman Empire could be depicted in a digitized four-dimensional space; a "volume" that grows as it moves through time. The Huns could be represented as a line that, upon entering the volume, moves around inside, weakening the integrity of the volume. The result would be a visual interpretation of the Fall of Rome.

Practitioners in other fields are already exploring such possibilities. Mathematicians are using computers to diagram pi in three dimensions in order to "climb around" inside this number.[14] Architects and musicians are exploring the abstract structures of information shared by their disciplines utilizing spatial diagrams.[15] Consider the higher-order skills needed to compose and interpret displays; consider their usefulness in an inquiry into the past. By "climbing around" in such spatial data structures, "historians" could uncover facets of the past hidden in a purely textual rendering.

Such information, however, must be viewed with caution. As an example, consider Joseph Minard's nineteenth-century display of Napoleon's march to and retreat from Moscow, popularized in Edward Tufte's *The Visual Display of Quantitative Information*. The chart conveys five variables of information simultaneously: size of the army, location, direction, temperature, and chronology. More significantly, the viewer can see the relationships between these variables. As a result, new vistas of information and interpretation unfold with this spatial display. However, Minard's display does not depict causation very well. The viewer is able to see *what* happens, but receives only minimal information as to *why* it happened. Thus, visual displays are not a superior substitute for other displays of information and must be used thoughtfully and critically.

Another contemporary example of these associative assemblages is museum displays. At the Campus Martius museum in Marietta, Ohio, Rufus Putnam's colonial house has been preserved, allowing visitors to walk inside and examine the location of household artifacts, the size of the rooms, the amount of lighting, and the enormity of the fireplace. This kind of spatial information can be conveyed through writing, of course; however, this visual display is better able to capture the simultaneous spatial relationships that would be linearized in a written account. By extension, if computer pioneers are correct and telepresence (the creation of digitally habitable places) is an attainable goal, there is every reason to believe that "retrospective virtual spaces" will be manufactured, designed by "historians" with an understanding of how space was organized in the past.[16]

Events from the past depicted via kinesic images, such as film, are another type of contemporary associative assemblage likely to have a prominent place in the emerging environment. Films, whether by Ken Burns or Oliver Stone, are not always well received by historians. The ire historians usually reserve for films (and filmmakers) stems in part, I believe, from the fact that visual association is an inherent part of the medium of film and is very difficult to critique through words alone.[17] If we are to evaluate and create such kinesic images, "historians" will need to become skilled at not only the assessment of the script but also the juxtaposition of images, visual composition, and the study of gesture, diction, and phrasing.

If "historians" desire to create "multimedia and interactive" displays of the past, we need look no further than dramatic presentations for our models. I recently attended such a presentation—*America's Women on Stage*—which used music, costumes, photography, and oral interpretation to tell the story of the suffrage movement that was every bit as "multimedia and interactive" as anything conveyed via electronic tools. Should "historians" of an electronic culture wish to display the past in this fashion (and I believe we should), we might wish to begin by exercising our performance skills.

Associative thought need not be visual. Steven Reich's musical composition *Different Trains* provides a case in point. The piece is a study in contrasts between Reich's biography—his parents were divorced, forcing him to travel by train across the United States—and the story of European Jews dislocated by train during the Holocaust. The result is an aural collage of train sounds and sampled voices of survivors, held together by the musical themes of the *Kronos Quartet*. Reich views these sounds as working in concert with visual images and describes this assemblage as "a new kind of documentary music video theatre." It is entirely plausible that future "historians" will display the fruits of their research through the medium of sound.[18]

These types of "cognitive artifacts" might become valid masterpieces worthy of credentialing by our profession. If this is to happen, we might begin to think of criteria and standards for judging these assemblages based not on technical wizardry but cognitive elegance.[19] Three- and four-dimensional digital diagrams or "visual essays" might be accepted as legitimate products of research. Meaningful virtual displays of artifacts might be accepted in lieu of a dissertation. In addition to mastering the secondary "literature" of a field, our apprentices might also be expected to master the secondary "pictures" or "sounds" of that field. While providing historians with new opportunities, electronic tools alone will not create these performance options. The determining factors are the creativity and cognitive virtuosity of our practitioners and the willingness of our profession to embrace the resulting assemblages.

I composed this manifesto out of concern that historians will simply ignore the larger implications of the electronic culture, especially its cognitive assumptions. I am also concerned that historians may uncritically embrace the electronic culture, lured by the buzz of the tools and their procedures, without understanding the proper use of the cognitive skills necessary to communicate with those tools. "Historians" might wish to begin to think about and represent the past via an expanded set of cognitive skills—to develop greater "cognitive flexibility"—as a strategy for anticipating the yet-to-be-created tools and procedures of the electronic culture. Such flexibility would involve teaching apprentices how to write, and draw, and move, to better use electronic tools to our (cognitive) advantage. Because new electronic tools and applications proliferate, it will not be possible for us to anticipate and prepare for every advance. Therefore, historians should not become so infatuated with tools and their procedures that we overlook the reason we use them: to enhance our cognitive skill.

Notes

1. See Howard Gardner, *Frames of Mind* (New York: Basic Books, 1983).
2. See Merlin Donald, *The Origins of the Modern Mind* (Cambridge: Harvard University Press, 1991).
3. For an expanded justification of this scheme, see my "Visualizing the relationship between speech, writing and image," *Comparative Civilizations Review* (Summer 1997), 77–98.
4. Rudolf Arnheim, *Visual Thinking* (Chicago: University of Chicago Press, 1969), 246.
5. Gerda Lerner, *The Creation of Patriarchy* (Oxford: Oxford University Press, 1986), 12.
6. I have found no better way other than this clumsy phrasing to convey this simultaneous process, unless I were to draw a picture. This sentence conveys the linear tendencies of the written word.
7. Of course, the "past" is often a construction based in part on the medium of representation. This fact has clear implications for history in an electronic culture: will we view the past as a non-linear, associational event in the new cognitive environment emphasized by the computer?
8. Horst Bredekamp, *The Lure of Antiquity and the Cult of the Machine* (Princeton, NJ: Marcus Wiener Publishers, 1995), 113.

9. J. David Bolter, *Writing Space: The Computer, Hypertext, and the History of Writing* (Mahwah, NJ: Lawrence Erlbaum and Associates, 1991), 113.

10. George Landow, *Hypertext: The Convergence of Contemporary Critical Theory and Technology* (Baltimore: Johns Hopkins University Press, 1992), 101.

11. Bolter, 113.

12. Mark Monmonier, *Mapping it Out* (Chicago: University of Chicago Press, 1993), xi.

13. William H. McNeill, *The Rise of the West* (Chicago: University of Chicago Press, 1963), v. 1.

14. See Stephen Hall, *Mapping the Next Millennium* (New York: Vintage, 1992), 247–264.

15. See Elizabeth Martin, *Architecture as a Translation of Music* (Princeton: Princeton Architectural Press, 1994), 64–67.

16. See William J. Mitchell, *City of Bits: Space, Place and the Infobahn* (Cambridge: MIT Press, 1995), 19.

17. Concerning the difficulty of confronting images with words, see Jay Rosen and Paul Taylor, *The New News vs. The Old News: The Press and Politics in the 1990's* (New York: Twentieth Century Fund, 1992), 61–62.

18. Thinking through sound opens up new possibilities for representing the past. Reich has also worked on a musical technique he calls "phase shifting," the juxtaposition of two or more tones that, when shifted, produce aural strobing effects. This idea could be an interesting way to think about and represent the thresholds between historical epochs.

19. To help create such standards, historians might begin to rely on Monmonier's *Mapping It Out* and Edward Tufte's *The Visual Display of Quantitative Information* (Cheshire, CT: Graphics Press, 1983) and not just Kate Turabian.

2

Will the Real Revolution Please Stand Up!

Gutenberg, the Computer, and the University

M. Daniel Price

Introduction

In looking at early modern Europe, we may be startled by the directive, "Will the real revolution please stand up!" There are so many revolutions, broadly speaking, from which to choose:

- New geographical discoveries with "strange new worlds" of peoples, plants, and animals.
- Several new forms of Christianity that no longer adhere to the ecclesiastical leadership of Rome.
- New forms of thinking and expressing created by the Renaissance and Humanism.
- Many cities and states beginning to develop capitalistic economies.
- New "paradigms" for looking at the world of nature stemming from the works of Copernicus, Vesalius, and others.

Then there is the revolution in communication brought about by the printing press. Elizabeth Eisenstein presents the introduction of print as a major, although often overlooked, revolution of the period in *The Printing Press as an Agent of Social Change*. Eisenstein is so impressed by the impact of the printing press that she seems to assert that the press was the necessary means of incorporating the achievements of both the Renaissance and the Reformation into the Western heritage.[1] In other words, without the press many facets of these movements that we accept as commonplace today, such as choices among forms of Christianity and

14

a general acquaintance with classical authors, would simply be topics of study for that particular era.

Let us look more closely at how the institution of the university responded to this new invention and see if the term "revolution" actually applies. To provide further perspective, I will compare and contrast the historical response of the university to print with the response of today's universities to the computer. Is there another revolution in our midst?

Point 1: The Universities and the Response to Print

During the first two centuries of print, much university instruction and reference centered on the world of ancient Greece and Rome. Seeing a ready market, early printers did not disappoint those who wanted more texts and different versions of familiar and unfamiliar authors. Editions of classical Latin and then of ancient Greek authors multiplied. By 1500, several hundred editions of Virgil and Cicero had been published, while in the following century, more than a hundred different editions of Aristotle, the study of whom was so critical to the university, were made available.[2] Often the publishers themselves took a lively interest in this literature and made sure that a wide variety of texts and authors were printed. Aldus Manutius of Venice owned several print shops in his long career and at times even sought a career at the university. He prided himself on his knowledge of the classics and possessed a great desire to share them with others. For instance, he did extensive work developing a clear and readable typeface for the Greek alphabet in order to place more readable versions of Aristotle and Plato into rapid circulation.

The impression that the arrival of the printing press made possible great change for the world of learning is confirmed by one of the most famous scholars of the era, Peter Ramus. By the middle of the sixteenth century, Ramus had completed a number of commentaries on Aristotle, which won him an appointment to the prestigious College Royale (the forerunner of the College de France), founded in the previous decade to provide a new forum for scholars working with texts in Greek, Latin, and Hebrew. In one introduction, Ramus asked the reader to exercise his imagination in order to appreciate the magnitude of change achieved during the past hundred years:

Let us imagine a teacher of a university who died a hundred years ago and had now returned among us. If he compared the efflorescence of the humanistic disciplines and the sciences of nature in France, Italy, and England as they had developed since his death, he would be shaken and astonished when he compared his own age with the present. He knew only human beings who spoke in a crude barbarian manner. Now he sees countless persons of all ages who speak and write Latin with elegance. . . . Now he would not only hear Greek being read with the greatest of ease, but he would encounter scholars who would be able to teach this language with the greatest expertise. . . . How could he not be astonished? It is almost as if he raised his eyes from the depth of the earth to the heaven and saw for the first time the sun, the moon, and the stars.[3]

Many twentieth-century scholars agree with Ramus's assessment. As he closes his final essay on the Middle Ages for the *Cambridge History of the University in Europe,* the noted historian of European higher education Walter Ruegg looks ahead to the next era and comments on the influence of print: "Thanks to humanism *and* its connection with book-printing (emphasis added), the world of knowledge and ideas in the universities expanded in all its historical depths and its diverse magnifications to an extent which could only be fully developed in subsequent centuries."[4]

Yet, when considering many aspects of the university for the early modern period, the term "revolution" does not seem to apply. For example, to reverse the direction of Ramus's time machine, a young man from Cambridge (or Paris or Padua) in the late 1500s would have found things very much the same if he had journeyed back in time to 1450. The young man would have gone to the same geographical setting for instruction and often to the same physical buildings. His instruction would have commenced at the same time and would have finished at the same time. He would have had the same degrees from which to choose, and he would have followed much the same curriculum for those degree choices. He would have followed the same primary means of communication—the lecture, repetition, disputation, and oral exams. Finally, instructors and students alike would have spoken the same language for instruction as did those in the previous century—Latin.

Equally important, the young man also would have been quite at home with the students from the earlier period, as they would have been from the same social class.[5] The university did not take initiatives to become more democratic, although greater access to information for a broader social spectrum was among the most notable achievements of the press, especially in Eisenstein's evaluation.[6]

Critics who respond, however, that the humanists of the late fifteenth and early sixteenth centuries made great inroads in the fields of grammar and rhetoric are correct. Erasmus had received a university appointment to teach Greek at Cambridge, and increasingly the young students were expected to have a mastery of classical Latin and more and more frequently of ancient Greek. It is precisely this development of rhetoric and the use of classical Latin, together with a general familiarity with classical authors, which Ramus found so striking. In the passage cited before, he also remarks:

> And how could one compare the darkness which once covered all the arts with the light and the brilliance of today? Of the grammarians, the poets, and the orators, only Alexander of Villedieu; and works like Facetius and Graecismus in philosophy; only Scotus and the Spaniards; in medicine the Arabs; in theology there were few; one does not know where they came from. Now, he would hear Terence, Caesar, Virgil, Cicero, Aristotle, Plato, Galen, Hippocrates, Moses, and the prophets, the apostles and the other true enunciators of the Gospel, and he would hear them speaking in their own languages.[7]

If we look to the curriculum, however, the chief group of studies at these universities was neither grammar nor rhetoric but philosophy. Philosophy was so primary that, while it was possible to have a university without a faculty of law or of medicine, it was not possible to have one without a faculty of philosophy, and for all practical matters that was the philosophy of Aristotle.[8]

Aristotle's position was so dominant that it was well over a hundred years after Gutenberg before a non-Aristotelian penetrated the faculty of philosophy at a university. Furthermore, when Francesco Patrizi was appointed to a chair at Ferrara, this did not come from the initiative of the university faculty seeking to broaden academic inquiry and enrich their discussion by adding another voice to their ranks. It was the continued patronage of the local Duke that led to Patrizi's appointment. Patrizi, for his part, was likewise not eager for dialogue, since he categorized the Aristotelians as heretics and went so far as to seek a papal ban on their teaching.[9]

During this period there were significant developments in the field of philosophy. Of primary importance was the renewed interest in Plato, but other philosophical approaches from the ancient world were also explored, including Stoicism, Atomism, Cynicism, and Epicureanism. Some scholars of the Renaissance have claimed that it was only now that the educated European had the opportunity to choose among a variety of ethical frameworks. Each framework was grounded on a "reasonable metaphysics" but was incompatible with the other systems, thus destroying the reign of Aristotle for the previous two millennia. Depending on one's view, the possibility of choice has led either to social confusion and chaos or, on the other hand, to an enhancement of individual freedom.[10]

The persistence of a single, dominant world view reflects one of the often ignored drawbacks to the rapid introduction of print—it was not simply new learning and scholarship that came to press, even though these works by-and-large occupy scholarly attention today. The works most frequently published in early modern Europe were the traditional and accepted views, and these publications sustained traditional ways of looking at things. In their pioneering work on the appearance of the book, Lucien Febvre and Henri Martin spell this out: "In fact, by popularizing long cherished beliefs, strengthening traditional prejudices, and giving authority to seductive fallacies, it [the press] could even be said to have represented an obstacle to the acceptance of many new views."[11] New discoveries and new opinions were more likely to be ignored than publicized, while reliance was placed on a conventional authority that was all the more available and widespread through the use of the printing press.

Finally, to confirm that the press was not an agent of change for the university of the early modern period, one can point to the general lack of initiative in the development of modern science. Apart from the faculties of medicine with their attention to anatomy and botany, those interested in the natural sciences seem to have left the university and sought support elsewhere (for example, private discussion groups, wealthy patrons, lectures of the College Royale, and so forth).[12]

To sum up for this section: Were there revolutions during the early modern period? Definitely! Was print one of them? Certainly! Did the print revolution significantly affect the university? It seems only minimally, since we do not discover significant changes in basic considerations. We find that instruction was at the same time, in the same place, with the same curriculum, in the same language, for the same social class. To put it rhetorically, the revolution of print, in so far as it applies to the early modern university, will have to sit down!

Point 2: The University and Oral Culture

The limited response of the university as an institution to the much greater amount of information made available through the printing press is not altogether surprising, since the university "conducted its business" within what may be described as a predominately oral culture. Granted, there were texts and readings, but the manner in which texts were treated reflects the more traditional uses of an oral culture. For example, in the quotation on page 17, Ramus usually refers to "hearing" (*audire* in Latin) rather than "reading" (*legere* in Latin) the ancient authors, which points to the continuing role of orality within this culture.

When studying cultures, anthropologists often make a distinction between those that are oral and those that are literate, in which at least some members are comfortable with reading and writing. The oral culture depends on the traditions of the elders for its very survival, since those traditions answer some basic and diverse questions such as "Where did we come from?" and "When do we plant corn?" Within the oral society, the teachings of a master or the wisdom of the elders are preserved and handed down ("tradition") from generation to generation. Since not all are eligible to become elders, the culture develops a defined social hierarchy.

When writing is introduced, some of the elders' authority is negated because anyone with the ability to read can appeal to the text. The text can allow for judgment by others, including those of other times and places. Because of this ability for the reader to distance himself from the message in the text, the written culture promotes abstract thought, and it does so in a broad and contentious fashion.[13]

The format and intention of the medieval university reflects many features of the oral culture. The oral dimensions of the university included lectures—that is, listening to the presentations by the local elder (or professor) of the teachings of the past masters. There were "repetitions," in which the student recalled what he had been given in the earlier session. There were public commentaries on the teachings of the professor in his role as elder through the practice of the "disputations." Here, the teacher expounded at length on a particular focus of the teaching (and did so sometimes for hours because of his prodigious memory). To gain entry into the society of elders (professors), one had to orally demonstrate a mastery of the teachings. The primary master for the central study of the university, both in the medieval and in the early modern era, was Aristotle.

In this discussion of oral cultures and the university, it is crucial to remember how the function of the university was perceived at the time. First and foremost, this entailed the preservation of past teachings. At all the various levels of education, there was an introduction to the knowledge that had been accumulated and commented upon by various authorities. It was then the task of both student and teacher to make sure that this "tradition" was absorbed and transmitted to the next generation. Only very gradually and over several centuries did the model of the university as a place of "scientific" research and inquiry come into play.[14]

The task of the university, therefore, was not so much to open new paths of inquiry as to pass along the wisdom of the elders. The university had its own format and rules, and these did not change with the introduction of print. "They thought of learning, not so much as a process driven inquiry, as a body of information controlled by rules."[15] For instance, the philosophers of the late fourteenth and early fifteenth centuries discussed at great length the concept of nomenalism, which considers the meaning of universal categories such "man," "matter," and "soul." Yet, nowhere was this concept presented as something new, creative, and personal—in other words, as a break with the tradition. Nomenalism was presented simply as a more accurate interpretation of the tradition.

To give another example, Pietro Pomponazzi taught philosophy at Padua toward the end of the fifteenth and beginning of the sixteenth centuries. With a commentary on Aristotle's "De Anima," he put forth the view that Aristotle had not demonstrated the immortality of the individual soul. Without stating as much, he seemed to imply that such a demonstration was not possible. This question aroused so much debate at the time that the council of bishops of Lateran V chose to give their interpretation of the tradition, declaring that in fact the immortality of the individual soul could be demonstrated by reason.[16] Subsequently, Pomponazzi went on teaching about other matters, and the issue seemed to be closed. For the community of philosophers, the result was to arrive at the correct interpretation of the primary master, Aristotle. One may note, too, the close link between the university and the Church, since it was the Church's Council of elders that rendered the correct view of "tradition."

Earlier we mentioned Ramus's appointment to the College Royale in Paris. This body had been founded in the late 1530s, when royal advisors convinced Francis I to take advantage of new advances in learning and establish royal professorships in Latin, Greek, and Hebrew. However, this institution did not become a rival to the University of Paris, since it could neither grant degrees nor teach in other subject matters. The University of Paris had charted out its own territory and preserved it.

With this background, it is easier to understand the reluctance by the university faculty to admit a non-Aristotelian into the circle of elders, since he would add a confusing, alternative wisdom. It is also possible to better appreciate the reluctance of the universities to promote the physical sciences, where the appeal to reason is countered by an appeal to experiment. The natural sciences do not lend themselves to an oral culture in the same fashion as philosophy or the arts. In this light, the remarks of David Olson about the impact of print on the culture of early modern Europe take on added significance. Olson observes that "the introduction of the press was important as an instrument of standardization, dissemination, and accumulation [of information], rather than as an agent of change of conceptualization."[17] Applying this statement to the university, the effect of the revolution of the printing press was to standardize, disseminate, and accumulate the work of Aristotle.

Point 3: Academic Discourse for a Broader Audience

Certainly print greatly facilitated academic discourse both within the university and among a wider educated audience. For instance, when Peter of Ravenna, who was teaching at the University of Cologne in the early 1500s, began to speculate about the possibility of salvation for executed criminals, the faculty called upon him to dispute his views within the university community. Peter, however, thought he would receive a better hearing if he appealed to a wider audience, and he began to publish a series of pamphlets defending his position. This presumes a literate audience capable of following the discourse and interested in pursuing this topic at a fairly sophisticated level of argument.[18]

A new intensity of academic discourse with much greater consequences took place when Martin Luther began to broadcast his findings and appeal to a larger audience. Since he started as a professor of New Testament at Wittenburg, he initially felt that he was presenting the fruit of his academic research. He also seems to have well understood the power of the press to "talk" with fellow academics and to carry the debate to the wider audience, especially in the "Sermon on Indulgences." In fact, it is estimated that one-fifth of the pamphlets written in Germany between 1500 and 1530 originated from his pen alone.[19] While his eventual triumph must be understood against the political backdrop of Germany at the time, the role of the press in announcing, then teaching, then confirming Luther's message among an educated audience was likewise a major factor for his success.

A third example of educated discourse comes from Erasmus, who made his living from his publications and could not have survived without them. Although he had taken various university appointments, he eventually left the university to pursue the life of a scholar in dialogue with his own generation and those of the future. Like Luther, Erasmus published a number of religious works. His *Enchridion* was a manual for the Christian layman, envisioned as a soldier doing battle against the evil of the world. Erasmus actively responded to many of Luther's charges in a series of pamphlets; in addition, he also wrote about the church fathers, especially Saint Jerome. In 1516, he presented a Greek edition of the New Testament, which he intended as a study version of the original texts.

Erasmus also extended the scholarly use of the press beyond religious issues. He composed grammars, and he published a continuing series of conversations on a variety of scholarly topics, providing his editorial comments on major events and disputes. With his *Praise of Folly,* he encouraged a skeptical view of many institutions of his day, including the church and the university. For instance, Folly (actually a name for himself) says this about the philosophy teachers of his day: "Nature has a fine laugh at them and their conjectures, for their total lack of certainty is obvious enough from the endless contention among themselves on every single point. They know nothing at all; they yet claim to know everything."[20]

Erasmus actively involved himself with many noted printers of the day. He collaborated with Manutius on the stylization of the Greek characters and was in constant correspondence with Froben about the appearance of his works, including his letters to notable academics. He anticipated his readers taking time to read and putting effort into that reading, pursuing his ideas in successive revisions and editions of a single text. As he often stated to his readers, he also viewed book printing as the highest of arts because it permitted a continuous dialogue with the most educated men of all time. It was thus by his conscious use of print that Erasmus sought to, and succeeded in, presenting himself as the archetype of the European scholar. [21]

As the preceding examples show, in the sixteenth century the press provided academics and scholars with new audiences and increased the broader exchange of ideas. It did so across a broad spectrum, from the case of Peter of Ravenna in a single instance, to that of Martin Luther on a single topic, to that of Erasmus, who utilized print as a universal scholar to engage others of his own time and those of the future.

Point 4: New Practices of "Going to College"

If we look at the university of today, do we see a revolution? To continue our theme, will the current "revolution" be able to stand up?

I want to examine today's revolution by walking through the experience of Jessica R., who lives and works in Juneau, Alaska. Jessica works full-time as a counselor at an alcohol clinic, and her round of activities does not provide the opportunity for attending the local college. She also uses a wheelchair, which would make regular attendance even more difficult. Jessica has chosen to complete her degree through a distant learning program.

Time of instruction or learning activity: Jessica accomplishes her instruction according to her personal schedule, day or night, seven days a week. She logs onto her computer and receives assignments, uploads files, conducts research, enters chat rooms—all on her own timetable and at her convenience.

Place of instruction: Jessica has a choice of location, again depending on her schedule and convenience—home, office, a hotel room while at workshops, or even the guest bedroom when visiting her parents in Seattle. From any of these locations, she can more than simply do "homework" assignments as she would if attending a traditional program. She actually "goes to school," since she pulls down the latest class discussion, receives and posts assignments, and interacts with her professors, her classmates, and her advisor. She even can even register and pay for her courses from any of these locations.

Delivery mode of instruction: She has access to the Internet and so has several print and image and sound resources; she makes use of various software packages and CD-ROMs to assist her learning in math, statistics, and college biology, including laboratory simulations.

Choices of courses: Jessica has the option of utilizing the world library, which lists hundreds of courses from dozens of institutions around the world.[22] Although in principle Jessica could plan her degree program with multiple offerings from multiple schools, she has chosen to concentrate on only two accredited colleges.

Choice of instructors: Since Jessica is not limited to one time slot or to one campus, she has more options regarding the instructors for the courses she is selecting. Currently Jessica is working with an instructor in San Diego, another in Boston, and a third in Houston, while her classmates from across the county likewise are working with faculty in several locations.

Curriculum: Parts of her curriculum directly take up topics related to the new electronic means of communication, including courses on such topics as: "The Computer and Society," "Introduction to Computer Science," and "Computers and the Law." By contrast, in the sixteenth century there were no courses on print and its effects on society. Today, there is even a software package designed for counselors to use in analyzing various types of personality and suggesting further steps of treatment. This could be an additional component of Jessica's practicum in counseling.

Discourse among academics: Jessica's teachers are professionals in their fields and are able to follow the latest advances and discussions and to converse with colleagues from around the globe through the use of various listservs. By electronic means, they also conference with each other about Jessica's academic progress. If she chooses, Jessica can also join discussion groups or simply "chat" with her classmates. In a traditional setting, some of the educational process occurs in hallways, the cafeteria, and on the mall; so too in the electronic forum that opportunity is provided.

Do we need further evidence of a revolution in our midst? If we do, we can simply turn to a college catalogue and find several courses and even majors, such as information sciences, which were not available thirty or forty years ago. There is even a chair of "The Computer and the Humanities" at Oxford. What would Ramus's professor from the fifteenth century, or even Ramus himself, have said about this?[23]

This past spring, in an interview for *Forbes,* Peter Drucker "prophesied" that the brick and mortar colleges of today will be gone in thirty years. "Uncontrollable expenditures, without any visible improvement in either the content or the quality of education, means that the system is rapidly becoming untenable."[24] However, he argues almost exclusively from economics, stating that the schools will price themselves out of existence. While that may or may not be true, what I am suggesting here is that quite apart from economics, the delivery system outlined above is sufficient in itself to make the college buildings of today obsolete for the education of tomorrow. This is a revolution!

Point 5: Toward New Habits of Learning and Thinking

This revolution is new and combines three cultures of communication, that is, oral, written, and electronic. Will this result in a new "episteme," or habits of thought? If we experience new ways of learning, will we not develop new habits of thinking? Will a new institution come forward to respond to such habits of thinking?

I want to pick out some major threads of this "revolution," and I am using the word "thread" by design, because the threads interweave with each other to compose the design and structure of the whole cloth. The threads include:

Active Learning

In this perspective, the educational experience focuses primarily on what the students are actually learning rather than on how much material is presented by the instructor. For example, in a course on the French Revolution, "active learners" would become familiar with the concept of revolution as a social event, rather than memorizing the dates and identities of those in the streets of Paris in 1791. They would then be able to apply the concept in analyzing other political and social events.[25] One should also note that a further consequence of this approach centers on the function of the teacher. To emphasize the focus on the student's learning, the role of the teacher shifts from that of the "sage on the stage" to that of the "guide by the side."

The concept of "active learning" is, of course, not new and has been the basis of much non-traditional education dating back to the 1960s. In many respects, it can be implemented quite well apart from the electronic culture. However, this kind of learning is particularly suited to electronic means. The use of hypertext requires the learner to be actively involved in his or her own learning, since it requires a constant series of choices about one's next step for learning. In another application facilitated by electronic communication, the use of e-mail can allow for the greater participation of the course members—the discussion can be carried by all, rather than just a few; and it can provide more frequent and more in-depth response from the instructor.

One principle of "active learning" is to move at one's own pace and not necessarily "to begin at the beginning." If a learner starts at one place, it is easy enough through the use of hypertext to go backward or forward or sideways. For example, in studying the French Revolution, one could start with the riots of 1789, then go back and see where they originated or go forward to see what will happen to the monarchy. The learner could also go "to the side" and see what was occurring elsewhere during that summer. In this approach, there seems to be a greater respect for the natural curiosity of the student and a trust that the student will eventually cover most, if not all, of the points of the exercise. Since the learner has the freedom to move in the direction of choice in this new "classroom," naturally one may choose to move sequentially through the course in the traditional manner.

Consider too the demonstration of learning. While it is an oversimplification to say that the demonstration of university learning has shifted exclusively from one medium to another, there is enough substance to see significant transition. At Oxford in the thirteenth century, a student demonstrated mastery of information primarily by oral exams, repetitions, and disputations. Gradually there was a shift to a greater use of written exams and, in the nineteenth century, to various kinds of writing assignments such as term papers, interviews, book reports, and chapter summaries, while the use of written exams continued.

Twenty years from now, the most common demonstration of learning could reflect the electronic culture. It could be a Web page composed of various hyperlinks to different media resources, such as film, graphics, print, recordings, and other Web pages. It could be something done entirely in "virtual reality." These kinds of demonstrations will be different from a traditional term paper and as a result call for different perceptions and temperaments, different responses and styles of instruction.

Active learning allows for, and even forces, the learner to choose the next step for his or her learning. In many ways, the choices can be more demanding and frightening because in a very immediate sense the learner realizes that she or he is responsible for the next learning activity: "Which icon do I click next?" and soon "Which voice command do I give?" Certainly there were choices about learning activities previously, such as "Do I go to the reference shelf or not?" The difference here is that electronic culture provides an immediacy of choice as well as a plethora of options. Many learners find it more demanding to respond to the screen, and what they have created on the screen, than to simply turn the next page of the book or to inscribe the next word on the page, and this is the point. Participation in the electronic culture for learning demands more, engages more, and empowers more than the traditional approaches.

The sense of empowerment is further heightened by the control that the learner has over the physical presentation of the material. With the click of a button, the text can be enlarged, demoted, or put into an altogether different typeface. The learner in this sense becomes the "co-author" or at least the co-presenter of the materials for study.[26]

True enough, a great revolution in education was heralded with the arrival first of audiotapes then of videotapes. Nonetheless, what distinguishes this revolution and marks it apart is the importance of the one in charge of the delivery machine. In electronic learning, it is the learner, not the instructor, who directs the learning.

Immediacy of Information

Anyone with more than an hour's experience on the Web can proclaim that not everything desired for learning is available on the net—yet. The scholar's dream, captured in the image of the library at ancient Alexandria which gathered all the information known into one accessible location, is still a dream. Yet it is amazing what now is available, especially if one knows how to navigate one's way.

Ten or fifteen years ago, if I were in a library and needed to check my reference, I interrupted my writing to physically get up and walk to the dictionary or the encyclopedia. When I was working on the section on Pomponazzi above, I wanted to check a date and went on-line. In a few minutes, I could access articles by Paul Kristeller (among the most noted historians of Renaissance humanism). I could observe a course on Renaissance history, and I could join a discussion group at the University of Bologna. What will this be like in years ahead? Space and time will no longer be significant factors; no need to go to Washington for archives or even down to the library to check the *Britannica*. Physical buildings such as the university classroom or library will no longer play such a large role in our thinking about learning.

Community of Learning

For the academic of the sixteenth century, print provided quicker access to the thoughts of a greater number of people, as with Erasmus and Luther. In the electronic culture, the community of learning is all the more inclusive, as the most common name for this communication—"the Net"—implies. Through the vast network of interactions and resources, the limitations of time and space are greatly reduced, if not entirely eliminated.

Recently I "attended" a conference hosted in Hawaii. I attended by way of e-mail, listservs, and MOOs and discovered people in Australia, England, and even Oxford, Ohio, some twenty miles away from my university, who are thinking along the same lines and share similar interests and questions.[27] Although some critics of the Net fear an isolation of learning because of the physical absence of others "going to class," quite the opposite is true. Participants engage in a much wider, even international, circle of learning. Through listservs today, I can "bulletin board" with colleagues on topics of choice. In the future, I will "bulletin board" through sound bytes or asynchronous video bytes. While personally I prefer the text format as more anonymous, the next generation could be perfectly comfortable with video bytes. If they choose, scholars and students could have simultaneous video conferencing at prearranged times. As Fowler poetically puts it: "No piece of hypertext ever sings solo; as part of a cacophonous choir, it is joined with all of the other nodes of the network, forcing the reader to make critical choices of what to access next."[28]

One of the most important ramifications for the community of learning involves the concept of the "social ownership of knowledge." Print encouraged, even demanded, the use of copyright, and promoted the individual ownership of knowledge. This claim seems to vanish when working with hypertext on the Net. The text is posted and copied and incorporated into other works with the press of a key.[29] As a result, the activity of both author and reader tend to merge in this format and move toward the creation of yet another document or presentation.[30]

Serious academic discussion of knowledge as a social process goes back at least to Thomas Kuhn and his book, *The Structure of Scientific Revolutions*. It was Kuhn who introduced the term "paradigms of thinking" to show that significant breakthroughs in learning are not created by a single genius such as Newton or Einstein, but by genius in dialogue with others about putting together available information into a new composition. As a result, the paradigm becomes a social creation.[31] By providing an immediacy of information and developing the community of learning, the Net seems to negate the individual claim for invention and ownership. The demand for new ways of thinking in this regard is summarized by the French historian of the book, Roger Chartier:

> The time has also come to redefine the juridical notions (literary property, author's rights, and copyright), administrative regulations and institutions ("depot legal" and national libraries), and libraries' practices (cataloguing, classification, and bibliographical description) that have been conceived and understood in relation to another form of production, conversation, and communication of the written word.[32]

If knowledge is regarded as social, and writing on the Net is presented as collaborative, there is a certain leveling of authority that takes place.[33] The community becomes neither an oral society tightly controlled by the elders, nor one of script in which some are given access, but, at least in theory, an entirely open one. In this consideration, there is again a reminder that the role of the teacher becomes not so much that of the sage but of the guide through the frontier of learning, often simply as a participant in the dialogue of the learning community.

Thinking and Sense Perceptions

In working with printed text, the reader (of English) moves the eyes from left to right, from the top of the page to the bottom, from the front of the book to the back. The block characters of print are uniform. Because the reader has to work (and work hard) to go in a linear movement through the text, he or she is encouraged into one way of looking at the text. Through its very format, one acquires the habit of regarding thinking itself as sequential, in which one idea always builds on another.[34] At the very least, we tend to identify academic discourse with clear, logical, sequential thinking and expression.

With the written text, I am working with something cast in lead on the sheet of paper; by contrast on the computer screen, the letters "dance" before me. The sensory perception itself is different, since electronic text is not stable, not cast in the lead of print; it is flexible, "restless," and prone to change. It can be more ephemeral than the printed text and so promotes the realization that knowledge itself is unstable, changing, and flexible.[35] With electronic text especially, one can move around within the text and then move out to various references. In effect, there are at least three new ways in which the reader could interact with text: through associative indexing or links, by making use of the trails made by successive use of links, and through sets or webs made by the cluster of trails. This ability to move so quickly outside of the text encourages the idea of knowledge at the disposal of the learner, so we are led back to the thread of "active learning."

Not only are different points of view more obvious with hypertext, but clearly stated beginnings and endings are not present. While the book has an opening and closing page, the hyperlinked text can "sing" forever. As a result, one has the sense of immersion into learning instead of clean, clear definitions with easily recognized finalities. Instead of using an outline with linear indentations and progressions, one is led to imagine thinking as a process of intersecting circles and tangents. "Hypertext does not only redefine the central by refusing to grant centrality to any lexia for more than the time a gaze rests upon it. In hypertext, centrality, like beauty and relevance, resides in the mind of the beholder. . . . This hypertext dissolution of centrality, which makes the medium such a potentially democratic one, also make it a model of a society of conversations in which no one conversation, no one discipline or ideology, dominates that of the other."[36]

At the same time, there appears to be a kind of trade-off in choosing to work with text or to work with hypertext. While hypertext allows the reader more control of where to go and what to do, the "where" he or she is going is not as clear and distinct as it is with the page of script or print; yet that difference may simply reflect the bias of one who was raised on print.

New "Customary" Tools for Learning: Sound, Graphics, and Film

Today the primary means of learning and research is text and the written response to the text. To a significant degree, each of the above threads remains based simply on text, either print or hypertext. Tomorrow, additional tools will be available and simply presumed. Consider what learning may be like with such new tools.

In the future, for instance, I could study Pomponazzi by starting a film about medieval Padua and stopping the film to ask questions, or perhaps listening to a recording of the decree from the council. I could make a reference to the textual resources and look up members of the council, then submit a sound byte to a colleague in Hong Kong about his Web page concerning the Renaissance papacy. So far, this has been very linear, and it could develop in a much different direction. Looking at the architecture of Padua could lead to questions about forms of thinking and their relationships to architecture and then to questions of public architecture, which may lead to investigating forms of city services, and so on.

Of course, there will be drawbacks and losses, just as script does not retain all the advantages of oral culture, especially in giving a sense of local community. With learning based on electronic culture, it could be those aspects of objectivity and length of study, which are presumed in written culture, would not be part of a new demonstration of learning. Certain features of the commonality of education may also be lost. For instance, Bolter questions if there will be a common list of classics, however defined, which the generally educated person will be expected to know.[37] While we will have a broader community, will we have something in common to talk about?

Gathering Together

To be true to my statements above, I would not dare to say that I am drawing these threads into a definitive piece of cloth which is fixed and determined. The above is part of the ongoing conversation. The immediacy of resources, the control over those resources, and the multiple sensations that will be called forth—all of these link together and allow us to imagine an entirely different format of learning and thinking than our present experiences allows us.

Imagine, however, what learning may be like in, say, thirty or forty years for the student, for the professional scholar, or for the generally educated lay person who has experienced learning exclusively in this fashion—not through a course or two as today, but whose entire gamut of learning, with all that is needed to act as a professional in his or her chosen field, including licensure or certification, has been done in this fashion. Surely different ways of looking at so many "givens" in our academic thinking, such as "tradition," "demonstration of learning," "sequential ordering," and so on, will follow.

What did the early scribes of Sumer tell the elders of the community about the strange new way for recordkeeping and of committing to tablets and papyrus their sacred traditions? Are we not in a similar situation, as we return to our university colleagues who are but literate and not electronic, and tell them of the strange new world we have visited?

As we look to the future, we can be sure of at least two things:

1. People will continue to learn. The accumulation, processing, and application of information will proceed. The next generation has an absolute need to process tradition, as well as to develop new information, new learning—in order to carry on with civilization and culture.
2. People will learn in new and different ways than in the past. The one who knows the past knows only that the future will be different. The process of gaining this information, of producing new information and sharing with other members of the learning community, of becoming "credentialed" by demonstrating mastery of particular information— all of this will be far different than what Pomponazzi, or Ramus, or you and I have experienced and identified as "the university."

Perhaps the university will make that transition, perhaps not. With this background, we can better understand, however, why new and far different educational institutions may arise to address these two certainties.

Perhaps the real revolution has yet to begin!

Notes

1. Elizabeth Eisenstein, *The Printing Press as an Agent of Social Change* (Princeton: Princeton University Press, 1979), 687–709.

2. Anthony Grafton, "The Availability of Ancient Works" in *The Cambridge History of Renaissance Philosophy* (hereafter as *CHRP*), ed. Charles Schmitt and Quinten Skinner (New York: Cambridge University Press, 1988), 778.

3. "Oratio de studiis philosophiae et eloquentiae conjugendis Lutetia habita anno 1564" in *P. Rami at Audomari Talei collectaneae prefationes, epistolae, orationes* (Paris, 1575), as reprinted in *A History of the University in Europe*, ed. Hilde de Ridder-Symoens (New York: Cambridge University Press, 1996), II, 305.

4. Walter Ruegg, "Epilogue: The Rise of Humanism" in *A History of the University in Europe*, I, 467.

5. Wilhelm Frijhoff, "Patterns" in *A History of the University in Europe*, II, 64

6. Eisenstein, 87.

7. Ramus, in *A History of the University in Europe*, 305.

8. Wilhelm Schmitt-Biggeman, "New Structures of Knowledge" in *A History of the University in Europe*, II, 489.

9. Brian Copenhaven, *Renaissance Philosophy* (New York: Oxford University Press, 1992), 189.

10. Ibid., 346.

11. Lucien Febvre and Henri Martin, *The Coming of the Book* (New York: Verso, 1992), 278.

12. Charles Schmitt, "Philosophy and Science in Sixteenth-Century Universities: Some Preliminary Comments" in *The Cultural Context of Medieval Learning*, ed. John Murdock (Boston: D. Riedel, 1975), 574.

13. Walter Ong, *Orality and Literacy* (New York: Routledge, 1982), 78–204.

14. Christoph Schwinges Rainer, "Student Education, Student Life" in *A History of the University in Europe*, I, 231.

15. Copenhaven, 348.

16. M. Daniel Price, "The Origins of Latern V's 'Apostolici Regiminis,' " *Archive Historicae Conciliorum* 2 (1985): 464–472.

17. David Olson, *The World on Paper: The Conceptual and Cognitive Implications of Reading and Writing* (Cambridge: Cambridge University Press, 1994), 58.

18. Charles Nauert, "The Clash of Humanists and Scholastics," *Sixteenth-Century Journal* 1 (1973): 9–10.

19. Mark Edwards, *Printing, Propaganda, and Martin Luther* (Berkeley: University of California Press, 1995), 2.

20. Desiderimus Erasmus, *Praise of Folly* (Harmondsworth, England: Penguin Books, 1971), 151.

21. Lisa Jardine, *Erasmus, Man of Letters* (Princeton: Princeton University Press, 1993), 189.

22. See the collection of course offerings from universities around the world on topics from accounting to zoology at http://utexas.edu/worldlibrary/.

23. For a thorough "report from the field" by a college teacher making this adaptation, see http://bingen.cs.csbsju.edu/tcreed. Tom Creed of St. John's University describes how he got started, what mistakes he made, and what suggestions he has for those willing to follow.

24. Peter Drucker, interview with Robert Lenzner and Stephen S. Johnson. *Forbes,* March 10, 1997 (reprinted on-line at http://nrsite.com/click.ng;spacedesc+RunOfSite_Forbes_4).

25. To see how this idea can be focused on the teaching of history as well as the debate that it can engender, see, for example, the spirited discussion in *Historical Perspectives* (March 1997): 23–30.

26. Roger Chartier, *Forms and Meanings: Texts, Performances, and Audiences from Codex to Computer* (Philadelphia: University of Pennsylvania Press, 1995), 20.

27. The papers from the conference, as well as much of the interchange, may be accessed at http://leah.kcc.hawaii.edu/org/tcc_conf.

28. Robert Fowler, "How the Secondary Orality of the Electronic Age Can Awaken Us to the Primary Orality of Antiquity" (http://www2.baldwinw.edu/rfowler/pubs/secondoral/index.html).

29. Doug Brent, "Oral Knowledge, Typographic Knowledge, Electronic Knowledge: Speculations on the History of Ownership" (htttp://rachel.albany.edu/ejournal/vln3/article.html).

30. Chartier, 20; Jay David Bolter, *Writing Space: The Computer, Hypertext, and the History of Writing* (Hillsdale, NJ: L. Erlbaum, 1991), 6.

31. Brent.

32. Chartier, 23.

33. George Landow, *Hypertext: The Convergence of Contemporary Critical Theory and Technology* (Baltimore: Johns Hopkins University Press, 1992): 88–100.

34. Ong, 75.

35. Bolter, 155; Richard Lanham, *The Electronic Community: Democracy, Technology and the Arts* (Chicago: University of Chicago Press, 1993), 7.

36. Landow, 70.

37. Bolter, 240.

Part II

Scholarly Communication and Publication in the Electronic Age

3

Participatory Historical Writing on the Net

Notes and Observations from Recent Experience

Timothy Messer-Kruse

The increasing trespass of computers upon the territory of the book has raised fears among antiquarians and book lovers, but is also opening up new possibilities for the enrichment of books themselves. For a decade now, electronic newspapers, magazines, and a flowering of amateur publishing ventures on the Web have assumed great importance in our culture. Computer companies have pitched their wares by appealing to the computer's kinship to the book. How many ads have we all seen of yuppies coolly typing away on a sun-drenched verandah or in the solitude of some verdant meadow? If we are to believe the advertisements, we live in an era of revolution and profound social change brought about by the innovation of wiring together the planet's microprocessors. Everyone, it seems, across the entire spectrum of learned opinion from the Pollyannas to the Cassandras, believes that the Internet is bound to shake the pillars of society, whether for good or ill. While Madison Avenue envisions the Internet unshackling workers from their cubicles, academics raise the alarm that our new technologies will undermine literacy and result in the death of the book itself.[1] The dean of the Graduate Library School at the University of Chicago repeated these fears to a conference called to consider the future of the book:

> The reality is that the printed book seems already to have been partially replaced. In the scholarly field, it is often no longer the book itself which is consulted but a substitute for the book. . . . In the popular field, the invasion is even more troubling, because such [new] inventions . . . supplant the book,

instead of merely altering its external form. When they vie with the book for attention at an identical time, these nonbook devices are likely to win, and that means that not only the book but also the reading act is being replaced as a means of communication. If we assume that these trends must necessarily continue and be aggravated, we have cause to fear that the book as we know it may some day disappear.[2]

Such were the fears expressed at the Future of the Book Conference way back in 1955.[3] Forty years ago academics condemned the triple threat of "the moving picture, radio, and television," much as contemporary critics caution us of the dangers of electronic communications. Contrary to the fears raised in 1955, neither movies, the radio, nor even the tube have done much to erode book culture in America over the past generation. The book is alive and well and will, I venture, continue to flourish as fiber optic cable unspools and modems hiss into the next century.

The appearance of these new means of mass communication have not undermined the importance of the book for the simple reason that the book form is not easily reproduced in a broadcast medium where time is at a premium and attention spans are not. Likewise, computers should not be viewed as the great usurper of literary culture, but as powerful adjuncts that may, if developed intelligently, enrich the meaning, role, and relevancy of books to increasing numbers of people.

In the field of publishing, especially in the field of historical publishing, there are several concrete ways that this new tool can deepen scholarship and even enrich the reading experience itself. Both cellulose and silicon have their own unique and complementary advantages. Books are portable, aesthetic, narrative, structured, authoritative, and durable, while computer networks are eclectic, ephemeral, decentralized, and nonlinear. Relative to the data file capacity of modern computers, the printed book is a puny compendium; yet, it is precisely this limitation that is the book's greatest asset, dictating as it does the logical narrative structure that leavens the rigorous development of ideas. Conversely, it is the steadily growing speed and depth of data storage and transmission that gives computing networks their great value as repositories of raw, unfiltered information. Clearly, any predictions of the future use of the book and the computer must be based on some division of labor between the two, rather than upon the replacement of one by the other.

Science has long since realized the benefits of this division of labor between print and networks, and scientists have for decades been exchanging data sets and engaging in collaborative research over computer networks, while continuing to publish important papers. Scholars in the humanities, however, have been slow to realize the benefits that these new electronic tools can provide; for them the Internet has become an extension of the mailbox and the card catalogue, but little else of real importance. For all of the billions being poured into networking and computerization, this is a ludicrous underutilization of resources—like using the newly invented radio only for civil defense drills and news bulletins. Thank goodness, we got jazz instead.

Within the humanities, the field that may best take advantage of the new electronic division of labor is history. Historians wear two hats, each suited to either of these two mediums of communication. At their best, historians are composers of literature, with all of literature's necessary attention to narrative, style, perspective, voice, and reader. For this the book will remain the ultimate product of the historian's art. Historians are also great scroungers and compilers of data, assembling mounds and mountains of discrete items of evidence, while searching daily for the next needle in the haystack. While truly great historical authors are rare and workaday writing dominates the annual outpouring of history books, the problems posed by the literary form have never been what distinguished the professional historian from the interested public. What made history a profession and gave it social authority was its monopoly on the gathering, sorting, and sifting of historical data. Due to the physical and economic constraints of publishing, it has until now only been possible for *historians* to publish their *interpretations,* not their sources. Of course, rigorous academic histories include numerous citations and notes, but these are merely catalogues of data, not the data itself. The interested amateur, not having the training, the means, or the time to track down sources is placed in the position of either accepting a historian's argument on logic alone, or even worse, on faith. In the best case, the interested amateur will compare the historical monograph to a review written by a historian equally versed in the data and, by means of triangulation, arrive at a more informed conclusion, even though the sources themselves remain beyond his grasp.

When the first professional historical associations were formed in the United States in the late nineteenth century, they had a more inclusive model of historical research than we have today. It was the vision of the founder of the American Historical Association, Herbert Baxter Adams, to create a public institution that would bring interested amateurs, univer-

sity academics, and local historical societies together into a single research community. Nevertheless, the professionals, in their eagerness to
raise the standing of their discipline within their own universities, succeeded in nudging the amateurs out by the turn of the century.[4] In spite
of all the talk over the decades of writing history for "everyman," or of
discovering the "usable past," or of tying history to "popular memory,"
the fact remains that a wide gulf separates academic debates from the
public historical dialogue.[5]

The historical profession's effective monopoly of historical information is one of the reasons that the public is so alienated from the debates
and conclusions of academic history. This monopoly is partially artifi-
cial and social, and wherever the public can easily overcome it, they do
so with great eagerness. The increasing attendance at historical sites,
museums, and "living" history centers indicates that the public hungers
for a direct encounter with historical sources, which in most cases takes
the form of an artifact, whether the Declaration of Independence in the
Library of Congress, the Wright flyer hanging from the ceiling of the
Smithsonian, or an iron historical marker by the side of the road. Textual
sources remain the exclusive preserve of professionals, not only because
of the cash and leisure required to travel to archives, but also because
there is a certain degree of technical competence that goes into being
able to find them. The addition of electronic indices to such arcanery as
the National Union Catalog of Manuscript Collections (NUCMC), census tables, and the archival finding aid have only made the old saying
that "a good historian is a good librarian" more true than ever.

Historians, having invested untold hours of research in digging out the
fragments of evidence they need to string together their arguments,
develop a certain proprietary feeling toward their documents. This is only
natural, especially when it is combined with the institutional pressures to
publish and specialize that foster competition among researchers. As a
result, history as practiced in America today is one of the most individualistic of all the humanities. Historical studies as a whole are impover-
ished as a result of the hoarding its institutional structures encourage
among its practitioners. Graduate students spend inordinate amounts of
time collecting primary sources that are already collected and collated;
researchers continually follow the same footnotes to the same original
documents in the same archives (with increasing wear and tear to the
sources themselves); and numerous potential cross-fertilizations and
synergys of evidence go unrealized because there is no systematic way

beyond the ancient footnote and bibliography of sharing sources.

The consequences of this hoarding of accumulated historical knowledge is sometimes tragic. One of the towering figures of historical studies in the nineteenth century was the great English historian, Lord John Acton. According to all who knew him, Acton was the best read, most erudite, and greatest historical mind of his age. When he died in 1902, his Cambridge colleague, Sir Charles Oman, went to see Acton's home before its furnishings were carted away:

> [T]here were shelves on shelves of books on every conceivable subject—Renaissance Sorcery, the Fureros of Aragon, Scholastic Philosophy, the Growth of the French Navy, American Exploration, Church Councils. The owner had read them all, and many of them were full in their margins with cross-references in pencil. There were pigeon-holed desks and cabinets with literally thousands of compartments, into each of which were sorted little white slips with references to some particular topic, so drawn up . . . that no one but the compiler could easily make out the drift of the section. . . . I never saw a sight that more impressed on me the vanity of human life and learning. A quarter of the time that had been spent on making those marginal annotations, and filling those pigeon-holes might have produced a dozen volumes of sound and valuable history—perhaps an epoch-making book that might have lived for centuries. But all the accumulated knowledge had vanished, save so far as that the dead books, without the link of live thought, were to go as a gift to Cambridge. And I said to myself, intensive research, even by the most competent researcher, is wasted, unless the results are put together and printed.[6]

Lord Acton, although known as the greatest historian of his generation, never published a single book in his career. What heights might his students and successors have climbed had they had ready access to his compiled sources and works in progress? What may have been accomplished had Acton possessed more than a row of dusty pigeon-holes to store his notes and musings? Why should the historical profession still be based on the Acton-model of the lone, heroic bibliophile, rather than upon a collaborative model of an engaged community of researchers?

The advances in computing and communication technologies over the past thirty years have laid the material basis for overcoming the Lord Acton syndrome that continues to plague the historical profession. It is now possible for the Lord Actons of today to share an unlimited number of their notes, ideas, and annotations with the entire world of interested scholars with minimal cost. Paperless publishing through the Internet theoretically offers the means for transcending a centuries-old model of historical scholarship and breaking down the barriers between academic and amateur historians.

A sizable proportion of practicing historians now record their notes and transcriptions of important documents in computer databases. The rapid improvement of OCR scanning devices and the exponential spread of networked computers have made it possible for much historical data, once locked away in historians' file cabinets and card boxes, to be made accessible to the public. Already this is being done in the voluntary and haphazard manner that is characteristic of the Internet. Today there are thousands of electronic texts, image archives, virtual museums, genea-logical databases, and listserv discussion groups available on-line. The task of the future will be to make these resources more accessible, rational, and integrated than they are today.

Most historical Internet sites, from those of university departments to on-line museums, are organized to send rather than receive informa-tion. History departments serve up faculty profiles, syllabi, and news-letters, while museums usually just digitize a portion of their collections and dump them on the Web. These sites are very useful in their own ways, but they do not take advantage of the medium's real strength, and that is its ability to allow for dialogue and the exchange of ideas. Nor do they take advantage of a division of labor with the traditional book.

In the summer of 1996, I initiated an experiment that in a very small way was an attempt to move beyond the typical "broadcast" mode of most academic Internet sites toward a more interactive and collaborative approach to history. In the course of researching a book on American radicalism in the mid-nineteenth century, I came across a roster of some 500 delegates (and their home towns) to the founding convention of the Equal Rights Party (ERP), an ephemeral political party that brought together suffragists, spiritualists, socialists, labor reformers, and pacifists in the presidential campaign year of 1872. Some of the names on this list, such as Victoria Woodhull, the presidential candidate of the Equal Rights Party and the first woman to run for that office, were familiar, but most were not. After determining that the great majority of people who attended this convention did not appear in the master biographical bibli-ographies, I realized that the task of tracking down sources that were locally held and scattered among fifty or sixty locations was more than I cared to tackle, but was just the sort of research that might best be done through an Internet collaboration.

My Web site, called the Equal Rights Party Project, contained the 500 or so names of the founders of the party arranged by geographic location.* It also provided a short history of the party, elementary tips and tactics for locating sources, and a variety of means, including an on-line form, for returning information. It invited anyone interested in history to look up the names of ERP founders from their communities in their local library, government records hall, or historical society. My role was to be one of editor, formatting the responses and updating the database.

After nearly a year of operation, the results are encouraging, but not what I had hoped for. The traffic on the site has been small—I would estimate that only about 500 individuals ever "visited" the site. This is not too surprising, as the subject itself is rather specialized, and I made only a half-hearted attempt to publicize the site, sending a small announcement to several H-Net discussion groups and making sure it was indexed on the major search engines, such as Yahoo!. Also, I made all the common mistakes of the Web novice—initially a few undetected bugs rendered some of the pages of my site inoperable; after six months of operation I changed servers and URLs, leaving an unknown number of hyperlinks to my site dead, and I was not as regular as I should have been in updating the site and posting fresh contributions. Although I have reason to be discouraged by the relatively small number of responses to the site, the quality of the responses I did garner convince me that collaborative projects have tremendous potential to reach popular audiences. Compared with the small number of total visitors, the proportion who have contributed to the ERP collaboration has been relatively high. Nearly one out of ten of those who accessed the site contacted me in some way about it, either to request further information, comment, or contribute in some way.

Most of those who have submitted information to be added to the site's database have been professionals, mostly librarians and archivists, and a few academic historians. Their submissions have been the most fruitful, but not the most interesting. The more intriguing submissions and queries have come from the general public. For example, a self-described "collector of campaign memorabilia" from Ballwin, Missouri, who chanced

---

*The Equal Rights Party Project site and the other collaborative projects can be found at: http://www.history.utoledo.edu.

upon the Equal Rights Party site, wrote me a very detailed letter, indicating that he had done an impressive amount of research into the question of the actual institutional lifespan of the party itself. (There is some question as to whether the party died in 1888 or 1892.) From this letter, I also learned that there is probably more Woodhull memorabilia in private hands than there is in all the musuem collections that I was aware of. On another occasion, an individual who claimed to be a descendent of Belva Lockwood (the second woman to run for president), and who was tracing his genealogy, requested a more detailed bibliography on works about her. In December 1996 the International Women's Day Celebration Committee of New Jersey designated the site one of its optional themes for students in the research essay competition, although I do not think that any high-schoolers took them up on it. Others have corrected spellings, sent criticisms and suggestions, and proposed links to other sites.

In the end, the Equal Rights Party History Project fulfilled its mission of bringing together a small group of individuals interested in the history of this ephemeral political party. This is but a small example of the potential of the Internet to broach academic and public boundaries. With traffic over the Internet increasing at 30 percent per month, the number of users of the Web doubling every six months, and the median income of the typical Internet user steadily declining from its early heights, this medium can only continue to bore deeply into popular culture and consciousness. The latest survey of World Wide Web user habits and trends showed that the Web is evolving into something more than a means of news or entertainment; it is being popularly used as means of interaction and communication. In that survey, a high proportion of the over twenty thousand respondents (close to half) indicated that they used the Internet to make contact with people who shared their interests.[7] Clearly, professional historians who continue to view the Internet as merely a means of broadcasting the fruits of their research, or as a new medium for traditional publication, are missing an important opportunity to participate in a new emerging forum for the exchange of ideas.

Amateur historians are already far ahead of professionals in the many creative ways that they have applied Internet technology to historical problems. Even a cursory search of historical sites will return a majority of local historical societies, geneological databases, civil war reenactors, antiquarian marketplaces, and personal pages filled with interesting and often surprising amounts of historical information. This segment of the virtual historical community will continue to grow and flourish with or without the input of academics. However, academics could do a great service to the public were we to use the Internet to tie traditional research to these on-line public circles of historical interest.

One place to start utilizing the Internet to open up the elite domain of academic history is by increasingly integrating electronic and paper publishing. A few recent books, such as the one co-edited by the organizer of this conference, are published along with a Web site where readers of the book can keep abreast of the latest news and trends in the field.[8] I hope to see an expansion of this concept in the future, wherein a books' very structure is interwoven with network supplements. Of all the integral parts of the book, our time-worn systems of citation are perhaps the most adaptable to electronic augmentation. It is certainly possible today for any traditionally published book to debut along with a Web site that reproduces the footnotes or endnotes of the book, but links each one to the original source document itself. I imagine someday coming across a controversial interpretation in a book and then being able to walk across the room, fire up my computer, and in moments examine the full context of quotes, related sources not excerpted, and even pages of commentary on the subject by both the author and his or her critics, which I can easily add to. Such a system of publication would go far in democratizing access to academic historical debates.

Of course, professional historians may be reluctant to relinquish the legitimating function of their footnotes. To the public, citations function not as a roadmap to fact but as a token of legitimacy and authority. Historians have long exploited this aspect of popular readership and hidden behind their footnotes like Oz at the controls of his visage. By jealously guarding its file cabinets and note boxes, the historical guild has preserved its privileges from the judgments of the public.[9]

Moreover, the ability of historians to innovate in this way will largely be determined by the willingness of universities and foundations to reform the existing system of incentives and sanctions to accommodate modes of research that are not individualistic. The collaborative model that I have presented here, and the technologies underlying it, are presently inhibited by academic systems of hiring, funding, and promotion that encourage research in the loner style of Lord Acton (although given his poor publication record, he might not do well today). If they cannot reform, the increasing gap between academic history and popular memory will only widen.

Notes

1. See Clifford Stoll, *Silicon Snake Oil: Second Thoughts on the Information Highway* (New York: Doubleday, 1995), passim.

2. Lester Asheim, "New Problems in Plotting the Future of the Book" in *The Future of the Book: Implications of the Newer Developments in Communication,* Lester Asheim, ed. (Chicago: University of Chicago Press, 1955).

3. For a concise example of more recent fears that computers will undermine literacy, see Edmund D. Pellegrino, "The Computer and the Book: The Perils of Coexistence" in *Books in Our Future: Perspectives and Proposals,* John Y. Cole, ed. (Washington: Library of Congress, 1987), 84–88.

4. John Higham, "Herbert Baxter Adams and the Study of Local History," *American Historical Review* 89 (December 1984), pp. 1225–1239.

5. See the special issue of the *Journal of American History* on the Enola Gay controversy for a good example of the disconnection of professional and public dialogues, *Journal of American History* 82 (December 1995).

6. Sir Charles Oman, On the *Writing of History* (New York: E.P. Dutton, 1939), 209–210.

7. See J. Pitkow and C. Kehoe, "Emerging Trends in the WWW User Population," *Communications of the ACM* 39, no. 6 (1996); and the more detailed data in the "Sixth WWW User Survey" of the Graphic, Visualization, and Usability Center, Georgia Tech Research Corporation, October 1996 (http://www.cc.gatech.edu/gvu/user_surveys/).

8. Dennis Trinkle et al., *The History Highway: A Guide to Internet Resources* (Armonk, NY: M.E. Sharpe, 1997).

9. See David Hackett Fischer, *Historian's Fallacies: Toward a Logic of Historical Thought* (New York: Harper and Row, 1970), 286–287, for more discussion of the "fallacy of references."

4

Scholarly Publication in the Electronic Age

Ellen Meserow Sauer

In this age of increasing monopolization of goods, services, and even information, where Microsoft = Software, Blockbuster = Movies, TCI = Cable, Netscape = Information, Intel = Microchips, and Barnes & Noble = Books, the Internet has great potential to shake things up. Simultaneously, like other previous technologies that promised to revolutionize education, it has an even greater possibility of relegating education to an even more superfluous role in American culture.

How does this relate to scholarly communication? Permit me to ramble a bit about the routes and structures of scholarly communication currently in place, in question, and under revision by the powers that be, and I will try to answer that question.

At first glance, global networked computer technologies appear to be the great leveler of scholarly roles. In institutions of higher education, at least, they certainly have shown us a route toward the Marxist dream of an open means of production and distribution more clearly than any other communication tool yet invented. Flattening perspective, such that both multinational mega-corporations and the average citizen with access to a computer have equal opportunities to represent themselves to the world in the form of "home pages," our current web refuses to merely broadcast information in the one-way, us-versus-them manner of paper publications, radio, and television. Culturally, the breakdown of this hierarchy of producer over consumer is an immense challenge, not simply a freedom which overnight will circumvent our traditions of separating the artist from the worker, the corporation from the everyman. By allowing each of us to act as student, scholar, author, editor, librarian, archivist, and publisher, a disintermediation of our educational culture has begun, a change with the potential to alter the very nature of American culture more radically than any other shift in information distribution and retrieval for centuries.

Such a change in the well-established roles and in access to technology will likely take some time to settle enough to be analyzed. While the book recently celebrated its 550 birthday as a medium of communication, the Web has just celebrated its fifth. However, the questions of reorganization have already begun. In the commercial world, they appear to surround strategies for making money through this technology. In the educational environment, however, the questions are more experimental: What does it mean to own information? Must we control information? Communication? When does intellect become property? Do we still need publishers? Do we still need libraries? What is a campus for? As the playing field looks more level (at least around the ivory tower, where access to networked computer technology is becoming a given), and as windows into previously shrouded or expensive operations are opened, organizations such as ourselves who stand between the producers and the consumers of our culture find ourselves required to re-evaluate our methods, examine our means of funding, question our definitions of property, and in some contexts, justify our own existence.

It is about these pressures that I would like to talk today, the pressures of being a publisher in the childhood of the electronic age. About being a non-profit publisher on a network that expects information to be free. About the structural possibilities for formal electronic scholarly communication in the world of higher education. And, finally, about methods in our new global context for collaborative university experimentation which take advantage of the skills and experience of all areas of our organizations, so that we can take on the opportunities of the global network without falling into its traps.

Without such collaboration, and perhaps without such mobilization, I am fearful of the other road toward a disintermediated culture we could find ourselves on. Among the possible outcomes of which we should be extremely wary is acceptance of the idea that any more consolidation of our information marketplace is desirable. The large list of corporate giants I gave earlier is microcosmically reflected in the arena of publishing: at present, only eight huge media conglomerates own most of the trade publishing ventures in the United States and only two multinational publishers own the majority of science, technology, and medicine journals.[1] These two arenas of traditional publishing are the most lucrative, and therefore the most outrageous, in that their methods for becoming profitable include turning information into infotainment, and pricing which severely affects the availability of funds for humanities scholarship.

To fully depict those situations for you, I will need to give a bit of the history of publishing over the last fifteen years and explain Johns Hopkins's role in it. I am hopeful that my experience with a collaborative university experiment in scholarly communication will offer one framework through which we can envision the future of scholarly communication. This is Project Muse [http://muse.mse.jhu.edu/]—the almost four-year-old child of a university collaboration at Johns Hopkins involving members of the Johns Hopkins University Press, the Eisenhower Library, and the Academic Computing Office on the Homewood campus.[2] In late 1993, discussions began on distributing the Press's paper scholarly journals electronically—in order to prepare the Press and its publications for the digital future, but also to participate in the serials pricing debate which was being waged at library conferences around the world. As many of you may know, over the past fifteen years multinational commercial publishers of science, technology, and medicine journals have escalated their pricing beyond all expected bounds, impacting library budgets in all disciplines and mediums radically, including purchasing of the university press's primary product, the scholarly monograph. To give you a bit of context, the average increase in price of the 134 periodicals in history over the past five years was 28 percent, applied to a base price, which on average in 1997 was about $82. In contrast, the average increase in pricing in the three journals in chemistry over the last five years was 51 percent, applied to an average price in 1997 of $1400.[3] I am sure you can see that with the limited literature in chemistry, cancellation of these three journals has been a difficult prospect for research university libraries. Instead, they have had to curtail spending on other resources.

So, having lost the certainty of a library base of sales for the majority of our publications, a base which had allowed some luxury in terms of the publishability of small, interdisciplinary studies, university presses and other small, non-association/membership-based publishing ventures have been increasingly pushed toward individual purchasers. Gearing our acquisitions and product toward at least a few trade, reference, and regional publications each season, bookstores, newsstands, departmental and classroom sales became the funding opportunities focused on, and more and more these days this focus fails. According to *The Nation*'s recently released special issue on publishing, the eight media corporations who publish the majority of trade titles in the United States have established, together with the superstore book chains which have put out of business many smaller booksellers, a quick-sale mentality, which caters to an audience that runs from *anything* scholarly, footnotes and indexes included.[4] At this stage in the game, most scholarly materials do not belong in such bookstores any more than they fit in during network television's prime time.

With known avenues for dissemination (i.e., funding), therefore becoming scarce and unfriendly, at Johns Hopkins we are experimenting with a reachback to a market that university presses used to rely on, libraries. As the Internet matured, library conferences world wide discussed the possibility of electronic journals decreasing the cost of the out-of-control science, technology, and medicine serials (called "STM journals"), allowing once again reasonable budgeting for all resources. Concern had been voiced, however, that in the hands of the same commercial publishers who had increased their pricing year after year despite the outcry, electronic journals would surely be priced outrageously. Confirmation came in STM journal publishers' public speeches, in which they claimed, should not e-journals be 200 or 300 percent of the price of their paper counterparts, in that they are two or three times more efficient and useful? In was in this context that Muse was prototyped, proposed, and given grant funding by the Mellon Foundation and the National Endowment for the Humanities. As we publish primarily history, literary theory, and social science journals, we were incredibly fortunate to receive such funding; grants for humanities resources are quite scarce and, in the booming electronic environment, often dependant on a short start-up phase toward a built-in cost recovery mechanism of some sort.

Working with that funding toward a cost-recovery plan, which would decrease the price of our already inexpensive journals but increase use by opening up networked access for entire campuses through a single library subscription, we launched in August 1995 with a set of five journals and a consortium of sixty libraries around the country (including Oberlin, Denison, and Kenyon in Ohio). Over the past eighteen months, we have brought on-line an additional thirty-seven journals, including such journals as *Reviews in American History, American Quarterly,* and *Eighteenth-Century Studies.* During this period we have also been enlarging our subscription base, which now includes systems as large as the California State Universities, the public and private colleges of Virginia, and the public library systems of Cleveland and Pittsburgh.

With almost 400 subscribing libraries now, we believe Muse's financial model to be on its way to the expectations proposed to our grant funding agencies and to hopeful librarians wary of the STM pricing to come in the digital future. Even more thrilling has been the impact we have had on electronic STM publishing ventures. Enthusiastic librarians, tired of announcing to their faculty cancellations due to rising prices year after year, have uniformly endorsed Muse's campus-wide access model, a model in which all use on campus is paid for by just one source, the library, at a rate which is less than that for the single paper subscription they have shelved for decades—no matter the size of the institution. In response, STM publishers have followed this lead, by-passing simultaneous user restrictions or password access, and even pricing their electronic access at or below the print journal cost.

This massive experiment has taught us a great deal about the riches of universities themselves and even showed us a bit about publishing through the refreshingly naive window of technology. Talk about leveling the playing field. Within the publishing arena alone, consider the fact that Muse has landed tiny Johns Hopkins University Press on panels with multinational commercial media conglomerates struggling for their start in e-publishing, and allowed us to watch as still others collapsed in false starts this year, as most of the major trade publishers shut down or fired their "electronic publishing" divisions in order to start again with "fresh" teams, who could see into the future beyond by-product CD-ROMs.

Further, it has taught us about intellectual property in the cycle of scholarly communication. In an era in which big information and software publishing are fighting hard to disable the 1976 "fair use" provisions of copyright law (with some successes and governmental backing), the knowledge afforded to JHUP in these university collaborations has allowed us to take a stance supporting fair use while demonstrating that we will not lose our shirts in the process.[5] Included in the single price for each project or journal we publish is much more than traditional "fair use." *All* campus use—classroom, archival, printing, downloading, electronic reference shelves, and on-line syllabi, even interlibrary loan—is allowed. In a time in which many publishers are finding the World Wide Web a quite insecure forum for distribution of what they consider publisher property, we have found our university and non-profit ties a unique perspective for working toward a mutual respect, which asks that scholars recognize that the Press is making no profit from the materials in Muse, but instead participating in the primary mission of a university—to facilitate and disseminate learning.

So, after wandering around a bit through my experience, let us go back to some analysis of the roles of the scholarly communication process of the future. One of the first and clearest conclusions available is that if this information revolution is ever to affect the higher education process of tenure, promotion, and general recognition of a contribution to scholarship, the effect will be gradual and slow. At the same time, however, the self-motivated production of electronic projects by faculty and students at higher education institutions is not escalating in a gradual or slow manner. While libraries struggle to approach the concept of cataloging the thousands of elaborate Web sites which arduously collect discipline-specific information, the hundreds of listservs and archives of listservs, a huge number of electronic texts, and a plethora of new electronic-only serial publications, scholars continue to create more and better forums for scholarly communication within and among disciplines.

What shall we do with all this energy and talent on campus? First, I think we have need of distinctions between informal scholarly communication, which adds to the richness and immersive quality of study, and formal, finalized, edited publications/projects, which are intended to contribute to the long-term, collaborative corpus of intellectual discourse. Then, in the face of the growing corporate presence on the Web, turning it quickly into an interactive TV rather than a means for open educational discourse, we need to organize the skills and talents on campus to facilitate both the informal and formal manifestations of electronic scholarly communication, so that recognition is available to both. Revision of our mechanisms of recognition will obviously be a necessity, in order to support the motivated structural foundation we will need to build to take on this challenge.

In answer to the questions, Do we need publishers?; Do we need libraries?; Is intellect property?; and so on, I say we have need of a vision that realizes the necessity of all skills available on university campuses to handle the information needs of the electronic age. Collaborative university planning in which libraries, university presses, and academic computing are all given a feasible chance to facilitate the scholarly process is the best strategy for playing on this new, disorienting playing field.

Notes

1. See Mark Crispin Miller, "The Crushing Power of Big Publishing," *The Nation,* March 17, 1997. On-line at http://www.thenation.com/issue/970317/0317mill.htm.

2. During the implementation phase of the grants from NEH and the Mellon Foun-

dation, which funded Muse (1995–97), the author was manager of the project at the Johns Hopkins University Press, directing all implementation aspects: staffing, production, systems, reporting, and much public speaking. She also participated in policy discussions from pricing to copyrights. Muse can be found at http://muse.jhu.edu/.

3. *Library Journal,* Periodical Survey, 1996–97.

4. Miller, "The Crushing Power."

5. Donald F. Johnston, *The Copyright Handbook* (New York: Bowker, 1978).

5

On-Line Reviewing
Pitfalls, Pinnacles, Potentialities, and the Present

Scott A. Merriman

The whole issue of the Internet has burst upon the scene in the past four years to much hype, interest, complaint, and hoopla. In many areas, however, the Internet seems to be more smoke than fire, as can be seen in a recent commercial for IBM in which we watch a sales team looking needlessly at a "flaming logo." Similarly, despite Vice President Gore's touting of the "information superhighway," it was revealed recently that the White House just installed its first computer in the Oval Office.[1] These missteps aside, the Internet is certainly revolutionizing the field of history, and the number of on-line historical resources is growing exponentially. Electronic book reviews are making a particular mark upon the field. Several on-line journals have been created specifically to provide reviews. These electronic reviews have received a great deal of positive press, and they unquestionably already have much success to trumpet. On-line reviews are not without their trials and tribulations, however, and it is in this light that this article will explore "On-Line Reviewing: Pitfalls, Pinnacles, Potentialities, and the Present."

To provide a comparative background, we will discuss some of the current problems faced by traditional print journals before turning to the electronic journals, which have been created to address the limitations of print.

Print reviews face several challenges, not the least of which is the increased competition from new journal formats. The main challenges for print journals concern time, content, and costs. Scholars have long complained about the lengthy delay between the appearance of a book and the publication of a review in a scholarly print journal. With gaps of more than a year between a book's publication and the appearance of a review the norm, this is clearly an area of concern to subscription journals in an environment of heightened competition. Production costs are another concern. The costs of shipping place a limit on the number of reviews which each issue can contain, which in turn limits the coverage that these journals can devote to each historical subfield. Since electronic journals are less constrained by issues of space, print journals are now under more pressure than ever to create innovative ways to address these issues. The costs of subscription also pose another obstacle. Despite the proliferation of specialty print journals, costs have not been kept in check by competition and have escalated significantly over the past decade. The advent of electronic media, however, now presents subscription journals with a variety of options for reducing costs (such as Project Muse discussed by Ellen Meserow Sauer). Competition from journals that charge no subscription fees is going to force print journals to take the new media's challenges seriously.

Having seen the problems that printed reviews face, we should now turn to on-line reviews. There are three different basic forms of electronic media which review books as their primary focus, or as one of their primary concerns. The first are the journals, which provide peer reviews done by specialists and which are available only through subscription. These journals are generally electronic versions of long-established print journals. A fine example of this type of journal, which I will call a subscription review, is *Reviews in American History.* The second type of journal also provides peer reviews done by specialists, but is available free of charge on-line. Without exception, these are new journals that have been created to specifically take advantage of the new opportunities presented by the Internet. Excellent examples of this genre, which I will call free access reviews, include *Reviews in History* and *History Reviews On-Line.* The third category includes reviews that are presented by discussion lists and are not affiliated with any particular "journal." The most well known example is the H-Net review project.

Each of these genres has some unique pluses and minuses. The subscription reviews seem to face the fewest problems. As the identical or nearly identical twins of print journals, however, these journals certainly inhabit an ambiguous terrain, and their primary hurdle may well be establishing a clear and viable relationship with their print siblings. This will certainly be crucial for subscription success, and the question of subscription will unquestionably be the Achilles' heel for these reviews.

Since they are funded by fees rather than institutional or charitable grants, they will be at the mercy of the market. Their success will depend on whether libraries and individual scholars judge them a worthy investment in a climate of hyper-competition.

Free access reviews avoid this problem; however, they have a significant problem with finances. Amidst the hype and hoopla, many have claimed that the Internet presents a costless medium for scholarly publication, and many items, including H-Net's reviews, are published free of charge. This does not mean that these publications are free of costs, however. Producing electronic journals entails a number of expenses. Significant hardware and software expenditures are required. There are heavy expenses for postage and correspondence (mailing the average scholarly book costs $1.50 in the continental United States; foreign postage charges are seven to ten times higher). There are still also editorial and production costs.

Thus, "free" electronic media are on tenuous financial ground. For example, H-Net's highly touted efforts have only been possible because of generous grants from the National Endowment for the Humanities, the support of Michigan State University (where H-Net is based), and the *pro bono* labor of hundreds of energetic scholars. Without the subscription charges of the subscription reviews, or the governmental and institutional grants supporting H-Net, a journal is reliant on outside funds or university subventions, and these are not always reliable. In this age of shrinking budgets and adjunct faculty (consult any edition of the *Chronicle of Higher Education* if you are not convinced), electronic journals are more apt to be labors of love for their editors than endeavors seriously supported by universities. Even the presidents of major organizations, such as the American Society for Legal History, do not always receive release time for their work. And there are only so many hours in a day.[2] Thus, while there are no costs for printing, there does not seem to be an overwhelming cost advantage for electronic journals, and university support is still essential for the long-term success of any such venture.[3]

Review projects sponsored by discussion lists face the same financial hurdles confronted by free access reviews, but they also have some unique problems. The first problem for reviews done by discussion lists is editorial consistency. For example, although they possess a significant technological advantage in providing timely reviews, there still is often a serious time lapse between when a review is written and when it is posted. Similarly, there is an issue of preservation. Not all discussion lists maintain archives of past posts, so reviews may disappear after their initial appearance, limiting their utility. Some discussion lists have attempted to counter this problem by creating Web sites that archive the activities of the lists, but again, there is a problem of editorial consistency. No rhyme or reason seems to exist for the posting or lack thereof. Even after a review has been electronically published, therefore, it can be lost in cyberspace.[4]

Another obstacle for discussion list reviews is simply that of time. We are all bombarded with a great many e-mail messages every day, and one wonders when the saturation point will come. A recent article in *Time* magazine noted that the number of e-mail messages had tripled over the past three years from 694 billion in 1994 to 2.6 *trillion* this year, and that the number would continue to climb so that by the year 2000 over 6.6 *trillion* e-mail messages will be sent. Consider the number of e-mail messages a person receives per day at this rate. With only 15 percent of the population possessing e-mail accounts, the average person receives about ten messages per hour at present. By the year 2000, this number is estimated to rise to about 12.5 per hour, or about one message every five minutes. The publishers and editors of discussion-list reviews, thus, must worry about their reviews being lost in the jetsam of the Information Superoverload.[5]

Another problem for discussion list reviews is that of indexing. Currently, some electronic reviews done by discussion lists, such as H-Net, do not have an index, even though they are publishing many reviews a year. Having to search through every review to see if one exists on your area of interest, or having to hope that a list in your area has reviewed every work and has posted every review, seems to be a tactic wishing for refinement.

A final problem with discussion lists is that of quality. Unlike their peer-reviewed cousins, discussion list reviews are not always written by specialists. The qualifications of their reviewers varies as widely as their subscriber rolls. This is not necessarily an absolute drawback. To the extent that these lists attract and appeal to a general audience, there should indeed be a place for reviews in different registers. For the university or college professor in search of a reliable academic review, however, the variable quality is a problem.

An issue central to all forms of reviewing is the current respect, or lack thereof, accorded to electronic reviews by tenure review and hiring committees.[6] Currently, it is safe to say that most print journals are accorded more prestige than electronic ones. This is for a variety of reasons, including the simple fact that print issues have been around longer than electronic versions. This has significant implications for the quality and development of electronic reviews, however. With a finite amount of time in each day, scholars can only devote so much effort to writing reviews that are to be judged irrelevant professionally. If we wish for electronic journals to continue and to be viable vehicles, we need to accord them the respect that they deserve. This does not mean that we need to accept electronic journals without question, but we should protest vigorously against anyone dismissing electronic journals simply because of their medium. In addition, we need to realize that multiple electronic journals can exist. There is no need for any one electronic media source to try to block out the existence of other electronic reviews. As electronic journals evolve and reliable editorial practices (such as careful editing and peer review) become the norm, it is hopeful that these issues will resolve themselves.

The outlook is not all gloom and doom for electronic reviewing, however, since electronic reviews can already claim a fair degree of success. We will end on a positive note, by looking at the four principle strengths of electronic reviews—democracy, speed, ease, and length.

First, for all forms of electronic reviews, the Internet allows much greater democracy and visibility in terms of reviewers. Often, electronic reviews offer young scholars an opportunity to contribute to the debates in their field that they might otherwise not have. In addition to being more democratic for individual reviewers, this is also more democratic for the field. For example, scholars in a subfield who may not be able to fund their own print journal can band together to produce on-line reviews at a lower, if not negligible, cost. Also, individuals who are not at Research I colleges with extensive libraries already can search the Net for information and read reviews of works in a staggering variety of fields.

Second, speed can be a plus for electronic reviews. Because electronic journals do not require the long publishing process involved in producing a print journal, reviews can be distributed to readers with much greater speed. As soon as the review is edited and loaded onto the electronic journal or mailing list, it is immediately available to everyone or at least everyone who has subscribed in the case of subscription reviews. Electronic reviews will still be subject to vagaries of human behavior such as missed deadlines, and the initial claims that reviews can be produced electronically just a month or two after a book's release may not be realistic in many cases, but there is no doubt that on-line reviews can be presented months before analogous print reviews appear.

A third advantage is the simple ease of distribution for electronic reviews. As soon as a mailing list is set up, reviews can be rapidly disseminated to all list members. One does not need to bother with the post office for the discussion list review. For the subscription reviews and the free access reviews, as soon as they are posted to a Web site, they are instantly available, and they can be consulted twenty-four hours a day, seven days a week.

The fourth major advantage is the possibility of much longer and more detailed reviews on-line. While print reviews are necessarily limited due to space constraints, often to 750 words or so, no such limits exist in cyberspace. One can set much longer limits for the reviews in each electronic journal, and these longer treatments allow for lengthy discussions of the issues, with detailed examinations of the relevant historiography. Unfortunately, the short, print book review allows only for summaries and a very limited amount of analysis. Granted, some critics of electronic reviews such as Christopher Tomlins (writing in the *Chronicle of Higher Education*) have claimed that electronic reviews tend to be "long winded, turgid, rambling, bereft of wit or flair."[7] This is an easily solved problem of responsible editing, however, and the example of successful print journals, such as *Reviews in American History,* which do encourage longer reviews, illustrate the potential for success. In short, the fact that space constraints are far less pressing in cyberspace allows for careful, considered, in-depth examination of works, which can be a valuable tool, if the reviews are written by specialists in the field, are full of well-articulated arguments, and are well edited.

In addition to its current pinnacles and problems, the Internet also has a lot of potential. It allows reviewing to join the multimedia revolution. A review can be hyperlinked to pictures of the book under review, to other reviews of the book, to ordering information, to feedback from the author, and so on. Many electronic reviews, including those on some discussion lists, such as H-Survey, and some free access reviews, such as *Reviews in History,* include the review, a reply by the author, and, sometimes, a rejoinder by the reviewer. No author would want to respond to every review of his or her work, so there is a saturation point, but the development of the review and simultaneous reply model is a beneficial one. The development of MOOs and the evolution of real-time video conferencing also present the possibility in the near future of real-time discussions between a book's author, an assigned stable of reviewers, and the larger reading audience.

There will be future hurdles. Access will remain a problem. These new mediums, after all, are only available to those with access to a computer hooked to the Internet. Also, as has been often asked, do people want to read reviews or books over the computer? Or, to put it another way, should electronic formats be the "only" way to go? Another problem is with the world outside of the United States. Many have noted that the United States is the current dominator of the Internet. All fields need to bring in those outside of the United States and have their input as well.[8] Since Internet access for scholars in countries outside the United States varies greatly, creative initiatives must be developed to avoid marginalizing those in other countries.

Electronic reviewing has made large strides in only a few years and has truly revolutionized reviewing. All interested groups need to see the past, understand the problems of the present, and plan for the future. Where it goes from here depends on editors of on-line reviews, administrators, academics, and the public. However, on-line reviewing's short history suggests that electronic reviewing and the Internet, contrary to popular hyperbole, is neither the undertaker for print reviews, nor a thing full of sound and fury, signifying nothing. Thus, understanding the past, on-line reviewing should go exploring into the future, revolutionizing what it needs to for success, but not what it wants to only for the sake of revolutionizing, and growing in partnership with print reviewing, not in destructive competition with it.

Notes

The author would like to thank Dennis Trinkle for all of his suggestions regarding this article.

1. Brian Hecht, "Net Loss," *The New Republic,* 216, no. 7 (February 17, 1997): 15–18.

2. Robert J. Haws, ed., "Help Wanted—Secretarial," *American Society for Legal History Newsletter* 27, no. 2 (Winter 1997): 6.

3. Christopher L. Tomlins, "Print and Electronic Book Reviewing Can Peacefully Co-Exist," *Chronicle of Higher Education,* August 9, 1996, A40. On a similar note, a story in *The Wall Street Journal* last year noted that Project Gutenberg, a project to put thousands of books on the Internet, had run into many different roadblocks and seemed to be running out of steam. This is due in part to the lack of the project's founder, Michael Hart, to find any "substantial funding." Thus, it is not just electronic reviewing that has trouble finding financial support. Robin Frost, "Net Interest—Web Weavers: The Electronic Gutenberg Fails to Win Mass Appeal," *The Wall Street Journal,* November 21, 1996, B12.

4. I should note that the slow rate of posting is not a limited occurrence. Of all the reviews that were distributed in March and April 1997 by the eighty-plus lists associated with H-Net, only six, all in March, were posted as of June 1997. Some lists are far more lax, with one list not having posted any reviews since September. Thus, the Web sites of H-Net, which is one of the largest, if not the largest, electronic reviewing project, do not post their reviews with the "lightning" speed with which the Internet is so often touted. And, if electronic reviewing is to prosper, this is one of the issues that must be addressed. (Personal survey conducted April 16, 1997. On H-Survey there are no reviews since September of 1996, which is an eight-month lag. On H-PCAACA there are no reviews since February of 1997, and it only has four from 1997.)

5. S.C. Gwynne and John F. Dickerson, "Lost in the Email," *Time,* April 21, 1997, 88–90.

6. Peter Shoemaker, "Writing History on the Web," http://www.contextus.com/thoughts/thougharchives/thought1.html (December 2, 1996).

7. Tomlins, A40.

8. Linda K. Kerber, "Ventures into Vietnam," *OAH Newsletter* 25, no. 1 (February 1997): 1, 5. See also "The Devil's in the Internet," *The Nation,* March 10, 1997, 8.

Part III

Multimedia Approaches to Teaching

6

The Enhanced Lecture
A Bridge to Interactive Teaching

Larry J. Easley

Although we all know instructors who still advocate the quill pen, most college teachers have embraced the computer revolution. Computers have replaced our typewriters, filing cabinets, and card catalogs. In the areas involving research, writing, and communication, computers have produced a more efficient method of doing the tasks we have been doing for years. For these tasks, at least, we use the technology without necessarily rethinking the basic elements of our craft. The use of computer-mediated instruction, however, is different, since acceptance of this part of the new technology does force us to revise many of our basic assumptions.[1]

In 1900, instruction in America's universities and colleges was essentially the same as it had been for generations, even though there had been some enhancements—most notably chalkboards.[2] In this classic lecture format, instructors dispensed information and students acted as the largely passive recipients. Even then, there was talk that new technology would revolutionize teaching. After seeing *Birth of a Nation* in 1915, Woodrow Wilson supposedly remarked that the new film media would soon replace the traditional history lecture.

Fifty years later, educators were still predicting a new age of learning thanks to technology. Some crude attempts at computer-assisted instruction were tried in the 1960s, and it was widely feared that computers would replace living teachers. Even then, those who understood the new technology assured their fearful brethren that, "using computers may make it possible for teachers to spend more time with students individually or in small groups."[3]

The scholarship over the last thirty years has been virtually unanimous in criticizing the lecture method as a teaching tool.[4] Despite the condemnations, the lecture method is as deeply entrenched as ever in history classrooms. Advocates of the lecture claim that it is an efficient method of delivery, is very familiar to faculty, permits easy presentation of new information, gives instructors control of the information, and allows lecturers to model thinking. There are, however, some real disadvantages to the method we so frequently employ. The lecture minimizes the role of the learner, requires someone with exceptional presentation skills, ignores the individual needs of the students, and provides little information about the understanding of the students.[5] What researchers discovered is that even though the lecture aids the recognition and recall of information, if the purpose of our teaching is the development of higher order thinking skills, other methods are more effective. We also know that throughout the lecture the concentration of both student and lecturer diminishes. If we plan for students to retain material we deliver after the first fifteen or twenty minutes,[6] we instructors must change our classroom techniques to correspond to the realities of the students we teach.[7]

If the assessment of Robert Barr and John Tagg is right, traditional lecturers may be out of time. "A paradigm shift is taking hold in American higher education . . . to a new paradigm: A college is an institution that exists to *produce learning*. . . . We now see our mission is not instruction, but rather that of producing *learning* with every student by *whatever* means works best."[8] The "instruction paradigm," they believe, promotes the delivery of information (usually in a lecture format) and the assessment of that instruction mode, *not* student learning. With all its flaws, the "instruction paradigm" is far from dead and will probably outlive most of those in the profession today. Inertia alone will ensure its survival well into the next century. If we begin making the transition now, however, graduates of the twenty-first century will have the pedagogical training for the paradigm shift Barr and Tagg recommend.

Bringing technology to the classroom is one way to do this[9] and, at the same time, to begin to make the shift to a learning paradigm.[10] While technology is not a panacea, it is a start.[11] If instructors begin using computer-mediated presentations to illustrate problem-solving techniques and textual modeling, and to act as the backbone for informational lectures, they are more apt to take the next step toward other technology-based interactive techniques. The Pennsylvania State University experience seems to follow this model. Their study found that initially faculty used the same methods in their teaching as they had before. Within two years, faculty who became involved in technology began switching to more interactive methods.[12]

Besides being a form that Nintendo generation students can relate to, the enhanced lecture is a "means to showcase the enormous variety of sources routinely employed by teachers in most disciplines."[13] Instructors should realize that when they make this shift, it will lead to new tools in the teaching/learning process, change the roles of teachers and learners, and require new methods of assessment.[14]

Those switching should also recognize that even with the preparations already underway at many universities, there is still much to do, including:

1. Change the nature of graduate training. Most historians educated in American graduate schools hope to enter the teaching profession, but they are not trained in teaching.[15] The examples of classroom teaching they do receive are usually static, with the roles, tools, and assessment unchanged.

2. Change the merit and promotion system. Although recently there has been a national effort to change merit and promotion criteria, most university reward systems give only lip-service to rewarding excellence in teaching; we all know where the priorities are. In its 1996 survey, the Campus Computing Project found 80 percent of public universities have technology resource centers, while only 8 percent made instructional technology part of their promotion and tenure criteria. The report concluded that "failure to promote or award tenure to faculty who invest time and effort into instructional integration sends a chilling message about the campus commitment to technology integration in instruction and scholarship."[16]

3. Build classrooms conducive to the new technology. If instructors wished to introduce multimedia techniques in the classroom, on most campuses they would face severe difficulties. In their rush to computerize, many campuses place the emphasis on networking the campus and insuring every professor has a desktop computer. Without presentation equipment, faculty will have little incentive to develop the skills necessary to use presentation software. There was a substantial growth in the number of computer classrooms built between 1994 and 1995, but the rate of growth dropped considerably in 1996. The Campus Computing Project found that 16 percent of colleges and universities had computerized classrooms in 1994. This grew to 24 percent by 1995, but remained stagnant in 1996.[17]

4. Increase training resources. Building technology-rich classrooms without faculty training is fruitless.[18] Steven Ehrmann notes that many people believe that if the hardware is purchased, faculty members "will easily, and quickly change their teaching tactics and course materials to take advantage of it. Thus, technology budgets seldom include enough funding to help faculty and staff members upgrade their instructional programs."[19] Departments that are serious about computer-mediated instruction should consider dedicating a graduate assistant to help faculty members in the creation of multimedia presentations and gathering graphic images.[20]

Although it seems a daunting task, the use of the computer in the history classroom has more potential and challenges than in most other disciplines. In one study, Albert Mehrabian found that only 7 percent of the successful communication between teachers and students came from the spoken word. He discovered that 55 percent comes from visual elements.[21] This can be especially valuable for historians, since the nature of the subject and the type of materials used to convey ideas and information are very visual. Historians should ask, "If I could do anything I wanted in the classroom, if technology was not a problem, what would I do to best illustrate the concepts I am trying to teach?" According to Alistair Fraser, anything is almost possible when you combine the power of new presentation software and the newest versions of Netscape. In his "classroom without walls," Fraser has proven that interactive graphics produced on the Web allow "computer visualization" of "mental models" that we previously tried to explain with words.[22]

Even historians at the fringe of this visual revolution can begin to create professional and interactive computer-mediated classroom presentations using software that is relatively easy to learn. Corel Presentations 7 and Microsoft PowerPoint for Windows 97 both meet this criterion well. Besides being bundled in an inexpensive suite, both allow publication of classroom presentations in a HTML format. Even if instructors do not have access to the Web in their classrooms, the Web version of the visuals allows students to review the material outside class.[23]

Although there are map programs showing contemporary nations, there are few historical map series available in a digital format. It is possible, however, to import a graphic of modern Africa, for example, change the fill color for individual nations, add explanatory text, and you have a functional map that illustrates your concept. You can also download maps from other programs such as World Atlas and, using the bitmap editor in WordPerfect Presentations, change the fill color, delete text, and change boundaries. By adding new text and enhancements, a map illustrating the start of the Arab–Israeli war can be inserted into the multimedia presentation. It is also possible to draw your own maps using WordPerfect Presentations or PowerPoint. A little practice drawing polygons and the addition of a few enhancements gives an effective map showing the military situation in Boston just before the Battle of Bunker Hill.[24] One enhancement I included was five sailing ships to symbolize the British navy. I originally drew this ship when putting together a presentation on the age of exploration and discovery. The caravel had been outmoded for more than two centuries in 1775, but students seldom notice that the little sailing ships in Boston Harbor are not British men-of-war. They would notice, however, if I included the modern destroyers you find in available clip art packages.

Effective charts can be drawn using Quattro Pro or Excel. One of the benefits of Windows suites is the fact that you can easily move materials from one suite program to another or link them to create an interactive slide. Changes in the spreadsheet will be transferred automatically to the chart in your classroom presentation.

For photos, drawings, and other similar materials, the scanner is the historian's best friend. Besides giving a sense of place and time in a presentation, photographs can stimulate effective interaction and help develop critical thinking skills.[25] If these images are going to be included in a public Web page or loaded on a university network, care should be taken to ensure copyright restrictions are followed. Although it is generally safe to use materials published before 1922, the seventy-five year guideline is not always safe.

According to the guidelines adopted two decades ago, educators operate under a "fair use doctrine" that allows "the fair use of a copyrighted work, including such use by reproduction in copies or phono records or by other means . . . for purposes such as . . . teaching (including multiple copies for classroom use), scholarship, or research, is not an infringement of copyright." Despite this guideline, there are four stipulations in the law that bear watching. According to the rules,

1. You may not convert the material from one medium to another.
2. Video materials can only be stored for forty-five days.
3. You cannot alter or edit the program.
4. You cannot transmit the material over a network.[26]

If these rules, adopted in the 1970s, were applied rigorously, they would certainly put a damper on most multimedia projects, but it was certainly not the intention of the framers of copyright legislation to prevent innovation. In the 1970s there was no way for legislators to predict the changes over the next twenty years. If copyright restrictions are a problem, it is possible to create a system of passwords to limit access to students enrolled in the class.

For historians, the advances implicit in the information technology revolution are both challenging and intimidating, but they represent the best possibility to climb the learning paradigm plateau. Introduction of a wider variety of visual and audio materials into an informational lecture and the introduction of computer-mediated methods into the history classroom will act as a bridge to more interactive methods.

Notes

1. Kyle L. Peck and Denise Dorricott, "Why Use Technology?," *Educational Leadership* (April 1994), 11–14; Peck and Dorricott believe educational institutions are building information "dirt roads" rather than highways—they are frozen at stage two, where the technology has been introduced but is not effectively used.

2. Alistair Fraser, "The Web, a Classroom *Sans* Walls," *Syllabus* (November/December 1996): 18–20.

3. William W. Brickman and Stanley Lehrer, *Automation, Education, and Human Values* (New York: School and Society Books, 1966), 20. For a similar discussion, see Nancy Stern and Robert Stern, *Computers in Society* (Englewood Cliffs, NJ: Prentice-Hall, 1983), 275–303.

4. For discussions of the research and excellent bibliographies, see Thomas Cyrs, *Essential Skills for College Teaching: An Instructional Systems Approach* (Las Cruces: New Mexico State University Press, 1994); and Robert J. Menges and Maryellen Weimer, *Teaching on Solid Ground: Using Scholarship to Improve Practice* (San Francisco: Josey-Bass, 1996).

5. Wilbert McKeachie, *Teaching Tips: Strategies, Research, and Theory for College and University Teachers* (Lexington, MA: D.C. Heath, 1994), 53–70; and William J. Ekeler, "The Lecture Method," in Keith Prichard and R. McClaren Sawyer, eds., *Handbook of College Teaching: Theory and Applications* (Westport, CT: Greenwood Press, 1994), 85–98.

6. Barbara Gross Davis, *Tools for Teaching* (San Francisco: Jossey-Bass, 1993), 99–146, has some excellent tips for preparing lectures and a review of several studies on student concentration. One study she cites claims student concentration drops considerably after only ten minutes; see also Wilbert J. McKeachie, *Teaching Tips—A Guidebook for the Beginning College Teacher* (Lexington, MA: D.C. Heath, 1969), 36; and Peter J. Frederick, "The Lively Lecture—8 Variations," *College Teaching* 34, no. 2 (Spring 1986): 44.

7. M. Lee Upcraft, "Teaching and Today's College Students," in Robert J. Menges and Maryellen Weimer, *Teaching on Solid Ground: Using Scholarship to Improve Practice* (San Francisco: Jossey-Bass, 1996), 21–41, which analyzes the changes in the

"average" college student over the last three decades and finds that although there have been tremendous changes, the teaching methods—particularly the lecture—have not adapted to meet the new challenges.

8. Robert B. Barr and John Tagg, "From Teaching to Learning—A New Paradigm for Undergraduate Education," *Change* (November/December 1995): 13.

9. Stephen C. Ehrmann, "Asking the Right Questions: What Does Research Tell Us About Technology and Higher Education?" *Change* (March/April 1995): 20–27, is an interesting discussion of the issues related to the new technology. Ehrmann believes the idea of "traditional" is hard to define, and "if you're headed in the wrong direction, technology won't help you get to the right place."

10. Barbara Means and Kerry Olsen, "The Link Between Technology and Authentic Teaching," *Educational Leadership* (April 1994): 15–18; the authors believe that "efforts to introduce technology in schools failed to have profound effects because the attempts were based on the wrong model of teaching with technology."

11. Kenneth Green and Steven Gilbert, "Great Expectations: Content, Communications, Productivity, and the Role of Information Technology in Higher Education," *Change* (March/April 1995): 18.

12. Judith Boettcher, "Technology Classrooms, Teaching, and Tigers," *Syllabus* (October 1995): 10–12.

13. Saul Cornell and Diane Dagefoerde, "Multimedia Presentations: Lecturing in the Age of MTV," *Perspectives* (January 1996): 1, 8–10.

14. Ehrmann, 26.

15. Cyrs, 14–15, and Vicki Hancock and Frank Betts, "From the Lagging Edge to the Leading Edge," *Educational Leadership* (April 1994): 24–29.

16. Kenneth Green, "Instructional Integration and User Support Present Continuing Technology Challenges" in *The Campus Computing Project* (Washington, DC: American Association for Higher Education, 1996). The project did find that there was a slightly higher percentage of formal rewards for efforts in developing instructional technology projects in community colleges and private colleges and universities.

17. *The Campus Computing Project* (1996).

18. Steven W. Gilbert, "Teaching, Learning, and Technology: The Need for Campus-wide Planning and Faculty Support Services," *Change* (March/April 1995): 47–52. Provides an informative and helpful guide to establishing roundtables and other forums to discuss technology and learning issues.

19. Ehrmann, 24.

20. "News, Resources, and Trends," *Syllabus* (January 1997): 8; indicates that Stanford University has developed an "Information Resource Specialist Program" to place consultants in departments to provide "discipline-specific" help to developers. Each specialist is an expert in the specific field as well as technology. For more information, see the Web site at: http://www-leland.stanford.edu/dept/SUL/irs/. Southeast Missouri State University hires students majoring in graphic art and computer science as design teams to assist faculty interested in integrating technology into courses. For more information, see their Web site at: http://economics.semo.edu/cstl.

21. Reza Azarmsa, "Technology-Mediated Presentation in the Classroom," *Syllabus* (January 1997): 10.

22. Fraser, 18.

23. Corel WordPerfect Suite is available to educators for $39.95. Microsoft Office for Windows 97 sells for $159. Earlier versions of PowerPoint can also be viewed through Web browsers by downloading viewers (http://www.microsoft.com/msoffice/mspowerpoint/internet/viewer).

24. Gerald A. Danzer, "Maps, Methods, and Motifs: Cartographic Resources for Teaching History," *Perspectives* (December 1995): 1–5.

25. Joseph M. Kirman, "Teaching Local History Using Customized Photographs," *Social Education* (January 1995): 11–13.

26. Adele Greenberg and Seth Greenberg, *Digital Images: A Practical Guide* (New York: McGraw Hill, 1995), 265–274, and Fred T. Hofstetter, *Multimedia Literacy* (New York: McGraw Hill, 1995), 174–178, are both excellent sources for a further discussion of the issue.

7

Options and Gopherholes
Reconsidering Choice in the Technology-Rich History Classroom

David B. Sicilia

The application of information technology in the history classroom is a controversial subject. And so it should be. It is controversial because it demands both fundamental reconsideration of pedagogical methods and large investments of human and capital resources. Often antagonisms have erupted between those who promote computer and network technologies and those they hope to covert. When the promoters are most aggressive and the uninitiated most recalcitrant, one hears some version of these opposing positions:

Technology Advocate: Newer is better; technology always enhances; this is how we remain current in our rapidly changing world; or—in its most pointed articulation, here quoted from a recent issue of *The Teaching Professor*—"We need to spend time and energy persuading one another that old ways of teaching never were effective, that they are certainly not effective now, and that they positively will not be effective in the future."[1]

The Uninitiated or Skeptical: Newer is not necessarily better; technology sometimes creates more problems than it solves; before I invest a lot of time in this, you must prove to me that it is more effective than traditional teaching methods in its own right, as well as positive from a cost–benefit perspective; or—in its most pointed articulation—this is yet another example of the misguided fascination with high-tech "gimmickry."

A careful consideration of these technologies, however, leads one away from these antipodal positions toward a more complex middle ground. As a first order of business, we should be asking whether information technology (IT)—intensive history instruction—is more effective than traditional methods. It may be, although we need to develop new ways of measuring effectiveness because the teaching/learning process with it is different. Virtually all of the studies are clear on this point: Teaching with technology is not harmful! Then why invest in these approaches? Because some of these modes may prove to be very effective, and if that is true we are obliged as teachers to find out.

Two things seem clear to me in approaching this subject. First, it is a mistake to lump together all technological modes of teaching and learning in terms of desirability and effectiveness. Appropriateness depends on what, where, who, and how many one is trying to teach. In other words, we must consider context, content, and intellectual process. Some technologies are appropriate for small classrooms, others for large lecture settings; still others are useful because they redefine the notion of the classroom itself as a physical place in which people assemble to learn during discrete periods of time. As for content, the fact that history is a humanity or social science rather than a "hard" science dictates a great deal about which technologies are appropriate. Most of us spurn the multiple choice exam and have little or no use for the digital simulation models or sophisticated mathematical applications that are finding wide use in the life sciences. Rather, our stock-in-trade is deductive reasoning, synthesis, and argumentation—modes of thinking that arguably can be nurtured by IT but cannot be automated.

With these constraints in mind, I would like to review a variety of information technologies and discuss some of their key strengths and weaknesses as classroom tools. Then I shall conclude with some more general remarks about the need for what I will deem "guided choice."

Within Four Walls

One result of the growing budgetary pressures in higher education is the burgeoning size of introductory and survey courses. At large public institutions, it is not unusual to find single-class enrollments in the hundreds. In the hope of ameliorating some of the obvious problems inherent in such settings—from alienation to logistics—many administrators are looking to multimedia technology for solutions. At my own institution, the main campus in the University of Maryland system, nearly every one of some forty large lecture halls will be outfitted with a kit of multimedia networking and projection equipment by next year.

A few instructors are experimenting with ways of infusing interactivity into these giant venues, but this is a difficult and expensive option, perhaps at best a goal for the long term. For now, we need to acknowledge that high-enrollment courses will remain essentially *passive* learning environments. Even so, I think that IT can enhance learning significantly in these settings; in fact, my experiences with IT in a range of history classroom settings leads me to conclude that IT in the large lecture class yields the greatest gains for the resources invested.

The instructor's basic tool in the large classroom is presentation software. This tool facilitates the orderly and clear presentation of key points, which together make up the lecture's intellectual spine. Moving beyond words, presentation software easily accommodates enhancements such as digital illustrations, sound, and—with powerful enough hardware—digital moving images. Also, presentation software can be used in tandem with other forms of multimedia (video recordings, video discs, and the like) without difficulty.

To be sure, instructors who employ these kinds of presentations (or productions, if you will) generally find they have imposed on themselves a greater degree of structure. Digression becomes difficult and awkward. On balance, I think this is a good outcome. It helps us deliver all the material that our syllabi promise to deliver. This is especially important in sweeping survey courses such as world history or Western civilization, where a single (albeit interesting) five-minute digression can wipe out an entire civilization!

It is important to note that these rigidities result from the use of the media, not the media itself. Presentations are as malleable as lecture notes. Those who revise lecture notes from one term to the next similarly will revise their presentations, without much extra effort.

Greater structure of lecture material has much larger consequences for students than for instructors. It is important to consider the dynamics of the interaction between lecture slides and the minds and notebooks of students. When presented with a set of concise, orderly, and attractive bullet points, the great majority of students will write down all of them. For some students, this is a great improvement over prior practice (which was to write down little or nothing). The presentation therefore provides an essential baseline for all students.

The bullet points qua notes, however, hardly are the sum total of what the instructor hopes to convey. One must take care, therefore, to communicate to students that bullet points are a minimal starting point rather than an endpoint. There are a couple of ways to communicate this message. One is to state guidelines and expectations *explicitly,* with statements such as, "Your notes should contain much more than what will appear on the screen"; or "These bullets are a starting point"; or "Some of these concepts will not be self-evident; you also need to pay attention to how I discuss and interpret them." The second way to shape the communication process is to *implicitly* convey the message that the slides are a starting point. Keep words on the screen to a minimum, and pace their appearance enough to allow time for listening and thinking. Watch students to see when they are recording on paper and when they are listening. As we all know, in the Information Age, the precious commodity is attention, not information.

On this note, one of the most powerful components of presentation software is its "build" function. By bringing up the bullet points on a slide one-by-one, this function encourages students to record key points at the appropriate places within their notes, rather than writing down the full list at the beginning (and therefore probably missing what the instructor says during the first minute of each slide).

Of course, one of the greatest attributes of the multimedia presentation is its aesthetic appeal. Color slides, sound, illustrations, and moving images are intrinsically interesting. For some critics of IT in the class-room, this is precisely the point. "Why pander to the proclivities of the TV generation?" they say. Insofar as a history professor produced multi-media course material of the same intellectual caliber as commercial television, I agree. Because I have never seen this happen and doubt it will, however, I suspect a form of contamination may take place in the opposite direction; that is, by sharpening the critical facilities of students in multimedia domains, the digital history instructor may raise standards and expectations about the popular culture media, particularly television.

For some subjects, moreover, multimedia is more appropriate than the written word, not only because people think and learn based on disparate media, but also because culture has been preserved in such different artifacts. It would be absurd to teach urban history without maps or history of technology without engineers' diagrams, for example.

Before I conclude with this topic, let me offer a few practical hints for designing multimedia presentations. First, use words, bullets, and slides sparingly. As a general rule, try not to exceed five words per bullet, five bullets per slide, and twenty slides per fifty-minute presentation. Second, sustain a consistent style. Resist the temptation to try every slide background, every method of building bullet points or transitioning from one slide to the next, and so on. This merely creates the impression of incoherence and confusion. Third, rely heavily on others for design and aesthetic judgments. With infinite possibilities available—in color schemes, font types and sizes, backgrounds, and so on—there are infinite ways to create slides that are horrendously ugly and difficult to see. One of the best experts to turn to is the software itself, which typically comes bundled with scores of attractive and functional templates. Fourth, move among media fairly often, but strive for seamlessness. There is ample evidence that a change in mode—from slides to lecture, from lecture to film, from film to words and pictures—helps sustain audience interest, but these transitions can be enormously disruptive if they are not smooth. Finally, have a backup plan.

It seems likely that multimedia instruction in large classrooms affects different student populations in different ways. While it is likely that the best students perform the best in both traditional and multimedia settings, I detect a larger positive impact on the lower-middle and bottom ranks. These students seem to benefit the most from the clarity and appeal of IT instruction. Some who might have earned Ds or Fs now manage to climb into the middling ranks. In that sense, multimedia teaching helps build the academic middle class from the bottom up. Does it therefore foster mediocrity, or proficiency? It depends on one's perspective, which in turn has a lot to do with one's institutional context. For large public institutions—where large classrooms dominate in the first place—improving the performance of marginal students is a laudable goal.

Moreover, introductory and core courses deserve this kind of attention. During their college careers, undergraduates generally experience dramatic improvement in their history offerings. In the first two years—precisely when departments are wooing majors and struggling with the problem of retention—the offerings are the most impersonal and (too often) the least engaging. The latter two years bring smaller courses, specialized offerings, and generally more pleasant experiences. Multimedia instruction can help reverse this neglect and thus enable historians to make a much better first impression.

Beyond Four Walls

Fortunately, large classrooms need not be completely passive environments. One of the least costly ways to bring a degree of interactivity to classrooms of all sizes is through electronic listservs and reflector accounts (a listserv whose owner determines membership). These discussion networks allow students to communicate with classmates—either the entire class or a subset—beyond the physical boundaries of the classroom. This can promote a sense of ongoing engagement that is especially beneficial for students at large institutions, those who commute, and those who work full-time, all of whom may find a virtual discussion community that is available around-the-clock preferable to no community at all.

These electronic nets can be quite useful for making announcements and distributing the work of both students and instructors. Here I will focus on the strengths and weaknesses of listservs and reflectors as discussion media. Most scholars are familiar with the mediated discussion groups operated under the aegis of H-Net. I have found non-mediated discussion groups preferable in both undergraduate and graduate teaching, however. Non-mediated listservs and reflectors are more democratic than mediated ones. They provide another conduit for discussion.

The chief attribute of these networks is that the subset of students who excel in face-to-face class discussions does not correlate neatly with the subset who excel in electronic discussions. A significant number apparently feel more at ease talking to the class through their computer screens than in person. Because learning correlates well with engagement, this is a finding of enormous significance.

There are drawbacks to electronic discussion groups. First, they can easily spin out of control. For some students, a listserv offers yet another opportunity to sound off with a string of declarations and unsupported assertions. Among the topics that have generated the most discussion on my modern United States survey listservs, for example, are prostitution, the decision to drop the bomb, and the impact of immigration on American society. Many of the entries on these "hot" topics were devoid of historical content or perspective. In the case of prostitution, many offered opinions on whether prostitutes were inherently good or bad, without referring to how this debate unfolded during the Progressive Era. Similarly, some considered the decision to drop the atomic bomb strictly in terms of whether they felt the Japanese "deserved it." So, some intervention from the instructor can be useful. I have tried to limit my intervention to this admonition: Strive to include historical content; consider how historical agents viewed these events and issues.

Intervention also can be needed when students "flame," spread misinformation, or otherwise make inappropriate remarks. Still, I have been surprised and impressed at how well peers keep this kind of thing in check. Sexist and racist remarks (whether intentional or inadvertent) often elicit a barrage of responses, which I suspect is much more discouraging of such behavior than words from the instructor. It is good practice to include a brief code of listserv conduct in the course syllabus and to communicate this simple concept: don't say anything on the listserv that you would not also say in person before the whole class and the instructor.

The most important drawback to this medium is administrative. In some institutions, listservs and reflectors are cumbersome to set up and load with student e-mail addresses. More serious is the problem of handling traffic. Even a moderately sized class (say thirty to fifty students) will generate a blizzard of messages if this kind of electronic participation is a component of course requirements. How to track and evaluate this work can be a massively time-consuming duty. For starters, we need better software. Beyond that, we need to reconsider what teachers do—and get rewarded for doing.

There are other ways to extend the boundaries of the history classroom beyond four walls and beyond four hours a week. These include Web-based courses, distant learning, on-line databases and archives, video conferencing, CD-ROMs, and what I will call "star chambers"—that is, technology rich environments that combine all or most of these technologies, such as the two multimillion-dollar teaching theaters on my campus.

Two examples of digital history tools—one a failure, the other quite useful—illustrate the importance of making technology serve methodology rather than the reverse. I begin with the strange tale of the history CD-ROM. One of the very first—and most costly—efforts to bring digital technology to the teaching of history was the development by leading publishers of history compact discs. On the whole, I think the history CD-ROM has been enormously disappointing. The main reason is that—not surprisingly—most publishers set out to create computerized versions of standard textbooks, with the addition of some bells and whistles (that is, sound and motion picture clips). As is common in the history of technology, these early developers fallaciously looked to an older technology (the book) to define the use of a newer one (the book-like CD-ROM). In doing so, they simultaneously underestimated the salience of the book as one of the most powerful learning tools ever invented and underestimated the special capabilities of the CD-ROM, particularly its enormous storage capacity and its hypertext capabilities.

Ironically, I think the CD-ROM is a much more useful historical tool when employed in a much less expensive and elaborate manner—as a portable digital archive. What we need are fewer digital textbooks with marginally useful bells and whistles and more collections of digitally reproduced primary documents. A well-assembled, searchable collection of documents on, say, women in the Progressive Era would offer under-graduates at colleges around the world an opportunity to visit a virtual archive. This archive would be large enough so that professors could assign research papers based on the collection year after year. Primary research on important subjects like this no longer would be the privilege of students in a few regions of the country.

Another tool long under development brings us even closer to the essence of the historians' craft. The "Great American History Machine" (now available on CD-ROM from Academic Information Technology Services at my university) is a massive compilation of county-level data on hundreds of topics throughout American history.[2] With this tool it is possible to create in a few moments a full-color map of the United States showing, for example, the religious affiliation of African-Americans between 1850 and 1890 or the concentration of workers in New England shoemaking in the 1820s. World-wide data is being added as well.

This technology comes the closest to anything that I have seen in emulating the way historians work. The history student begins by learning the general scope of the information available. She or he then poses historical questions, looks for patterns in the results, poses new questions, and so on, and begins to fashion an argument from the patterns. Using this tool can be an exciting, iterative process of historical investigation and problem solving, made possible through historians' close interaction with the evidence.

Reconsidering the Virtues of Choice

I shall conclude on a cautionary note. It is now a widely accepted proposition that new digital hardware and software are transforming the way we teach. In fact, many now argue that IT has made the terms "teacher" and "student" obsolete. The proliferation of digital technology is bringing a new emphasis on collaborative, student-centered learning. Instead of teachers imparting knowledge to students through a largely one-way exchange, students are encouraged to take an active role in shaping both what they will study and how they will study it. As the teaching specialists on my campus like to phrase it, the digital professor should be the "guide on the side," rather than the "sage on the stage."

The reason for the change is choice. Digital technology, by making more and more information available, is giving us more and more choice. And—the argument goes—choice is good, choice is a democratizing force, choice gives us control. This is the central message from our celebrated technologists, from Nicholas Negroponte to Bill Gates. These advocates of a digit-rich existence suggest that more choice will make us shrewder consumers, better informed citizens, and, yes, more highly motivated, life-long learners. To be sure, some point to ancillary problems with the digital revolution, such as the potential for "information over-load." But none seems to have fundamental reservations on the notion that the proliferation of choice, thanks to the proliferation of digital information, will bestow great benefit on society, including higher education.

I see a problem. It stems from my observation that people do not always act—or even know how to act—in their own best interest.

As a starting point to reconsider the virtues of boundless choice, let's consider the world of Bill Gates, as reflected in the home of Bill Gates. Each visitor to Gates' multi-million-dollar, high-tech home is assigned an electronic badge. Before entering the mansion, the visitor chooses a number of preferences, which are then coded into the badge. Then, as the visitor walks through the house, sensors detect the badge and adjust the immediate environment accordingly—by raising or dimming lights, playing certain music selections, even changing the artwork on the five dozen digital wall palates throughout the house. In this way, a customized environment follows the visitor wherever she goes. What other home offers such choices, and such a degree of control?

In his book of autobiography and prognostication, *The Road Ahead,* Gates explains how he endured school by pursuing his own interests and how he now wishes the Web had been around in his school years so that he could have done so even more intently.[3] *The Road Ahead* offers Gates's vision of how technology will transform our lives in a wide variety of areas, including higher education. To be sure, he is uniquely situated to learn of new developments in IT as they unfold; and a large part of his job is to predict the course of the industry's future. In reading the book, however, I was struck by the severe limitations of Gate's vision. There is little sense of context, and he often misuses history. More troubling, Gates exhibits every sign of being a technological determinist. In his view of the past and his scenarios for the future, technology moves ineluctably, following an internal logic; it is not socially constructed, that is, shaped by assumptions and historical momentum, imbued with values, politics, and power. How might Gates have come to understand the relationship between technology and culture in this way? A good liberal arts education.

As we incorporate information technology into the liberal arts curriculum, we are inclined to allow—even encourage—students to submerge themselves in a digital ocean of choice. The trend clearly is away from lockstep learning and toward individualized project work. Will we be able to nurture the intellectual growth of students as they dig one topical gopherhole after the next? What kind of citizens will we get if students pursue narrow interests (as Gates did and wishes he could have done even more)? After all, the purpose of a liberal arts education is to expose students to a broad range of subjects, not only to help them explore a range of interests but also to cultivate well-rounded, broad-thinking citizens.

Matthew Arnold argued that education should convey "the best that has been thought and done in the world."[4] In recent times, deconstructionists have unmasked power relationships within the structure and meanings of texts and empowered readers as makers of meaning. Technology can be a powerful tool for destabilizing hegemonic paradigms and assessing marginalized cultures and perspectives. My intent is not to protect a particular canon against the decentering effects of information technology but rather to warn of the risks in the purely interest-driven, student-defined investigation that information technology seems to enhance. In all of the liberal arts, but especially when exploring the vast terrain of history, students need guided choice rather than boundless choice.

Notes

1. Charles E. Kupchella, "Starting a Dialogue: Technology as a Solution," *The Teaching Professor* 9 (January 1995), 1.

2. American History Machine CD-ROM (College Park, MD: University of Maryland, 1997).

3. Bill Gates, *The Road Ahead* (New York: Viking Press, 1995): 247–252.

4. Matthew Arnold, *Literature and Dogma* (London: Thom Nelson & Sons, 1873), preface.

8

Constructing History with Computers

James A. Jones

Introduction

Although the origin of the 3x5 index card has been lost to history, its impact on professional historians has been profound. Scholars of all but the current generation readily swap accounts of laboriously hand-printing and organizing their collections of 3x5 cards, storing them in their freezers to prevent loss in a fire, and writing dissertation chapters from sets of cards. Perhaps more importantly, the 3x5 card determined how we structured our ideas about history. With its limited surface area and ease of handling, the 3x5 card encouraged the analysis of historical data as discrete morsels of information that we sorted into categories to examine for patterns that explained what happened.

My own foray into dissertation writing examined the social impact of a railroad in West Africa. The primary sources were located in three different countries—France, Mali, and Senegal—and my lack of funding obliged me to alternate sessions of data-collection with periods of labor to finance my research. In between trips, I read from secondary sources in the United States and tried to keep track of what I'd learned and what I still needed to discover.

To organize all of the bits of data as they came in, I resorted to a modified version of 3x5 cards. Instead of producing physical cards, I typed my information into a personal computer and used it to organize my material into virtual index cards, or what I have come to call "electronic notecards." Over time, I streamlined the note-taking process to allow the computer to perform as much of the sorting and labeling as possible. This led me to discover how to use macros, how to export data from one software program to another, and how to organize everything so that I could retrieve it easily.

The Computer Methods Course

In the spring of 1995, I introduced a course called "Computer Methods of Historical Research" at my university. The original goal was to teach students the method that I had devised for organizing a large research project, but we quickly discovered that the course served other purposes as well.

Our research focus that semester was on a local cemetery, chosen because students could reach it on foot and because the cemetery's directors granted us permission to visit the site. After verifying that all of the students in the class possessed some basic word-processing skills, we inspected the cemetery and devised our plan. Each student became responsible for collecting the information from gravestones in part of the cemetery and entering it into the computer in a predetermined order.

Since the cemetery belonged to the Society of Friends, all of the gravestones were uniform and contained exactly the same information— name of the deceased, birth date, and death date.[1] To that, we added information about the location of each grave within the cemetery, using a system of our own to preserve information about family relationships implied by the proximity of graves with like surnames.

After the data on more than one thousand graves was collected and transcribed, I showed the students how to import it into a spreadsheet, use the computer to calculate each person's age at death, compute basic statistical indicators, and construct an age pyramid for the population as a whole. We then used U.S. Census data to obtain national averages against which to compare our findings. We discovered that our population—Quakers from the county seat of Pennsylvania's wealthiest county—had a life expectancy that was considerably higher than that of the nation as a whole, especially in the late nineteenth century. We spent the rest of the course attempting to explain why, and eventually learned about diets, labor conditions, alcohol consumption levels, and medical practices that were prevalent in the United States during the last two centuries. A by-product of our research was the production of a printed index, which we furnished to the directors of the cemetery. They already possessed an index which listed the graves in the order in which they were occupied, but our index, sorted by name, made it easier to respond to inquiries about individual graves.

A year later, I taught the course again, and this time we focused on the county register of death certificates for the years 1893–99. With a larger class and some additional preparation,[2] we managed to construct a database of over 7,100 people that included their gender, marital status, age at death, cause of death, place of death, and other details. Once again, students learned elementary statistical techniques and how to export their data from one program to another, and they also gained experience handling fragile, handwritten documents. From our data, we produced an index that will extend the life of the register by reducing the need to handle the original volume.

To prepare their research papers, students were to find and explain a pattern linking data in two columns in our spreadsheet. For instance, one student examined gender and age at death to write a paper that attempted to explain why males had a shorter life expectancy than females. Another student compared causes of death and place of death to write a paper on mortality in Phoenixville, a steel town with a large immigrant population. The most ambitious paper was a study of errors in the register of death, which incorporated data from the Quaker cemetery study of the first year with data gathered during visits to other cemeteries.

The third offering of this course featured several innovations. First, I created a Web site to deliver data from the previous years to students, thereby eliminating a great deal of diskette handling as well as reducing the risk of spreading a computer virus. Second, instead of allowing students to choose their own research topics, I made them select something related to the history of Riggtown, a neighborhood located near the university. Not only could students walk there, but two lived in the neighborhood and all had friends who lived nearby in off-campus housing.

The Results

After three years, the results have been extremely encouraging on many levels. Students received practical computer training, plus "hands-on" experience in the conduct of original historical research. Moreover, since they were guided in the selection of their research topics and we held weekly meetings to discuss our progress, our research became truly collaborative and not just a collection of individual papers.

Within my department, there has been growing acceptance of the value of the course, as my colleagues have been forced to rely on computers for advising and office communications. Colleagues who work closely with public school teachers have become my strongest supporters. Faculty in other departments—notably urban affairs and geography—have found our data useful, and university administrators have encouraged the expansion of this course.

The most exciting results have occurred in the community. After some initial inquiries, a number of people offered to serve as subjects for interviews by my students. Others loaned me pictures and objects from the past, and more than one hundred current and former residents of Riggtown attended a public lecture where I presented the results of our research. I received an invitation to serve on the borough's bicentennial celebration committee, and a member of the borough council has indicated her desire to support publication of our work. This summer, current and former residents of the neighborhood will gather at the local baseball diamond—now a city park—for the first Riggtown reunion since World War II.

Is This Good History?

On most of the levels that matter to me as an educator and borough resident, this project has been a success. However, as a professional historian, I still have to ask," Is this really good history, or are we merely cataloging facts?" Even worse, is there a possibility that we have introduced distortions by treating history as the sum of discrete facts rather than the result of continuous processes?[3]

This question is not new. In the nineteenth century, Leopold von Ranke admonished historians to show history as it actually occurred *(wie es eigentlich gewesen)*. That led generations of historians to treat facts derived from original documents as the only basis from which to write "objective" history. This new "objectivity" combined with Hegelian determinism to produce new historical approaches like positivism and Marxism.[4] By the twentieth century, the objectivity of history based on facts came under fire, as scholars examined how facts and documents were produced, and how they were used by historians. For example, various interpretations of the French Revolution have been linked to the political views of their authors,[5] and later interpretations were clearly influenced by the outcome of the Russian Revolution.[6]

History consists not only of facts, but also of conscious decisions about which facts are relevant. For example, many people crossed the Rubicon River, and each crossing produced a fact. Only one crossing—that by Julius Caesar—has been elevated to the status of historical fact, thanks to historians who employed it to compose theories about the evolution of the Roman Empire.[7]

Using the computer, we greatly increase the number of facts at our disposal by making them easy to record and retrieve. By sorting our facts into categories, we construct a framework within which to seek patterns in our facts. From those patterns, we generate questions that suggest the need for new categories, and in that way, our project grows and leads us in new directions.

For example, my research on local history yielded an 1893 newspaper clipping that referred to some people who "scavenged coal lumps at night using lanterns, from around the locomotive turntable located at Chestnut and North Matlack Streets. They were tempted by the regular coal pile nearby, but railway guards kept them away."[8] I found this during my original search for information about the railroad and treated it as evidence of poverty in the adjacent neighborhood, so I placed it in two categories, "railroad" and "poverty." As my research progressed, I realized that coal scavenging was not normal behavior and added the notecard to the category of "effects of economic depression." It could also be filed under "law and order," because of the reference to railway guards, and if my study of the railroad ever moves forward, the same fact will appear in categories dealing with "railroad operations," "railroad equipment," and "public perception of the railroad."

Conclusion

The act of identifying categories leads directly to the construction of historical hypotheses, and hypotheses prompt us to seek additional facts. The result is a dynamic exchange between research and theory. If biases appear in the results of this process, it is not the computer that creates them. They are the product, as always, of limitations in the sources and in the imagination of the historian. Incorporating electronic technology can indeed produce good history.

Notes

1. Article V in "Constitution of the Friends Burial Society" (17 August 1871), in Chester County, Pennsylvania Archives, *Corporation Book* 1, 372–374.

2. For instance, I placed my laptop computer at the archives, so that students could enter their data directly into a computer, instead of copying it by hand and transcribing it at home.

3. The literature is still limited, but two authors have addressed the question directly. Janice Reiff and Daniel Greenstein consider computers to be useful for organizing data,

but only Reiff thinks that sorting and comparing data leads to useful insights. Janice L. Reiff, *Structuring the Past: The Use of Computers in History* (Washington, DC: American Historical Association, 1991), 29; Daniel L. Greenstein, *A Historian's Guide to Computing* (Oxford: Oxford University Press, 1994), 106–108.

4. Edward Hallett Carr, *What Is History?* (New York: Vintage Books, 1961), 5–6.

5. See the introduction to William Doyle, *Origins of the French Revolution,* 2nd edition (Oxford: Oxford University Press, 1988).

6. Carr, *What Is History?,* 28–29.

7. Ibid., 9.

8. *Daily Local News* (West Chester, PA), November 11, 1893.

9

Tom Swift Jr. Meets Clio

Reflections on Teaching Freshman History in a Mobile-Computing Environment

John D. Thomas

In 1954 Grosset and Dunlap published *Tom Swift and His Flying Lab,* the first of what became a series of thirty-three adventure stories featuring the estimable boy scientist, Tom Swift Jr. The series was conceived by Harriet Stratemeyer Adams, the daughter of Edward L. Stratemeyer, who, as the creator of the Bobbsey Twins, Tom Swift (Sr.), the Hardy Boys, and similar series, had all but invented modern juvenile pulp fiction earlier in the century. The Tom Swift Jr. books were very much a recasting of the genre for the baby boom generation: the series' warm embrace of postwar science and technology was calculated to appeal to children whose interests were being shaped by the angst and optimism that so characterized the 1950s and early 1960s. In chapter one of *The Flying Lab,* for instance, Tom happily explains the high-tech features of his atomic-powered airplane to an admiring visitor; a suspicious, clue-laden missile crash-lands in his research compound; and someone tampers with the Swifts' sensitive radar equipment. Tom Swift Jr. is in his element.[1]

Science and technology may have been Tom's metiers, but they weren't mine. As a child I had little interest in them. Being stuck with a Tom Swift Jr. book to occupy me on a rainy Sunday afternoon was my definition of privation. The truth is, I was a history kid, more interested in reading adventures about where we thought we'd been than where we thought we were going. If I'd been asked to celebrate a popular-culture icon, I'd have chosen the beginning, also in 1954, of Walt Disney's Davy Crockett phenomenon,[2] which for the next ten years or so helped to blaze a trail of romantic frontier adventure I eagerly followed. Clio, the muse of history, has introduced me to more reliable historical guides than

89

Disney in the decades since my childhood, but the course I've traveled was fixed those many years before. Tom Swift Jr. could have the future; I wanted the past.

The introduction of notebook computers to my history classroom at Acadia University has caused me to reassess my neat dichotomy. Having grappled with the complexities of a "notebooked environment" during the past year, I now have more than a grudging admiration for Tom's ability to glide from crisis to crisis, for his unbounded competence with technology, for his cheerful willingness to embrace change, and for his conviction, more often implied than stated, that the course he has embarked upon is indeed noble, just, and true. Can I, who have followed Clio's call for these many years, learn from Tom Swift Jr.?

This article reviews the introduction of mobile-computing technology to Acadia University and discusses its impact on a freshman history class. It is based on the observations of the instructor and the results of four surveys students completed during the year.[3] Historians have concluded that microcomputers can make significant contributions to the teaching and learning of history. They note that computers facilitate the development and presentation of census material, historical simulations, and supplemental instructional resources.[4] Can the use of notebook computers in a mobile-computing environment make a particular contribution to the teaching and learning of history? The answer is yes. As the experience of History 1306A0 attests, the introduction of this technology encouraged the development of an increasingly student-centered, active-learning curriculum by facilitating the birth of what came to be known as the studio class. As well as attending weekly lectures and tutorials, students participated in studio classes, working directly with primary sources through the medium of document-analysis and historical-simulation exercises. Notebook-computer technology facilitated not only the design and presentation of these exercises but also their monitoring and evaluation. The result was an enriched teaching and learning experience.

The Acadia Advantage

Acadia University is a small, predominately undergraduate, liberal arts university located in the town of Wolfville, Nova Scotia. Established as Horton Academy by the Baptist Educational Society of Nova Scotia in 1828, the school received a charter as Acadia College in 1841 and became a university in 1891. In 1966, when the United Baptist Convention of

Atlantic Canada relinquished control of Acadia, it became a publicly funded institution. Like other such institutions during the past decade, Acadia has weathered cutbacks in public support and increases in student tuition. In 1996–97, Acadia's 3,500 undergraduate students paid a base tuition of $3,670 (Canadian). International students paid an additional fee of $3,535, and all students enrolled in The Acadia Advantage paid a surcharge of $1,200.[5] In 1997–98, less than 50 percent of the university's budget is expected to come from provincial and federal sources.[6]

The "Acadia Advantage" is an academic program that integrates mobile computing into the undergraduate curriculum, supported with an $11,375,000 Mobile Computing and Enriched Teaching Fund. The university launched AA, as it is more commonly know, in 1996. In September of that year, 365 business, physics, computer science, and arts students, approximately one-third of the freshman class, received notebook computers issued by the university and enrolled in courses designed for their use. In September 1997, all freshmen will be required to register as AA students, and by September 2000, the entire undergraduate student body will be part of the program. The AA tuition surcharge meets the costs to the program of the student notebooks and accompanying software. The Mobile Computing and Enriched Teaching Fund is part of a larger long-term development campaign that targets governments, corporations, foundations, and individuals for support. The Fund provides financing for faculty computer hardware, software, and training; the establishment of a user support center; the creation of a teaching support center; the installation of an advanced computer network infrastructure; and the wiring of all classroom desks, residence rooms, offices, and campus common areas.

The genesis of AA lay in the late 1980s, when Acadia's administrators recognized that the decline in public funding would eventually leave the university without the ability to satisfy the growing demand for information and information technology. In 1988, at the request of the university, the university librarian and the director of the Computer Centre undertook a joint administrative leave to investigate the question of information access. Basing their conclusions in part on the experience of institutions in the United Kingdom, the United States, and Canada, they produced a report subsequently endorsed by the Senate and Board of Governors in 1991, "The Global Library: Strategies for Managing Information Technology at Acadia University." During the years to follow, the university moved on many of the recommendations of the report. Acknowledging that one of its key functions was to provide electronic access to resources around the globe, the university assigned the task of supervising the development of action plans for information-technology applications to the University Planning Committee. On the advice of an external review of the computer facilities, the university also established an Information Resources Advisory Committee to act as a consultative body. The most visible results of these initiatives included the introduction of computer-assisted teaching strategies in several disciplines and the provision of a number of new or improved services, among them the expansion of computer laboratories for students, the upgrading of computer hardware and software for faculty, the fiber-optic wiring of many major buildings on campus, and the installation of data drops in several classrooms and a student dormitory.

By 1995, the growing capabilities of electronic-classroom and mobile-computing technology suggested a particular focus for the Acadia initiatives: the creation of a campus-wide networked environment in which students and faculty would have access to the university computing system and the Internet from their preferred locations. Key to the environment would be the adoption of a standard mobile computer. In September 1995, Kelvin K. Ogilvie, the President of Acadia, and a leading proponent of the initiatives, established the Acadia Advantage Committee, composed of representatives from across the campus. The task of the committee, which took its name from the ten-year development campaign the university would soon launch, was to investigate the concept and bring forward recommendations that could be put before the university community. During the several months to follow, committee members visited the University of Minnesota, Crookston, which had become a mobile-computing campus, Wake Forest University, which was in the process of launching a mobile-computing program, and IBM's academic support and courseware development center in North Carolina. Recognizing that the costs of creating a mobile-computing environment would be considerable to Acadia, but also recognizing that corporations would find it advantageous to play a role in the development of the first such environment in Canada, the university also investigated the possibility of forming industry partnerships with interested parties. By the beginning of the new year, the Acadia Advantage Committee was ready to take its proposal to the university.

In March of 1996, following its passage through the university decision-making process, The Acadia Advantage was born. Under the direction of a project manager and an Acadia Advantage Implementation Team, the university prepared special materials for prospective students, developed a support program for "first wave" faculty who would be teaching AA courses beginning in September, established the Acadia Institute for Teaching and Technology, playfully known as The Sandbox, and instituted a User Support Centre. Three industry partners, IBM Canada, MT&T, and the Marriott Corporation, Canada, entered the program in supporting roles, and the university undertook to further upgrade its computing system. The task included providing the remaining unwired dormitory rooms and key locations on campus with data drops, constructing six fully wired electronic classrooms, and more generally developing an electronic infrastructure capable of supporting an integrated information technology network and high-speed link to the rest of the world.[7]

Perhaps the most important construction the university undertook in the weeks and months following the launch of The Acadia Advantage, however, was in the realm of argument: in particular, prospective students and their parents had to be persuaded that Acadia had indeed embarked on the right course of action. Three interrelated arguments in support of the program found expression in AA speeches and promotional literature and on the university Web site. The first argument emphasized the cost efficiencies that would follow the implementation of a coordinated and focused plan such as AA. It acknowledged the inequality of access to information students currently faced, noted the high cost of computer hardware, software, and their rapid obsolescence, and hinted at the affordability of the AA tuition surcharge in light of these factors.[8] The second argument addressed the very practical issue of computer literacy. "It has been predicted that by the year 2000, 95 percent of all jobs in Canada will likely require enhanced computer proficiency," the university informed prospective students. "We want you to be competitive in this new and changing marketplace . . . [by using] today's technology and develop[ing] the advanced analytical skills you will need to adapt to ever-changing study/work environments."[9] The final argument, and the crux of the university's appeal, focused on the role of The Acadia Advantage in helping the university provide an enriched liberal education. Under the impress of the program, the university library would become the "library of the world" and notebook computers the tools to facilitate learning inside and outside the classroom. Acadia, in sum, would "provide leadership as a national centre for the application of information technology to undergraduate education."[10] Three hundred and sixty-five students seem to have agreed. Following the Labor Day Acadia Advantage kick-off, the students received the IBM ThinkPad computers they would call their own until the close of the academic year, spent several days in introductory training, and began their AA classes.[11]

The Acadia Advantage History Course

The Department of History designated History 1306A0, a two-semester, full-year survey of Canadian history, as its Acadia Advantage offering. The class of twenty-three students in the first semester and twenty-two in the second semester met in a raised lecture style, fifty-seat "smart" classroom that offered full access to the university computing system and the Internet. Students sat in ergonomically-designed chairs at tables that ran the width of the classroom. Each table was equipped with electrical outlets and technology access ports (TAPs) placed at one-meter intervals. The instructor used a podium at the left front of the classroom that included a TAP, a notebook computer port and monitor, a TAP for a second notebook computer, and controls for a digital projector which broadcast images and stereo sound from the podium-based notebooks and video cassette tape unit on a 3x3 meter screen and speaker unit located at the front of the classroom. The classroom was also equipped with blackboards and an overhead projector and screen, and a telephone link to the User Support Centre.

Students and the instructor used IBM ThinkPad 365 ED notebook computers. They were equipped with a 586C 100/33 MHz 3.3 volt processor (Pentium equivalent); 10.4" VGA DSTN Display with 1 Mb VRAM and 256 color support; PC2 compliant integrated 16-bit audio with Sound Blaster Pro support and MIDI compatibility, internal microphone and speaker, external audio jacks, and MIDI/Joystick port; 2 Type II or 1 Type III PCMCIA Slot; Built-in infrared allowing users to transfer files, synchronize files, or print documents to other IrDA-equipped notebooks, desktops, PC Organizers, and printers; TrackPoint III integrated pointing device; full-size 85-key keyboard; 12 Mb RAM; 540 Mb Hard Drive; Quad Speed CD-ROM (internal); IBM Home and Away Credit Card (dual function Ethernet/14.4 modem); external floppy disk drive. Software included: Windows 95; CRT terminal emulatorm (telnet); NewsXpress news reader; Pegasus Mail; Netscape; WS FT32 (FTP client); Microsoft Office Pro (Word, Excel, Access, PowerPoint, etc.);

HTML Assistant Pro.[12] During the first week of class students purchased a copy of Norton Textra Connect, a word-processing program that allowed them to work independently or collaboratively on assignments posted to them by the instructor and to submit the assignments for comment and evaluation. The instructor's copy of Textra Connect included a marking menu and options for organizing student group work. With the exception of the mid-terms, the examinations, and the initial report in the first term, students were encouraged, but not required, to submit all of their written work through Norton Textra Connect, some twenty-four assignments in all by the end of the course.

History 1306A0 is a requisite for students majoring in history, and one of three sections of the introductory Canadian survey course offered by the department. Although the sections do not share common assignments or examinations, they are governed by common teaching objectives. Students should learn to understand the relevance and intrinsic merit of acquired knowledge; identify and address problems of historical significance; acquire critical reading and thinking skills; develop clear oral and written expression; clarify the values at work in specific historical contexts; and develop an interest in life-long learning. These objectives seem to be appropriate for Acadia freshmen and, perhaps, for most Canadian first-year students. Available evidence suggests that in terms of high school academic achievement, Acadia freshmen are broadly representative of other freshmen across the country.[13]

For these reasons the instructor was particularly interested in a curriculum that stressed skills development, particularly critical reading and writing skills, and oral presentation skills. The relatively small number of students in the class made this focus possible. Each semester, students were required to deliver a seven-minute oral presentation on a course reading and illustrate their presentation with PowerPoint slides; write essay-form mid-term tests and examinations; complete a minimum of two written reports on the course readings; and submit several short assignments individually or as part of a group. During the first semester students completed seven such short assignments. With the exception of the first, which introduced them to Norton Textra Connect, and an assignment near the end of the semester, which tested their mastery of several course readings, the short assignments asked students to answer questions on a document relevant to the course of study and to submit their analysis via Norton Textra Connect at the end of class. For instance, students analyzed a story from an 1840s *Every Boy's Own Book* to understand the nature of conservatism in mid-nineteenth century British North America, and they examined an engraving from an Ontario county atlas published in the 1870s to understand settlement patterns, persistence, and land use in rural Canada.

The competence with which these document-analysis exercises were conducted encouraged the instructor to make significant changes to the curriculum and methods of instruction at the end of the first semester. The least apparent change to the students was the increased complexity of the major written assignments, beginning with the second report. In past years these assignments had required students to write a thesis statement, precis, and critique for each of two articles on a controversial issue in Canadian history. Increased exposure to the students' writing made possible by its electronic submission via Norton Textra Connect persuaded the instructor that the students could handle three-article assignments, and this became the standard load for the major written assignments in the second semester. For obvious reasons, the instructor chose not to tell the students in so many words that more was being expected of them than of students in past years.

More obvious to the students were the changes in the classroom. The class met Monday, Wednesday, and Friday in an hour-long time slot, 8:30–9:30 A.M. During the first semester, the instructor lectured on Monday and Wednesday, using PowerPoint and CD-ROM presentations, overhead transparencies, and video recordings to illustrate the lectures. The final class hour on Friday was a tutorial focusing on the student-centered activities of the course: the student presentations, the reading discussions, and the document-analysis work. In essence the two-hour lecture/one-hour tutorial division was the same teaching format the instructor had used with introductory classes of a similar size in past years. The generally high quality of document-analysis work, the ease with which the instructor could evaluate the assignments, and the feeling that the Friday tutorial was much too short to accomplish its objectives, however, suggested the need for change. The results of the class survey the students completed in December confirmed the need. As Table 9.5 shows, most of the students in the December survey reported being pleased or very pleased with the document-analysis work they were performing in class. As Table 9.10 shows, however, a majority also reported that they should be using their notebooks "more" or "much more" in class than was presently the case. These elements combined to suggest the need to further refine and develop a computer-assisted strategy that was coming to be known at Acadia as studio teaching.

Studio Teaching

Although "studio teaching" may be a new term, it gives expression to methods of instruction as old as teaching itself. It can be defined as the creation of a workshop or laboratory environment in which students work with the raw materials of their discipline under the close supervision of the instructor. Notebook computers and supporting software and hardware can make significant contributions to this form of learning. Presently, two streams of studio teaching are evident at Acadia. Physics, for instance, has instituted an introductory course section built entirely on the concept, while other disciplines, including history, offer course sections with a studio component. In History 1306A0, the refinement of the studio teaching concept required changes to the weekly class schedule and the in-class methods of instruction. While the Monday and Friday classes continued much as they had in the first semester, the Wednesday class underwent significant modification. Beginning in the last week of the first semester and continuing throughout the second semester of the course, the instructor lectured in the Monday class, the Wednesday class became the studio class, and the Friday class remained a tutorial devoted to student presentations and the discussion of course readings. As Table 9.6 shows, the December survey indicated a high level of student satisfaction with the first-semester group work, so for the Wednesday studio class the instructor assigned students to permanent two-person or three-person studio groups based primarily on the first-semester groupings and on student performances generally: whenever possible, students who seemed to be working well together were left together; when first-semester groups had to be reduced in size or when students requested a change, the instructor assigned students working at the same level to the new studio groups.

Twelve assignments lay at the core of studio class curriculum. They included three skills-development tasks, three role-playing activities, and seven document-analysis exercises. The skills-development tasks focused on three problems the instructor had identified in the first semester: students' unfamiliarity with the university library; their reluctance to use their notebooks for note taking in the classroom and for note taking on the course readings; and their need to develop an analytical approach to the Internet. The first such task sought to familiarize students with the basic features of the library by posing a series of questions keyed to their surnames and answerable by accessing the university computer cataloguing system and by visiting the library reference and reserve sections.

Although the students worked on this assignment in groups, they submitted their work individually via Norton Textra Connect.

The second skills-development task sought to improve students' computer note-taking abilities by asking them to submit a description of their techniques via Norton Textra Connect and to enter into a dialogue by commenting on the techniques of the other members of their group. As Table 9.4 shows, student use of Norton Textra Connect to submit their work grew appreciably between December and April. So, too, as Table 9.2 shows, student use of notebooks for note-taking in class also grew considerably during the year. As Table 9.3 demonstrates, however, the aversion to using computers for note taking out of the class remained, although students were more interested in the practice in April than they had been in December. The non-Acadia Advantage history students surveyed showed even less interest in the practice.

The final skills-development task sought to help students develop the capacity to evaluate Web sites critically by asking each group to test a Web site evaluation form and assess "The Great Chicago Fire and the Web of Memory" Web site. Groups concluded that the simpler the Web site and the evaluation forms were to use, the more useful they were to them.[14]

The studio class role-playing activities included one Norton Textra Connect on-line discussion and simulation, and two classroom simulations. The former, a discussion of three interpretations of the evacuation of Japanese Canadians in 1942, asked students to evaluate the readings and then to assume the voice of a wartime federal cabinet minister and argue a course of action of the students' choosing. Because the students were preparing papers on the issue, but perhaps also because many of them had completed similar on-line discussions in their English courses and had learned to support their opinions with specific reference to the readings, the level of discussion was high. The two classroom simulations may have lacked the polish of the on-line simulation, but they certainly made up for it in energy. In the first simulation, groups took on the roles of government, official opposition party, minority opposition party, department of defense, department of external affairs, and the department of finance at the outbreak of the Korean War. The purpose of the simulation was to give students a sense of the many and varied domestic and international political considerations that go into policymaking in times of crisis. The second simulation asked each group to take on the role of a United Nations human rights research team and write a memorandum on the Canadian Multiculturalism Act, 1988, dividing the memorandum into three sections: the historical background to the passage of the Act; the contents of the Act; and an analysis of the Act, accompanied by recommendations to the UN secretary general. The purpose of this simulation was to develop the students' analytical skills and to help them learn to recognize the relevance of historical knowledge to policymakers, as well as to understand the nature of official multiculturalism in Canada.

Finally, a series of six document-analysis exercises, known collectively as the "Today and Yesterday" series, comprised the largest component of the studio class curriculum. Student role-playing was also a feature of these exercises. The initial assignment informed students that they had embarked on a writing and publishing career, concentrating on Canadian history. The first task of each group was to create a corporate name and logo and prepare a newspaper vignette on a turn-of-the-century issue, using an image and document from Canadisk, a CD-ROM collection of historical images and documents available on the Internet.[15] The newspaper vignette they prepared should educate readers about the historical issue and comment informatively and imaginatively on its relevance today. For that reason, "Today and Yesterday" became the title of the series of newspaper vignette subjects the instructor prepared for the class, each vignette subject drawing on a curriculum issue and commenting on its relevance in contemporary Canada. During the weeks to follow, students completed vignettes on "The Maple Leaf Forever," Canada's first national anthem and a poignant illumination of late Victorian jingoism; a letter home from a soldier in Flanders, an excellent illustration of early twentieth century family roles and the construction of gender; the landscape paintings of the Group of Seven, a quintessential example of the birth of a national school of art; the manifesto of the League for Social Reconstruction, which neatly summarizes the causes of the Great Depression and foreshadows the coming welfare state; and a 1958 "Northern Vision" election speech of Prime Minister John Diefenbaker, a document as indicative of postwar optimism about the economic potential of the north as it is mute on the environmental and human costs of northern development.

Like the other components of the studio class, the "Today and Yesterday" exercises could have been taught in a conventional classroom, but the studio classroom made the exercises considerably easier to deliver, monitor, and evaluate. Typically, the instructor prepared an exercise the afternoon before class, checking the veracity of Web sites students would have to visit, "cutting and pasting" the required images and documents, composing the instructions, and posting the exercises via Norton Textra Connect. At the beginning of the studio class the next day, the instructor informed students of any resources they would need to bring to future studio classes, screened particularly good examples of group work from the previous studio class, and introduced the current exercise. As the groups worked on the assignment, the instructor had the option of monitoring their progress via his notebook computer from the console at the front of the class, or of visiting the groups and discussing the assignment in person. Needless to say, the latter option was the more effective form of intervention. At the end of the class the students acting as secretaries of their respective groups posted the completed exercise. The instructor then critiqued and returned the exercises before the following studio class, and the cycle began anew.

From the instructor's perspective, the studio classroom work of both semesters, but particularly the second semester "Today and Yesterday" series, was the most dynamic component of the course. By working in a studio environment on documents that illustrated particular historical issues and possibly shed light on contemporary issues, students became historians. They examined the raw materials of the discipline, they formed conclusions based on their primary research, and they reported the results to their colleagues and to the instructor. On occasion they were called upon to defend those results in class. It was one of the most stimulating teaching experiences of the instructor's career.

Students were more reserved in their judgment, but nonetheless positive about the studio class experience. As Tables 9.5 and 9.6 show, respectively, the level of student satisfaction with document-analysis work and group work remained high in the second term. Open-ended comments on the departmental history course evaluation in answer to the questions "what are the best features and worst features of the course?" are more revealing. While eleven student comments can be interpreted as endorsements of the studio work, lauding it explicitly or commending the intensive use of notebooks in the classroom, another six are critical, in particular questioning the relevance of the document-analysis work to the rest of the course, and noting the difficulty of completing assignments in a one-hour time slot. To complicate the analysis, four students contributed answers to both questions. Clearly, the instructor will want to take these issues into consideration when he plans the curriculum and teaching strategies of future notebook courses.

Acadia Advantage Results

What does computer-assisted learning in a mobile-computing environment offer students? Table 9.1 suggests that AA student satisfaction with computers increased as the year progressed, although the number of students reporting in the very top category declined in the April survey. AA students also reported a higher level of satisfaction with computers in both surveys than did the non-AA history students surveyed. Tables 9.7, 9.8, and 9.9 suggest, respectively, that the majority of AA students want to take as many AA courses as they can in their sophomore year, that most look forward to using computers intensively when they graduate, and that the degree of satisfaction with the AA program increased between the December and April surveys. Clearly, for students in the social sciences and humanities, programs like The Acadia Advantage would have to be invented if they didn't already exist.

Does enrollment in Acadia Advantage translate into higher academic achievement for students? The absence of common measures among AA and non-AA sections in History 1306 make this an impossible question to answer. What can be said is that the AA section recorded a median grade of B–, while past sections of the course taught by the instructor recorded four medians of C+ and one B–. Several studies in other disciplines at Acadia, including psychology, anthropology, and physics, offer better evidence. A psychology honors thesis investigated the use of notebook computers in introductory psychology and anthropology courses, focusing on the length of time students took to begin using notebook computers as study aids in an effective manner. In the psychology course, AA students and non-AA students scored similarly on the first test, while the non-AA students scored better on the second test. The thesis suggested that the need to learn how to use notebook computers disrupted the productivity of the AA students. On the third and fourth tests the AA students improved their scores. In the anthropology course, AA students and non-AA students scored similarly on the first test, while the final course marks favored the AA students. The thesis concluded that instruction in the use of notebook computers impeded the instructor's ability to cover course material initially because of the time required to provide support and instruction in the use of notebook computers. "Study results showed that ThinkPads should probably be understood first as an application before they are used as a study tool."[16] Even broader research has been conducted in physics. Preliminary test results indicate that the performance of AA students was "better than the lecture section in all areas. This may be due to one or a combination of factors: the teaching methodology, the background preparation of the students, the differences in class size, and the use of technology."[17]

What does computer-assisted teaching in a "notebooked environment" offer instructors? To be sure, it is a major investment in time and requires considerable organizational skills. Unless instructors are technological wizards, or hopeful of sanctification, they should attempt no more than one new course preparation a semester. They should count absolutely on technological glitches and the embarrassment they cause. Every effort must be made to ensure that in-class exercises can be completed in the time allowed them; that documents and simulations illuminate the major themes of the course; and that students not become fatigued by group work. Not the least of instructors' concerns is the constant introduction of new technology into the teaching and learning environment on the one hand, and the reluctance or inability of publishers to produce useful software on the other. Instructors will suffer considerable stress in this environment, and they will be expected to counsel similarly afflicted students. At times instructors will ask: "Who will heal the healer?"

By the same token, instructors who embark on teaching in a mobile-computing environment will find it a stimulating and rewarding one. True, very few of the teaching strategies this instructor followed required notebook computers, but the work of the course was conducted more efficiently and effectively because of them. The notebooks, together with the small size of the class, enabled the instructor to establish a balance between instructor-centered "passive" learning and student-centered "active" learning. Students learned history by listening, but they also learned history by doing. The balance is important.[18]

How can we help students read, write, and think critically? How can we reveal to them the excitement and relevance of historical study? A "notebooked environment" can help us do it. Writing in 1987 on the question of computer-aided instruction, Richard C. Rohrs concluded that "Exposure to interdisciplinary research, problem solving, and modern technology should enhance . . . [students'] training as historians, make their skills more marketable, and better enable them to cope in modern society."[19] A decade later, the development of mobile-computing technology makes those aims more easily attainable than Rohrs might have imagined. Tom Swift Jr., it turns out, is not such a bad role model after all.

Table 9.1

Student Satisfaction With Computers Expressed in Percentages

	AA students: December survey	AA students: April survey	Non-AA students: February survey
Very pleased	22	9	12
Pleased	43	45	28
Satisfied	30	45	56
Unsatisfied	4	0	4
No. of students	23	22	25

Question asked of Acadia Advantage (AA) students: I'm [unsatisfied, satisfied, pleased, very pleased] with my notebook computer.

Question asked of Non-AA students: I'm [unsatisfied, satisfied, pleased, very pleased] with my/the Acadia computers. Percentages have been rounded.

Table 9.2

AA Student Classroom Notebook Use Expressed in Percentages

	AA students: December survey	AA students: April survey
Almost always	26	55
Often	9	23
Sometimes	13	14
Never	52	9
No. of students	23	22

Question asked of students: I [never, sometimes, often, almost always] use my notebook for making notes in class for History 1306. Percentages have been rounded.

Table 9.3

Student Notebook Use Outside Class Expressed in Percentages

	AA students: December survey	AA students: April survey	Non-AA students: February survey
Almost always	4	14	4
Often	9	18	8
Sometimes	30	36	35
Never	57	32	54
No. of students	23	22	26

Question asked of students: I [never, sometimes, often, almost always] use my notebook for making notes outside of class on my History 1306 readings. Percentages have been rounded.

Table 9.4

AA Student Submission of Written Work via Connect Expressed in Percentages

	AA students: December survey	AA students: April survey
Almost always	57	77
Often	30	14
Sometimes	4	9
Never	9	0
No. of students	23	22

Question asked of students: When given the option, I [never, sometimes, often, almost always] use Norton Textra Connect for submitting written work for History 1306. Percentages have been rounded.

Table 9.5

AA Student Satisfaction With Document Analysis Work Expressed in Percentages

	AA students: December survey	AA students: April survey
Very pleased	17	5
Pleased	43	59
Satisfied	30	36
Unsatisfied	9	0
No. of students	23	22

Question asked of students: I am [unsatisfied, satisfied, pleased, very pleased] with the Web site and document analysis work we do in History 1306. Percentages have been rounded.

Table 9.6

AA Student Satisfaction With Group Expressed in Percentages

	AA students: December survey	AA students: April survey
Very pleased	26	27
Pleased	48	36
Satisfied	17	32
Unsatisfied	7	5
No. of students	23	22

Question asked of students: I am [unsatisfied, satisfied, pleased, very pleased] with the group I'm in for document analysis in History 1306. Percentages have been rounded.

Table 9.7

AA Student Demand for AA Courses Expressed in Percentages

	AA students: December survey	AA students: April survey
Almost always	43	64
Often	39	5
Sometimes	9	14
Never	9	14
No. of students	23	22

Question asked of students: I [never, sometimes, often, almost always] want my second year courses to be AA courses. Percentages have been rounded.

Table 9.8

Student Desired Use of Computers After Graduation Expressed in Percentages

	AA students: December survey	AA students: April survey	Non-AA students: February survey
Almost always	43	27	23
Often	43	59	46
Sometimes	13	14	31
Never	0	0	0
No. of students	23	22	26

Question asked of students: After I graduate and begin a career or continue in school, I [never, sometimes, often, almost always] want to be using computers. Percentages have been rounded.

Table 9.9

AA Student Satisfaction With AA Expressed in Percentages

	AA students: December survey	AA students: April survey
Very pleased	13	9
Pleased	39	55
Satisfied	48	23
Unsatisfied	0	14
No. of students	23	22

Question asked of students: All in all, I am [unsatisfied, satisfied, pleased, very pleased] with Acadia Advantage. Percentages have been rounded.

Table 9.10

Student Perceived Use of Computers in the Course Expressed in Percentages

	AA students: December survey	AA students: April survey	Non-AA students: February survey
Much more	17	5	0
More	48	36	44
About the same	35	59	56
Less	0	0	0
No. of students	23	22	25

Question asked of AA students: I should be using the notebook [less, about the same, more, much more] in History 1306 than I do.

Question asked of Non-AA students: I should be using a computer [less, about the same, more, much more] for History 1306 than I do. Percentages have been rounded.

Notes

I would like to thank my colleagues Doug Baldwin and Kathleen Burke for permitting me to conduct a survey in their sections of History 1306 so that I could develop comparative tables. Pat MacNutt contributed her word-processing skills at a critical time. Bruce Cohoon, Director of the Office of Public Affairs at Acadia, kindly shared the contents of his filing cabinet with me so that I could better understand the history of "The Acadia Advantage." Tom Regan, Dean of Arts, and Maurice Tugwell, Acting Vice President (Academic), provided travel funds, making it possible for me to attend the symposium for which the initial draft of this article was written. Finally, I wish to thank the students of History 1306A0, whose stamina, patience, and good humor made me feel just a little bit like Tom Swift Jr.

1. Victor Appleton II, *Tom Swift Jr. And His Flying Lab* (New York: Grosset and Dunlap, 1954); Jeff Duntemann, "Tom Swift, Jr.: An Appreciation," http://www.coriolis. com/jeffd/tomswift.htm; Edward L. Stratemeyer, *The Cambridge Biographical Encyclopedia,* http://www.biography.com/cgi-bin/biography/biography-request.pl?page+biography/data/s/s.1321.

2. Paul F. Anderson, *The Davy Crockett Craze: A Look at the 1950s Phenomenon and Davy Crockett Collectibles* (Hillside, IL: R & G Publications, 1996).

3. The instructor has taught introductory-level history for thirteen years: seven as a teaching assistant at York University and six as a course director at Acadia. The four surveys students completed included the departmental history course evaluation by the students of History 1306A0, the Acadia Advantage notebook section of the course, completed in March 1997; two identical surveys completed in December 1996 and April 1997 by the same students; and the survey conducted in the non-notebook sections of History 1306 in February 1997. The results of the last three surveys are reported in Tables 9.1–9.10. Because the students of the notebook section were all first-year students, only first- and second-year students were included in the results of the last survey. Acadia is preparing a base-line study of The Acadia Advantage, results of which are not yet available.

4. Evan Maudsley et al., ed., *History and Computing III: Historians, Computers and Data* (Manchester and New York: Manchester Press, 1990); Nicholas J. Morgan and Richard H. Trainor, "Liberator or Libertine? The Computer in the History Classroom" in *Humanities and the Computer,* ed. David S. Miall (Oxford: Clarendon Press, 1990), 61–70; Richard C. Rohrs, "Sources and Strategies for Computer-Aided Instruction," *Historical Methods* 20, no. 2 (Spring 1987): 79–83; David Miller and John Modell, "Teaching United States History with the Great American History Machine," *Historical Methods* 21, no. 3 (Summer 1988): 121–134; P. Jeffrey Potash, "Systems Thinking, Dynamic Modeling, and Teaching History in the Classroom," *Historical Methods* 27, no. 1 (Winter 1994): 25–39; Trudi Johanna Abel, "Students as Historians: Lessons from an 'Interactive' Census Database Project," *Perspectives* 35, no. 3 (March 1997): 1, 10–14; James B. M. Schick, "The Decision to Use a Computer Simulation," *The History Teacher* 27, no. 1 (November 1993): 27–36; Vernon Burton and Terence Finnegan, "Developing Computer Assisted Instructional (CAI) Materials in the American History Surveys," *The History Teacher* 24, no. 1 (November 1990): 67–78.

5. All references to dollars are to Canadian dollars; *Acadia University Calendar 1997/8* (Wolfville, Nova Scotia: Acadia University, 1997), 21.

6. Budget Presentation by Gary Draper, Director of Budgets, Acadia University, to the Students' Representative Council, Acadia University, 26 January 1997.

7. Acadia University, *Decisions For The Decade Campaign Overview* 4 (June 1996),

1–21; Kelvin K. Ogilvie, "Kick-off Dinner, 22 January 1997, Montreal, The Acadia Advantage," Office of Public Affairs, Acadia University, np; "Acadia Advantage Project Progression," Office of Public Affairs, Acadia University, nd; Interview with Kelvin K. Ogilvie, April 28, 1997.

8. "Kick-off Dinner," np.

9. "The Acadia Advantage Questions and Answers," Acadia University, http://admin.acadiau.ca/library/acadvant/q&a/q&a.htm.

10. *Decisions For The Decade,* 12–15.

11. Students had the option of paying an additional fee and keeping the computer for the summer months as well.

12. In April 1997, students and faculty in the program upgraded to an IBM ThinkPad 365XD.

13. Generally, scholastic aptitude tests play no role in the admissions process of Canadian universities. *Macleans,* a weekly newsmagazine, publishes average high school entry percentages to universities as part of its annual issue on higher education. The average is 79 percent across Canada; the average for Acadia is 81 percent. *Macleans* 109, no. 48 (November 25, 1996): 36.

14. Learn North Carolina, "Evaluating Web Sites: Questions to Ask," http://www.learnnc.iat.unc.edu/documents/Web-eva.html. No Web sites on Canadian history can match "The Great Chicago Fire and the Web of Memory," http://www.chicagoohs.org/fire/intro.

15. *Canadisk,* http://schoolnet.carleton.ca/cdisk.

16. "The Acadia Advantage Update March 27, 1997: Studying The Acadia Advantage," http://admin.acadiau.ca/library/acadvant/update/970327, 1–2.

17. P.J. Williams, Cyrus MacLatchy, Philip J. Backman, Duncan Retson, "Studio Physics at Acadia University," http://admin.acadiau.ca/library/acadvant/physics.htm.

18. For an extended discussion of active learning, see *Perspectives* 35, no. 3 (March 1997): 23–30.

19. Rohrs, "Sources and Strategies for Computer-Aided Instruction," 82.

10

The Future of Teaching History Research Methods Classes in the Electronic Age

Leslie Gene Hunter

Introduction

The theme of the inaugural Cincinnati Symposium on Computers and History is "The Future of History in the Electronic Age." It is clear that technological changes are affecting how scholars access information. Historians need to train their students to do research in new ways to deal with the electronic age. As James B.M. Schick explains in his book, *Teaching History With a Computer: A Complete Guide for College Professors,* technology is providing new links between historians. "With it the relative isolation of scholars and the need for pilgrimages to document repositories may diminish as academia enters the global electronic community that links major corporations and government agencies."[1]

Great libraries have been at the center of traditional universities, but all students and faculty have not been able to use those resources. Parker Rossman notes in *The Emerging Worldwide Electronic University: Information Age Global Higher Education* that "one of the signs of the worldwide electronic university is an emerging global electronic research library system that is beginning to increase that use." Although this is only a dream at the present for some countries, "many students and faculty already participate in its beginnings."[2]

This individual historian is more inclined to look backward than forward, and has no clear vision about what the teaching of history using technology will be like in a decade or two. It is possible, however, to describe the modest changes that have occurred in the teaching of an upper-level class on history research methods at Texas A&M University–

Kingsville in just the past three years. The class is not conducted completely "on-line" but has mixed aspects of traditional pedagogy with some necessary emphasis on utilizing computer technology.[3]

Class Organization

The title of the class ("Methods of Historical Research") was chosen to fit the short spaces in the university catalog and in the printed schedules of course offerings. It is somewhat misleading. The class is a compound of three related topics: the philosophy of history, methods of historical research, and the use of computer technology by historians. It is taught only during the fall semester and meets once a week for three hours in the evening in a networked computer laboratory with access to the Internet.

An attempt has been made to keep the three "threads" of the class—philosophy of history, research methods, and computer lab—as related as possible. For each of the sixteen weeks of the class, the syllabus lists the essays to be read about the philosophy of history, chapters to be read concerning research methods, and the topic to be dealt with in the computer lab. The attempt to relate the three aspects of the course can be seen, for example, in the syllabus assignments and topics listed for the fourth week:

Fourth Class: Tuesday, September 24, 1996
    Philosophy of History Discussion:
        Augustin Thierry, "National History and Nationalism"
        Thomas Babington Macaulay, "History and Literature"
    Research Methods: Chapter 4, "Finding the Facts"
    Research: Computer Lab—Bibliography Searches on Library Catalogs

During the course of the class discussions, the professor tries to guide the students eventually to consider what the readings and computer activities mean for their individual research projects.

Philosophy of History

The first major component of the class is historiography and the philosophy of history. For each week the students read essays by notable historians on topics about the writing of history and share their comments about the readings on a computer "conference."[4] Students can use the computer labs on campus or access their account on the university computer from their homes, dorms, or apartments. During the week before the class meeting, the students discuss the readings "on-line." The first two years that the class was taught, the discussions were conducted on a VAXNotes conference using guest accounts on a computer at another university.

For the third year, the Texas A&M University–Kingsville Computer Center established a list ("H-Methods") restricted to members of the class. A considerable lead time is necessary to prepare for teaching such a class. At this university it is necessary to start early to get the computer staff to establish the list before the first class meeting if the students are to get full benefits of the list. It is also necessary for the professor to learn the functions and operations of being a list manager—well before the class starts! During the first class meeting, the first lesson on the computer is to explain e-mail and lists, and to assist the students in subscribing to the H-Methods list.

Each week the professor posts a question concerning one of the essays for the students to discuss for the upcoming week. He usually posts it (distributes it to the list) early on the morning after the previous class. The question concerns some aspect of one of the essays the students are to read for the week. When students log on to the university's computer system, they find the question included in their e-mail. All replies which the students make to the list are distributed to all members of the class. The discussion by the students of the topic is a continuous, asynchronous conversation lasting up to the time of the meeting of the next class. At the end of each week, the postings on the list for that week are archived so the students can retrieve questions or comments on that topic for further reference.

Student participation in the dialogue on the list varies as greatly as if the discussion were held in a traditional classroom. Some students are very active, posting numerous answers and adding questions and comments about postings by other students. Other students are "minimalists," adding only one posting a week. There are interesting variations from the participation expected from students. Some of the students who would usually be outspoken in class discussions are also active on the list, but some articulate students seem uncomfortable about the technology and participate much less on the list than they would in a classroom setting. Most interesting, however, is that some students who are reluctant to talk in class become very active in the discussions on the list. The capability of composing their answers, pondering about what they are saying, and then editing their answers before posting seem to make some usually reticent students more willing to contribute. Handicapped students, who might otherwise be self-conscious, have generally been especially active on the list.

The professor observes the discussions on the list but does not actively participate. Occasionally, he sends e-mail messages to individual students about some aspect of their posting, but does not post comments about an individual student's answers on the list for everyone to see. The discussion is meant to be by and for the students, with the professor an omniscient but silent observer. Students often encourage and discourage each other, moving the subject along, eliciting further comments, or bringing the dialogue back to the topic when someone strays. In general, the students discussions are much more civil than discussions on many of the lists on the Internet. Students seem to self-moderate the list. There was only one occasion when a student made a personal, unnecessary, and unacceptable comment—to which several students made replies, discouraging further such comments.

At the beginning of each class meeting, the professor tries to solicit further observations about comments posted during the week. The professor also asks students about their reactions to other aspects of the reading and to the other essays read but not included in the posted question. Some of the students who were reticent "on-line" feel more comfortable talking in a classroom setting and actively contribute more to the discussion. Because the students have already written answers to one question about the reading, they seem to have more completely internalized the material. Many seem to know the subject better for having organized and written about the subject. It is as if they had completed a take-home essay examination each week. During the class discussions, the professor asks the students frequently how the topics being discussed relate to their individual research projects.

Research Methods

A second major component of the class deals with the methods of history research. Each week the class is assigned one or more chapters in a textbook on researching a topic for history.[5] Most evenings the students discuss aspects of the readings about doing research and describe progress on their research projects. Each student is expected to research and write a paper on a topic agreed to with the professor as an exercise in philosophy and methods. They are to investigate the topic, locate documents, interpret the information, synthesize their conclusions, and demonstrate their mastery by writing a term paper. This component is expected to be a "history laboratory"—demonstrating that they are familiar with the philosophy of history, history research methodology, and resources available to historians by computer technology.

The professor also assigns himself a research topic so that he can participate in the discussion—describing developments on his project during the semester as the students report on their progress. This is intended to be teaching by example. It is hoped that the students will discover a logic to the professor's pursuing particular avenues of information and will be able to apply the same approaches to their own research. Although it may be embarrassing for a professor to admit that some weeks his research has not been fruitful, it is a valuable and reassuring lesson for students, who are just learning about the frustration of research, especially in archives and with primary sources.

To help prepare the students for their research papers, part of one of the early class meetings is a tour of the South Texas Archives (a division of the James C. Jernigan Library on the Texas A&M University–Kingsville campus). The archives are used extensively by many of the history classes as a teaching "lab" for research in history. Over the years a variety of projects have been developed to introduce history majors especially, but also general undergraduate students in U.S. history survey classes, to the qualities and utility of archives. History classes have used the South Texas Archives to research a variety of local subjects: the Kingsville Original Townsite Project,[6] the Tombstone project,[7] La Castaña Project,[8] and the seventy-fifth Anniversary History of Texas A&M University–Kingsville project. Even if students locate archival collections relevant to their topics on the Internet, they still need the skills to locate the specific documents at an archive.

Although students might be familiar with library research techniques, they are usually unfamiliar with archival research, which requires different and additional research skills because of the unique way in which the materials are categorized and filed. In addition to the tour of the South Texas Archives, a reading is assigned to the students, "Historians and Archivists: Educating the Next Generation."[9] The tour and the reading are intended to give students a better understanding of what they should know about archival practices in order to do research successfully. Lists of potential topics that might be successfully researched in these archives are accumulated with the assistance and cooperation of the archivist. In this way the archivist can be of more assistance in teaching students how to ask for assistance in an archive.

Computer Technology

A third major component of the class is a weekly laboratory presentation about some aspect of computer technology, followed by a hands-on application of that skill. During the course of the semester, the students are expected to employ e-mail during the list discussions; obtain documents by File Transfer Protocol (FTP) from the National Archives, Library of Congress, Texas State Library, or elsewhere; use on-line public access catalogs; subscribe to one H-Net list (in addition to the H-Methods list on the campus); discuss history subjects on Newsgroups; demonstrate Gopher, Archie, Jughead, and Veronica searches; and employ WAIS and WWW searches. The emphasis and examples used involve history resources available, not other amusing but not relevant features of the Internet.

The professor has been interested in finding a book focusing on the history resources on the Internet. For the computer laboratory component of the class, there are many books dealing with the Internet in general, which could be used as textbooks. Many of these books, however, are technical, very large, expensive, and often deal with a great deal that is not *necessarily* useful to history students. For this part of the class there has been no textbook, but there are a series of handouts for the students. By the end of the semester the students will receive approximately thirty-five handouts, totaling 100 pages.[10]

If the topic of the evening is public access catalogs, for example, approximately thirty minutes will be devoted to an explanation and demonstration by the professor followed by a step-by-step handout for the students to use to access several catalogs. One handout includes the steps to access the University of California System (MELVYL) and other university catalogs. At first the students are taught to telnet to the libraries because many are able to connect to the university's computer from home but lack PPP accounts. Later in the semester, they access the catalogs using Netscape Navigator and the World Wide Web. During the practice session following the professor's demonstration, the students search

MELVYL for books relevant to their personal research subject and e-mail the results to themselves as a beginning for their bibliography.[11] Another handout is devoted to doing periodical literature searches in Wilson indexes at the Texas A&M University Library and in UnCover at CARL (the Colorado Alliance of Research Library).[12]

Because the students are doing original research on limited local topics so that the documents will be available in the archives, most of their sources are not found "on-line." Much of the background and larger context for their topics, however, is found in the library catalogs, databases, or other information on the Internet. As archives continue to automate, more documents will be electronically available in the future from even the smallest archives.

Each class session covers topics on the philosophy of history, methods of research, and computer resources for historians. The syllabus lists the philosophy of history readings, topics to be discussed about research methodology, and computer activities for each class. There is at least one step-by-step handout for each evening's class dealing with the computer lab topic for the student to add to a ring binder. In addition to the step-by-step computer handout, frequently there are handouts on other relevant topics. Some examples from the syllabus of the subjects and activities for some typical weeks are as follows:

Sixth Class: Tuesday, October 1, 1996
  Philosophy of History Discussion:
    Henry Thomas Buckle, "Positivistic History and Its Critics"
    Karl Marx, "Historical Materialism"
  Research Methods: Chapter 6, "Handling Ideas"
  Research: Computer Lab—Armadillos, Gophers, and Javelinas

Ninth Class: Tuesday, October 22, 1996
  Philosophy of History Discussion:
  G. M. Trevelyan, "Clio Rediscovered"
  Henri Berr, "Specialization and Historical Synthesis"
  Research Methods: Chapters 10–11, "Plain Words" and
    "Clear Sentences"
  Research: Computer Lab—Archie, Jughead, and Veronica

It is not possible to perfectly match the three components of the class for each evening. For the fourth week, the overall topic deals with sources.

An essay on "History and Literature," a reading on "Finding the Facts," a discussion of documentation, and a computer search of public access catalogs work well for one evening session.

The students begin with an "on-line" discussion of the essay by Macauley on "History and Literature" in the week before the class meets. When the class meets, there is a review of the list discussion. The next part of the class that fourth class evening is an analysis of documents. There are three handouts: two handouts on documents and one handout about connecting to public access catalogs. The professor introduces the students to the section on "Teaching With Documents" in the publication of the National Council for the Social Studies, *Social Education.* He distributes to the students a copy of General Dwight D. Eisenhower's D-day message to General Marshall, June 6, 1944.[13] Another document distributed is an account of the confession of a young French woman accused of witchcraft in 1652.[14] The class analyzes the documents, considers problems of using sources, and then also discusses the information in the textbook on "Finding the Facts."[15]

For the last part of the class, the students practice telnetting to the library catalogs of the University of California, Dartmouth, Harvard, Texas A&M University, and the University of Texas.[16] Computer addresses can change quickly, and the ones included in a handout one semester often become outdated by the next time the class is taught. The emphasis in this exercise is upon doing literature searches for research topics. Obviously, other public access catalogs could be used instead of the ones noted above. Frequently the professor asks the students to consider how to apply what they have just learned to the data they are locating for their individual research projects.

Other Computer Lab Topics

Class discussions of essays by historians and of research methodology are traditional for such a course and do not need further elaboration. The computer laboratory emphasis upon on-line resources for historians is not so traditional. On one evening the computer lab segment of the class deals with the topic of File Transfer Protocol (FTP). The students connect to computers at remote sites such as the University of North Carolina, Library of Congress, Marshall University, Mississippi State University, and elsewhere to retrieve documents.[17] In addition to the step-by-step handout for that evening class, a copy of an article by Michael J.

McCarthy, "The Historian and Electronic Research: File Transfer Protocol (FTP)," is distributed to students.[18] Another laboratory session deals with lists and listservs, and the students subscribe to one of the H-Net lists appropriate for their interest in history. The professor gives a lengthy description, distinguishing and warning about the difference between the list and the listserv. One handout for that evening is a copy of the article on H-Net lists in *History Microcomputer Review* by Kelly Woestman.[19] In late October, the computer lab exercise deals with Web sites, and the examples used that evening are timely, dealing with the election. The class uses Professor Woestman's article on political candidates, parties, and political issues on Web sites and Newsgroups.[20]

The students also learn how to telnet to sites which have a menu of options so that the student can connect to many different libraries in the United States and at universities in foreign countries.[21] At Texas A&M University–Kingsville, the majority of the students in this class are Mexican-Americans and bilingual, and many are interested in Latin American history. They learn how to log on to the Rio Grande Freenet and to use it as a convenient gateway to Latin American sites through the Latin American Network Information Center (University of Texas).[22]

On another evening, the lab is devoted to Archie, Jughead, and Veronica searches. A demonstration is given in which "Veronica" at Universidad Nacional Autónoma de México (UNAM) is used to search for everything in which the word "museum" appears in the title. After several minutes, Veronica displays the first 200 items, but also shows that she had located a total of 3,582 sites, including Maritime Museum of the Great Lakes, Gold Prospector Museum, National Railway Museum. The students then spend the rest of the lab session trying Archie, Jughead, and Veronica searches of their own. During the course of their explorations, the students search for their individual research topics by searching for "slavery," "railroads," "Civil War," "ranching," or some other relevant term.

For one evening session, the handout is devoted to "virtual reference desks." There are many, many sites and routes to these types of resources. The example used is accessing some of the resources through the Rio Grande Freenet. From that base, the students examine dictionaries, encyclopedias, U.S. Census Data, Project Gutenberg, the complete works of Shakespeare, and so on.[23]

The computer lab session devotes an evening to an introduction to the World Wide Web. Web sites are popping up overnight like mushrooms.

It is not possible for this paper to include an extensive list because there are so many, and new ones are being added daily.[24] The students receive a handout of several sites to visit and are encouraged to explore for sites relevant to their topics. There is too much to cover more than just a basic introduction to each type of activity, such as FTP, Gopher, or the WWW, in each computer lab. For each of the topics introduced in the computer lab sessions, it is expected that the student will continue to explore this aspect of technology for historians in the week following the class and throughout the remainder of the semester.

Sites on the Internet and the technology to access them change so fast that handouts become dated before the next time the class is offered. The handouts used in the fall 1994 semester were seriously dated by the fall 1996 semester. The professor would like to prepare all handouts before the class begins so that students can purchase a complete set from a photocopy store across from campus. It has proved almost impossible to prepare that far ahead for the class. Handouts prepared for a specific topic in the summer, when the professor has the "leisure" to review the overall organization and materials for the class, have become partially obsolete by the time the class session devoted to that topic meets in November or December.

Future Teachers

Because many of the students will ultimately obtain certification and become secondary school teachers, useful teaching resources are pointed out during the computer lab. One evening the computer lab segment of the class explores Gophers and the handout is entitled: "Gophers, Armadillos, and Javelinas." The "Javelina Gopher" is the name for the Gopher of Texas A&M University–Kingsville (the javelina being the school mascot). "Armadillo" is the name of the Texas Social Studies Gopher.

After the professor describes and demonstrates Gophers to the class, the students are given a step-by-step handout taking them to "All the Gopher Servers in the World." From there they access "AMI—A Friendly Public Interface," where they explore "History" with sub-topics including Genealogy, Historical Documents (Queens City Public Library), History (University of Virginia), Library of Congress (LC MARVEL), North Carolina State University Library Gopher; RiceInfo (Rice University), Texas A&M, Washington & Lee University, and so on. From the Javelina Gopher the students are shown how to go to the Dead Sea Scrolls Exhibit,

Holocaust Archives, Soviet Archives, Vietnam Era Documents, etc. The Armadillo has a variety of projects and files useful for secondary social studies teachers. There are directories and sub-directories on Library Services and Resources; Super Projects!!!; Texas History and Geography; Famous Texans and Immigrants to Texas; multicultural topics; Texas Community Profiles; and other subjects.[25]

This secondary emphasis upon how students can utilize some of the resources for teaching public school social studies classes recognizes that many history majors will become school teachers. While the students explore Web sites, several examples of possible "virtual field trips to museums" are given—such as the Air and Space Museum of the Smithsonian Institute—which would be suitable for junior high school students.[26]

One computer lab session devotes a considerable amount of time to the use of simulations for teaching. A copy of the current issue of *History Computer Review* is shown to the students. Examples of software programs and CD-ROMs are described, and the literature survey section of articles relevant to historians is pointed out to the students. For example, the spring 1996 issue of *HCR* contained sixteen reviews. After a description of some of the reviews, a number of software programs and CD-ROMS are demonstrated to the class, and the students spend a major part of one evening exploring those programs. The students also learn that there are numerous postings during any week on the "H-Net List for Teaching College History and Related Fields" which are helpful to teachers. During the course of the semester, the professor forwards interesting and relevant postings from some of the lists to which he subscribes to the H-Methods list to be distributed to the e-mail box of each student in the class.[27] Reviews of new software, notices of new Web sites, or references to sources of information for research are the subjects most often "forwarded" to the H-Methods list.

In the next fall semester when the class is offered, there are other topics which can be added to these dealing with teaching. For example, reviews of Web sites, which will become a feature of *History Computer Review,* can be shown to the students so that they can see reviews of sites relevant to historians.[28] In addition, students in this class can also receive a copy of a recent article, which shows them how to set up a history-based Web site for their students when they become teachers.[29] There is also a template for students to build their own Web page, which can be shown to these future teachers.[30] Undoubtedly, there will be new Web sites of use to history students doing research which will be added in the upcoming months.

Research Paper

The topic of each student's research paper is posted on the H-Methods list, distributed in a handout, and mentioned frequently during the weekly discussions. Therefore, each student quickly learns what others in the class are researching. The computer lab seems to provide for more collaborative learning than a traditional class. It is obvious that those students more comfortable with the technology help the less "computer literate." But as the semester progresses, as they discover Web sites, bibliographies, lists, and so on, all students share them with their classmates. There seems to be considerable help by students on each other's research topics. There is more cooperation, source sharing, and suggestions by students for each other than in classes without the computer.

Students share with each other not only during the class evening meeting, but also during the week. The university archivist has observed students pointing out to their classmates file folders and boxes of information relevant for their research. Some students have asked the archivist to point out certain documents when a specific classmate shows up at the archives. Students share information on the "H-Methods" list to all in the class and individually by sending personal e-mail messages directly to each other. When the student mentions a problem in research to the professor, he is often able to refer the student to a classmate doing research on a tangential topic.

Students submit a rough draft of their research paper in the tenth week of the semester. The professor makes substantial suggestions, deletions, additions, and corrections to the papers and returns them to the students. All students rewrite their papers and submit the final version on the fourteenth week of the class. Some students are asked to make additional changes and to submit their papers to a scholarly journal to see if they can be published. Although it is not expected that all of the students who submit their papers for publication will be successful, it is an opportunity for the professor to convince those students to do one additional rewrite. Some of the students have been successful in having their research papers published,[31] and one of the sample research projects which the professor was doing at the same time as the students were doing their papers has also been published.[32] The paper demonstrates the extent to which the student has learned about the philosophy of history and the methods of history research and counts for one-half of the grade for the semester.

Final Examination

The final examination is a "scavenger hunt" on the Internet. To prepare the students for the final exam, there is a sample Internet scavenger hunt during the twelfth meeting of the class. For the practice session, all the students have the same scavenger hunt questions, are permitted to use their handouts, and are encouraged to cooperate and assist each other if necessary. The practice Internet scavenger hunt includes seven items: a literature search for a book on a public access catalog; a bibliography search for an article; a Gopher search for an oral history article; the retrieval of a document from the Soviet Archives; a search for an historical document at the Library of Congress; a Veronica search of Gopher space for a subject; and a Web search for an article. The students compose answers to the questions and e-mail their answers to the practice final exam to the professor.

The actual final examination is individualized for each student and is distributed to the students and submitted by them through e-mail. Students are not to share information during the actual final. The student is required to write an essay about some question concerning the philosophy of history, retrieve documents from a remote site, do a bibliography search in an on-line library catalog, and answer questions from information at the National Archives. The bibliography questions are related—at least slightly—to the individual student's research project. For example, one student was asked to identify when Abraham Hunter purchased land in Illinois and what price he paid per acre.[33]

The grade for the class is weighted for different components of the class. The student's class participation and discussions count for 10 percent; the quality and quantity of the student's weekly participation on the H-Methods list, 25 percent; the final examination, 15 percent; and the research paper is worth 50 percent of the grade.

Conclusions

This class continues to evolve. Surely, next fall semester there will be further changes, perhaps different textbooks, and new handouts. The search for the perfect textbook is never-ending, like the quest for the Holy

Grail. Several new books have been published recently that may be selected as a textbook for the computer lab sessions. In future years there may be a decrease in the number of handouts distributed. One new book appears to be an especially good textbook candidate for the computer lab part of the class—*The History Highway: A Guide to Internet Resources.*[34] There is also a briefer book, *History on the Internet: A Student's Guide,* which comes "bundled" with a freshman survey textbook that offers a short introduction to the subject.[35] One new introduction to locating information on the Internet is also brief enough to be suitable as a general textbook for the computer lab—*NetResearch: Finding Information Online.*[36]

For the introduction to historiography and the philosophy of history component of the class, there are more possible textbooks than the selection of readings from historians. A brief introduction, *History and Historians: A Historiographical Introduction,* could be used.[37] A more substantial textbook, *Historiography: Ancient, Medieval, & Modern,* could also be used.[38] Undoubtedly, there are other books which could be selected, or a series of articles could be assigned for readings. Whatever the readings, the most important aspect is to get the students to read, reflect, comment, discuss, and inwardly digest the information about the nature of history—and incorporate that into their own research.

For the first two years, the professor printed out the VAXNotes discussion at the end of the semester and gave a spiral-bound copy to each student. This gave the students the opportunity to look back over the topics discussed and to see their own answers to each question. But the number of students taking the class has increased, and the volume of student discussion on the H-Methods list is so high that it would require approximately thirty copies of over 100 pages in length. It was useful, however, the first two years, to look back at the progression of the postings by the students. It surprised the students to see how their discussions became more sophisticated, confident, and lengthy as they became comfortable with the computer technology.

The rapidly evolving technology will surely continue to cause annual changes in such a course dealing with the use of computers by historians. In just three years, there have been shifts in emphasis. The use of FTP, Gopher, Archie, Jughead, and Veronica were dealt with more in the first two years and considerably less the third year. The World Wide Web was dealt with less the first year and more each year thereafter. Surely that trend will continue.

Technology poses some new problems and challenges for a class taught in a computer laboratory setting. In none of the first three years this course has been taught have the computer facilities been close to ideal. The lab should be physically arranged so that the students can work at individual computers and also see a projected display from the computer on which the professor is demonstrating. Lacking such an arrangement can be extremely frustrating, forcing the professor to move from computer to computer to demonstrate the same operations repeatedly. An arrangement of computers in carrels, with limited visibility to the rest of the lab, is an especially difficult environment in which to teach this type of class. It is desirable that there be one computer for each student. The success of the class enrollment has reached the point where either two sections of the class must be offered or else students will have to "share" a computer, a much less desirable development for demonstrating "hands-on" type of activities. Teaching any such course will be considerably affected by the laboratory situation and layout and computers, networking, and resources available through the specific university computer center.

There are new computer and electronic versions of ancient problems professors have always faced. Using technology permits students to stray from the topic under discussion in new ways. There are now electronic methods of passing notes, and other computer variations of deviant classroom behaviors. Inappropriate e-mail messages, not related to historical topics, can easily be sent by students in the class. The content of some of the e-mail messages in the class apparently are not related to the subjects of philosophy of history or research methodology. On occasion, students seem to exchange jokes and distribute other interesting postings found on the Internet, which they usually do not share with the professor! There can be searches on the World Wide Web for topics not suitable or at least irrelevant to history subjects being discussed. Students are extremely versatile in finding unusual Web sites. On occasion, students have accidentally blundered into material on the Internet which was offensive or embarrassing to them.

Some students begin the class seriously advantaged by being computer literate. By the end of the semester, the advantage seems to be less serious. The majority of the students seem to catch on relatively quickly, especially if assisted by their peers. Most students do not seem to be intimidated by the technology. The students look forward to the class, even though it is a required course for all history majors. The class has increased in size each year because several non-history majors have been opting to take the class as an elective.

Students definitely enjoy the technology, even those who begin with a limited knowledge about computers. The subjects of researching and writing papers are something they have been exposed to in the other history classes but without the computer research component utilized in this class. The students come to dislike—and do not well anticipate—the length of time it will take to do the research for their paper. There are new electronic distractions and ways to procrastinate. The "Emerging World-wide Electronic University" has some of the same problems as the older traditional universities.

The global electronic university poses new challenges for historians. Different topics and approaches need to be included in classes to teach undergraduate majors the craft. The class described above has changed in each of the three years it has been taught in a computer lab setting. This is only a modest beginning. A decade from now it will certainly be even more different. The changes are relentless; one author has noted that there are over one thousand new Web sites being added to the Internet each day![39] The "search engines" used on the Internet when the University of Cincinnati holds its Tenth Annual Symposium on Computers and History will probably make those currently used seem primitive. A decade from now, the topics in the class described above will surely seem laughable and perhaps even quaint.

Historians must prepare the next generation of students, especially those who will become teachers themselves, to be comfortable with new ways of doing research and locating information. Historians do not have the luxury of simply ignoring the Internet. As one historian noted: "The resources are too rich and valuable." There are documents, databases, Web sites, library catalogs, electronic journals, and lively discussions by scholars and students of history. "The Internet is quite simply the most revolutionary storehouse of human knowledge in history."[40] There is, in fact, what Parker Rossman has labeled an "emerging global electronic research library system" emerging.[41] James B.M. Schick concluded his work on *Teaching History With a Computer* with the observation:

> The sooner historians take up the challenge of computer-assisted instruction, the more effectively will they reach today's students. By pressing for the establishment of computerized links among historians and with primary and secondary sources, history professors will significantly improve research

possibilities for themselves and their students and discover new ways to disseminate their findings. The use of simulations and other techniques to recreate the past will broaden the discipline's appeal and reveal new fields for scholarship. Finally, the computer offers historians the opportunity to improve the communications and cognitive skills of students, a task both important and necessary to society and the university.[42]

Notes

1. James B.M. Schick, *Teaching History With a Computer: A Complete Guide for College Professors* (Chicago: Lyceum Books, 1990), 207.

2. Parker Rossman, "Contributions to the Study of Education, Number 57" in *The Emerging Worldwide Electronic University: Information Age Global Higher Education* (Westport, CT: Greenwood Press, 1992), 61.

3. Leslie Gene Hunter, "Decade of Change," *History Microcomputer Review* 11 (Fall 1995): 50–52.

4. Fritz Stern, ed., *The Varieties of History: From Voltaire to the Present* (New York: Vintage Books, 1973).

5. Jacques Barzun, *The Modern Researcher,* 5th ed. (New York: Harcourt, Brace & World, 1993).

6. For example, a grant was received from the Texas State Historic Commission to publish a history, which included many of the papers by the students of some of the significant structures located in the Original Townsite. See: Cecilia Aros Hunter and Leslie Gene Hunter, eds., *Historic Kingsville, Texas: A Guide to the Original Townsites* (Kingsville: Kingsville Historical Development Board, 1994).

7. The Tombstone Project was a survey of the local cemeteries, with the students compiling all the information on the epitaphs to be entered into a computer database for students to manipulate to arrive at historical conclusions. For an example of this type of project, see Stephen E. Daniels, "Databasing the Cemetery: Using Microcomputers to Analyze the Past," *History Microcomputer Review* 7 (Spring 1991): 17–24.

8. La Castaña is Spanish for "the trunk." Students were assigned to locate and survey sources—especially Spanish language documents—which might be in the possession of their families, friends, and neighbors that would document the history of South Texas.

9. Edwin Bridges et al., "Historians and Archivists: Educating the Next Generation," *American Archivist* 56 (Fall 1993): 730–749.

10. Although students were not required to purchase it as a textbook, it was suggested that a good reference for them to use for further information was Ed Krol, *The Whole Internet: User's Guide & Catalog,* 4th ed. (Sebastopol, CA: O'Reilly & Associates, 1994).

11. Telnet://MELVYL.UCOEDU or 192.35.222.222. After searching for author, subject, title, word, and displaying the results, they typed "mail to XXXX," with the XXXX being the complete e-mail address of the student.

12. Telnet PAC.CARL.ORG or 192.54.81.18.

13. "D-day Message from General Eisenhower to General Marshall," *Social Education* (April/May 1994): 230–232.

14. Peter Charles Hoffer and William W. Stueck, *Reading and Writing American History: An Introduction to the Historian's Craft* (Lexington, MA: D. C. Heath, 1994), 10–11.

15. Barzun, Chapter 4 "Finding the Facts," in *The Modern Researcher*.

16. Telnet://MELVYL.UCOEDU or 192.35.222.222. Telnet://LIBRARY.DART-MOUTH.EDU or 129.170.16.15. Telnet://HOLLIS.HARVARD.EDU or 130.103.60.31. Telnet://ACS.TAMU.EDU or 129.194.103.14. Telnet://UTXUTS.DUTEXAS.EDU or 128.83.216.12.

17. University of North Carolina (FTP://sunsite.unc.edu); Library of Congress (FTP://seq1.loc.gov); Marshall University (FTP://byrd.mu.wvnet.edu); and Mississippi State University (FTP://FTmsstate.edu). Note: addresses can change quickly.

18. Michael J. McCarthy, "The Historian and Electronic Research: File Transfer Protocol (FTP)," *History Microcomputer Review* 9 (Fall 1993): 29–46.

19. Kelly A. Woestman, "Net Survey: Navigating the Internet," *History Microcomputer Review,* 11 (Fall 1995): 93–99.

20. Kelly A. Woestman, "Navigating the Internet," *History Computer Review* 12 (Spring 1996): 35–60.

21. For example, Sonoma State University has options of connecting to many universities in each state plus libraries in twenty countries. Telnet://VAX.SONOMA.EDU and login as "OPAC."

22. Telnet://RGFN.EPCC.EDU or 192.94.29.9. Logon as "visitor." In the #9 Libraries option, there is a connection to the Latin American Network Information Center (University of Texas).

23. Telnet://RGFN.EPCC.EDU or 192.94.29.9. Logon as "visitor." Choose Option #9 Libraries.

24. For a very comprehensive list, see Dennis A. Trinkle, et al., *The History Highway: A Guide to Internet Resources* (Armonk, NY: M.E. Sharpe, 1997), 23–198.

25. Leslie Gene Hunter and Donald Perkins, "Since When is an Armadillo a Gopher?" *The Social Studies Texan* (Fall 1993): 29–30.

26. Smithsonian Air and Space Museum: HTTP://www.nasm.edu.

27. H-Teach@H-Net.MSU.EDU.

28. See Kelly A. Woestman, "Evaluating WWW Sites," *History Computer Review* 13 (Spring 1997): 58–91.

29. See George Cassutto, "Setting up a History-Based Web Site for Your School," *History Computer Review* 13 (Spring 1997): 27–39.

30. See Andrew T. Stull, *History on the Internet: A Student's Guide* (adapted for history by David A. Meier) (Upper Saddle River, NJ: Prentice Hall, 1997), 54–56.

31. See, for example, James N. Krug, "The Kingsville Railroad Depot," *The Journal of South Texas* 8 (1995): 40–52; Carla Chapa, "*Las Notas De Kingsville* 1944–1963: The Voice of the Mexican American Community," *The Journal of South Texas* 9 (1996): 93–101; Michelle Riley, "Texas College of Arts and Industries, East Campus: 1946–1951," *The Journal of South Texas* 10 (1997): 88–105; and Eden J. Straw, "Texas A&I Campus Traditions, 1925–1996," *The Journal of South Texas* 10 (1997): 121–136.

32. See Leslie Gene Hunter and Cecilia Aros Hunter, " 'Mother Lane' and the 'New Mooners': An Expression of *Curanderismo,*" *Southwestern Historical Quarterly* 99 (January 1996): 290–325.

33. In 1832; $1.25 an acre.

34. Dennis A. Trinkle, et al., *The History Highway.*

35. Andrew T. Stull, *History on the Internet.*

36. Daniel J. Barrett, *NetResearch: Finding Information Online* (Sebastopol, CA: Songline Studios and O'Reilly & Associates, 1997).

37. Mark T. Gilderhus, *History and Historians: A Historiographical Introduction,* 3d ed. (Englewood Cliffs, NJ: Prentice Hall, 1996).

38. Ernst Breisach, *Historiography: Ancient, Medieval & Modern,* 2d ed. (Chicago: University of Chicago Press, 1994).

39. Woestman, "Evaluating WWW Sites," *History Computer Review* 13 (Spring 1997): 58.

40. Dennis A. Trinkle, *The History Highway,* xi.

41. Rossman, *The Emerging Worldwide Electronic University: Information Age Global Higher Education,* 61.

42. Schick, *Teaching History With a Computer,* 210.

11

Using Multimedia Computer Technology to Teach United States History at Medgar Evers College, City University of New York, from Three Perspectives

Professor, Teaching Assistant, and Undergraduate

Barbara Winslow, Kacy D. Wiggins, and Marisol Carpio

I. A Novice Uses Computer Technology to Teach the United States History Survey
Barbara Winslow

Beginning in July 1996, I participated in a National Endowment for the Humanities–sponsored seminar organized by the American Social History Project and the City University of New York (CUNY) Graduate School and University Center, called "The New Media Classroom: Narrative, Inquiry and Technology in the U.S. History Survey." The purpose of the seminar was to bring together university, college, and high school faculty to explore the possibilities of using computer technology in teaching U.S. history and American studies. The seminar, which lasted a week, continued through the 1996–97 academic year and the participants continue to discuss issues both electronically and at seminar meetings. This paper discusses my first attempt at using computer technology to teach a United States history survey course, HIST 200: Growth and Development of the United States.[1]

To provide some background, I am a historian at Medgar Evers College/CUNY—an embattled and underfunded urban public institution. I am teaching a United States history survey course in a computer lab which is not yet fully equipped, to students who are not history majors, of whom most have little or no computer experience, few, if any, have home computers, and not all have time to use the computers at the school. In addition, I have little experience and a lot less confidence in using computer-based multimedia technology. My situation is probably a common one, especially for faculty teaching in state-funded, urban, and other public institutions.

Based upon my two-semester experience, this paper will discuss some of the problems raised in using computer technology to teach a United States history survey, including: developing an appropriate classroom style for a multimedia computer lab, assessing the advantages and difficulties of using CD-ROMs and the Web for research and writing, and discussing the wisdom of untenured faculty embarking on experimental courses such as this one.

During the New Media classroom seminar, we were given an enormous amount of information to digest. Along with all the technological and historical information, I found that three very strong common sense items had made a lasting impression upon me as I developed my course for the fall:

1. Don't try to include too many computer assignments and exercises the first time your course uses computer technology.
2. Do your computer assignments early in the course; if they don't work out, you can always fall back on the more traditional assignments and exercises.
3. COMPUTER TECHNOLOGY CAN BREAK DOWN, AND IT WILL BREAK DOWN. In other words, *always* have a back-up plan ready and prepared for your class when you are using computer technology.

With these points in mind, I began preparing my class. Since I do not have a great deal of expertise in computer technology, I used my NEH stipend to hire a history graduate student, Kacy Wiggins, who had worked with the American Social History Project (ASHP) and was familiar with the material. Mr. Wiggins came to class once a week and provided both historical and technological assistance. I ordered two CD-ROMs, *Who*

Built America, produced by the ASHP, and *The American Pageant,* a CD-ROM based on the textbook by Thomas Bailey. I also prepared a questionnaire for my students, so that I could have a clearer idea about the technological expertise of the class.

I had three basic concerns regarding this class: 1) Would students be interested and/or excited about using computers in a history class? 2) Would students feel like they were "guinea pigs," that is, subjects for a professor's experiment? 3) And finally and most importantly, would computer technology be an effective way to develop students' critical thinking, reading, and writing skills?

The results from the fall semester survey helped me understand the students' computer expertise (or lack thereof). In a class of twenty-one, only one student wrote that this was their first time using a computer. About half used computers (but not word processors, CD-ROMs, or the Internet) at work; the majority, including work-study students, did not regularly use the computers at the college. The overwhelming majority had never used CD-ROMs, and only one knew how to use the Internet. I asked students who had e-mail accounts to send me messages. Only one student sent me messages, but even she did not communicate on a regular basis.

Problems developed from the first day of class because few students had any real computer experience. I had to go over the ABCs of computer technology. With the lab technicians, we went over the functions of the computer: how to use the mouse; how to scroll; how to insert a disk; how to insert a CD-ROM; how to put the syllabus on a disk; and how to make directories on a disk. There were usually one or sometimes two technicians who were very supportive and always available. However, in a situation where five or six computers could not be booted up, there simply were not enough technicians to solve the problems. In other words, a lot of class time was wasted because of technological glitches.

Students were often and justifiably impatient and angry with technological glitches. Quite often during a class session, anywhere from one to four computers would not work. The computer lab did not have curtains, and the walls are not large enough for video projections. We (meaning the students and myself) handled these technological problems with a sense of humor. Because I always had a back-up plan, had promised the students that technological glitches would not adversely affect their grades, and had warned (promised) them from the beginning and repeatedly to expect technological problems, the level of computer frustration stayed low.

As in all classes, some students were very proficient and a few were not at all. I encouraged the more experienced students to work with those who needed help. This helped create an atmosphere of camaraderie. While waiting for the CDs (which were replacing a textbook and map book) to arrive, I had to rely on the more traditional teaching methods of lecture and discussion, based upon assigned readings on reserve in the library. I also sent the class to the Smithsonian Museum of the American Indian, where they further familiarized themselves with aspects of computer technology, while at the same time learning about aspects of Native American life and culture.

Once the CD-ROMs arrived, the pace and interest of the class improved. The students were excited by the CD-ROMs, and this was reflected in both the quality of class discussion and the writing. However, there were still technological problems. It took a while for the technicians to get the CD-ROMs installed; during the first semester, the computers in the lab were not set up for audio, which made running *Who Built America* difficult, if not impossible. Finally, the technicians were able to solve some of the problems, and by the spring term all the computers were equipped with headphones.

Because of the problems inherent in teaching at a 'commuter' school and given the level of the class's computer skills, I would give in-class time for working at the computer. However, as far as the students were concerned, there still was not enough in-class time for the CD-ROMs. Mr. Wiggins and I were there to help the students navigate the CD-ROMs, but it took at least two class periods to go over each CD-ROM. To make the time more productive, as I showed students the different features of each CD-ROM, I gave a presentation on a particular area of United States history that we were studying. The students also were given two computer assignments that were graded on content as well as style, and they were given four other computer assignments that were not graded. These assignments were the most successful in terms of the students' interest and writing. (See appendices.)

The value of these CD-ROMs for our history courses is that they contain text, photographs, time lines, bibliographical and archival materials that our library does not have. *The American Pageant* is much less interactive, but it is useful as a basic history text. The *Who Built America* CD-ROM contains audio materials, including speeches from W.E.B. Dubois and Booker T. Washington, as well as selections from ordinary sharecroppers and garment workers plus clips from popular music of the time. *WBA* also contains video clips of, for example, a black regiment during the Spanish-American War and suffragists marching for the vote.

The most exciting use of the CD-ROM for the fall 1996 class was the assignment dealing with the Triangle Shirtwaist Factory fire (see Appendix F). In this assignment, the journalistic accounts are so vivid and so well written that the students all but experienced the horror of the tragedy. The students voiced their outrage at the working conditions, the lack of safety, and the horror of the young garment workers' deaths. The papers they wrote reflected their emotional connection to the material. In the spring, the most provocative assignment so far had been comparing and contrasting the lives of Chinese immigrants with that of southern African-American sharecroppers. The students read a sharecropper's contract with the owner and compared it with a Chinese woman's prostitution contract.

The students told me that they preferred the computer assignments over the "traditional" written assignments—the essay using primary sources, the time line, and the research paper. I believe this preference is due to a number of factors: 1) the novelty of using computers, 2) four of the six computer assignments were not graded (although, if the students did not complete each written computer assignment, their grade would be adversely affected), 3) the "traditional" assignments are somewhat more difficult for the students because they entail researching original documents, writing from primary sources, preparing bibliographies, and writing formal essays and research papers. I believe the three "traditional" assignments are imperative for the class and should be continued along with the newer computer assignments.

The value, however, of the computer assignments, is in part due to their novelty. The students enjoyed playing around with the CD-ROMs. Students came into the lab early to work; often when I would go into the lab during non-class lab hours, I would find my students working on their papers, and I found their papers more original. I believe these ungraded computer assignments are a way to get students to write, perhaps even to enjoy writing, and even to enjoy history! The students' evaluation of the course also indicated that they enjoyed using computers, but more because of the importance of learning new technology as opposed to learning history. Typical comments included, "I believe this class can benefit other students who want to improve their computer skills. With this class I learned how to use the mouse, open the CD-ROMs, and I became familiar with many computer functions"; "The experience on the computer enhanced my computer literacy"; and "Since everything now in everyday life includes computers, it is good to introduce it to history."

In the spring term, I was teaching the course again. This time, the computer lab was equipped with headphones which would access the *WBA* CD-ROM, and the computers were linked to the Internet. Progress! However, due to a series of errors by the dean and the registrar, thirty-eight students enrolled in a computer lab class with twenty-four stations. Since on average about four computers often do not work, doubling up on computers became a fact of life. This infuriated some students, who dropped out. Other students began to complain that there was not enough time in class to finish the assignments or that the computer lab was not accessible, given their time and work schedules. Suggestions to use other CUNY computer labs or the public library did not provide much of a workable alternative.

I spent the first month of the spring term (February) using the *American Pageant* CD-ROM; the students also went to the Smithsonian Museum of the American Indian. In March, we used the Internet exclusively. We began with a formal presentation from David Jaffee, assistant professor of history at City College/CUNY, who talked a little about the Internet and the Web and then took us to a Web site called *The Valley of the Shadow* (http://jefferson.village.virginia.edu/vshadow2/). This Web site is a collection of documents from two neighboring counties in the 'free' North, Pennsylvania, and the slave South, Virginia. I used this Web site so that the students could get a glimpse into people's daily lives, as well as examine the differences between the 'free' and slave states. This was the first time students used the Internet. Some students got on to the site immediately, others could not; three students were stuck with computers that were not working. Once the students got into the site, they became very excited and began to enjoy working their way through *The Valley*.

At first the students were impatient with what they felt was the waiting and the slowness of everything. We constantly reminded students that research takes time. We suggested they compare the time it took to bring up *The Valley of the Shadow* with the time it would take them to go to a library, order the materials, and wait for someone to deliver the materials. I also reminded them that the use of the Internet was one way to go to the National Archives or to libraries and museums anywhere in the world.

Once the students began using the Internet, they got very excited. I gave them lists of Web sites, and every day at the beginning of class, I had students click on to a particular Web site concerning such themes as Jackie Robinson, the Spanish–American War, or Women's Suffrage.

Using the Internet and Web resources also means that faculty have to explain and discuss new issues regarding research, in particular, how to assess the academic merits of a Web site. Just as anyone with some resources and an imagination can get a book published, so can anyone create Web sites. In assessing the merits of a book or a journal article, students should be aware of the author's publisher, the author's credentials, and the author's documentation of that particular book or article. The same methodology holds true for assessing Web sites. Just because something is published or put on the Internet does not make it a reliable source, let alone "true." Students learned how to devise a research strategy using the Internet, as well as how to use Web citations bibliographically. All this increased their knowledge of research methods.

The fall 1996 student responses to the course were very positive. No one complained about using computers or cited all the various problems incurred in class as a problem with my teaching. The spring 1997 evaluations were also very positive, but there were more complaints about the lack of working computers, the time that had to be spent in the computer lab, and the reliance on CD-ROMs as the text.

Next fall, I hope to continue teaching the United States history survey in the computer lab. I have also asked my chair and academic dean if I can teach the honor African-American history class using the computer lab, and I plan to develop my own Web page as a way to create an even more interactive class with my students.

So much for the narrative. What can be generalized from this experience? At the beginning of the New Media Classroom seminar, we, the participants, went over our ideal United States history survey, discussing the obstacles to achieving that ideal and the potential for technology to solve some of the obstacles. Looking back, I can see that technology can be particularly useful in limited ways. Multimedia computers are another tool in the tool kit. They can give us, teachers and students, a wider resource base—we can, for example, visit a Web site on a Sumerian god! This is especially important for those of us who teach in institutions with limited resource facilities.

Using a computer lab forces a professor to change their teaching style. With computers one can't resort to the traditional lecture format. I found that I spent a great deal of time walking around the classroom, visiting each terminal, and speaking directly to students, and they spoke directly to me. It also meant that on those days, I gave less historical lecture and more technical help. This process of dropping the traditional lecture format in lieu of a more interactive classroom dynamic is occurring in non-computer classrooms as well.

What, then, are the advantages and disadvantages for using this new technology in the classroom? I cannot say with any certainty that teaching history using multimedia computer-based technology enables me to pass on my love of the subject to my students any better than the traditional classroom format. There is no evidence that this new technology helps students to understand U.S. history, either in terms of content or methodology, any more than a traditional classroom format; nor is there any evidence that students' performances on state-wide tests or the GRE will be improved as a result of using computer-based multimedia technology.

However, there are advantages for students in taking such a course. They learn basic computer skills, especially with CD-ROMs and the Internet. (Remember, the overwhelming majority of the students we teach in a United States or world civilization survey are there because the course is required or fits into their schedule. Few plan to become professional historians.) At this point in time, because of the novelty of computer technology and because of the way in which historians are using this technology, students will learn some history and will gain some familiarity with technology. Once students are on-line at their colleges, e-mail creates the possibility of encouraging more student writing and a more interactive relationship with the professor and other students. Finally, the Internet takes the student out of the classroom and into museums, libraries, and other resource institutions that would otherwise be inaccessible.

What advice can I give to junior and untenured faculty who wish to use computer technology to teach United States history courses? First, I recommend that before anyone embarks on such a project, they must have the support of their department, chair, academic dean, and provost. If you do not have such support, I encourage you to develop expertise with computer technology, but bring it to the classroom after tenure. As we all well know, the academy is often quite suspicious of or indifferent to innovation. Some faculty may not appreciate the new technology and may bring their indifference or hostility to bear on faculty evaluations. For example, at my college, one colleague developed a CD-ROM on the Harlem Renaissance, complete with audio as well as video movie clips. There was a huge fight on the College Tenure and Promotion Committee as to whether or not this CD-ROM should be accepted for his promotion!

Second, if you are going to develop history courses in computer labs, you need your institution's support because what you will need more than anything is *time*. Of course, we all need more time—time away from grading papers, sitting through meetings, and performing some of the less liked academic chores. Finding appropriate Web sites, making links to other Web sites, and creating an interactive syllabus, however, takes time in front of the computer. Because I do not have a computer in my office, I sometimes hold office hours in the computer lab to help students with their computer-based assignments.

Finally, if you wish to use computer technology to teach history courses, I encourage you to do what you already have done and are doing by reading this book—make connections to faculty across the country who are doing this. The New Media Classroom of the American Social History Project, for example, has a discussion group. Other faculty have created their own Web pages and discussion groups, and already there are a number of publications which provide Internet resources for historians. As a result of this seminar, I have shed my computer-Luddite status and even have started my own Web page, http://ourworld.compuserve.com/homepages/purplewins.

Appendix A

HIST 200.003
Growth and Development of the United States
Spring 1997
03 credits; 03 hours
Class meets Mondays/Wednesdays 10:30–11:50 A.M., room 2013
    Computer Lab
Professor: Barbara Winslow
Telephone/messages 270-5066
Internet: 74641.401@CompuServe. com
Office Hours: Mondays 2:00–4:00 P.M., Tuesdays 4:00–5:45 P.M.,
    Wednesdays 4:00–6:00 P.M. or by appointment

This is your syllabus. Do not lose it. Bring it with you to each class session. There will be additions to the syllabus.

Course Description

This is a course studying the economic, political, social, and intellectual development of the United States from the beginning of the earliest societies. The course focuses on the intersection of class, race, ethnicity, gender, and sexuality on all U.S. institutions. Emphasis is placed on Native American and African-American culture and thought, the Constitution and the Bill of Rights, immigration and ethnicity. Films and museum trips will enhance the course. This course uses computer-based multimedia materials.

Course Objectives

The course will enable students to understand and analyze how social, economic, and political forces affected the development of U.S. institutions. In particular, students will study the development of Constitutional thought. Students will familiarize themselves with geography and understand how geography affects economic, political, and social development. Students will learn research methods and how to analyze original sources. Students will learn to utilize and develop a time line. Students will learn how to use computers, CD-ROMs, the Internet, and the World Wide Web for reading, researching, and writing history.

Required Readings

Melton A. McLaurin, *Celia: A Slave*. Purchase at the bookstore. Robin D.G. Kelley, "Kickin' Reality, Kickin' Ballistics: Gangsta Rap and Postindustrial Los Angeles," in *Race Rebels: Culture Politics, and the Black Working Class* (handout). "A Strange New World: Europeans' First Contact with the Indians" (handout), Deborah Grey White, "Reflections on the Community of Slaves in the Ante-Bellum South" (handout).

Required CD-ROMs

The American Pageant, by Thomas Bailey; *Who Built America,* The American Social History Project. Both CD-ROMs will be purchased from the professor. All students must purchase a formatted, 3.5 hard density disk for use in the class.

Course Requirements

Students must come to class regularly. It will be difficult if not impossible to pass the course if you are inexcusably absent more than four times. An *excused* absence occurs when the student speaks to me before the class period. Students are expected to come to class prepared to discuss the required readings and be prepared to be called upon. Students are expected to complete all the written and computer assignments. Media used in this class will be on reserve in the media center in case you miss a media presentation.

Policy on Late Papers and Assignments

You must contact me *in advance* if for some good reason your assignment cannot be handed in on time. If you miss a movie shown in class, or if you wish to see it again, all media will be on reserve in the media center. Assignments handed in late will be dropped 25 percent of a grade *each day* the assignment is late.

Computer Lab

Our class meets in the computer lab. We will be doing assignments and research work on the computers during part of class time on Wednesdays. This way, students will get hands-on instruction about the Internet, the Web, and CD-ROMs. There are a few rules regarding the computer classroom: 1) No food or drink allowed. Students who do not follow this policy will be asked to leave the class and will be given an A (absence) for that class period. 2) You are to treat the computers carefully and follow instructions of your professor and technical staff. 3) All students must check their disks for viruses *every* time they use a computer. If you fail to do so, and if you submit a disk with a virus onto a machine, you will get an F for the course. 4) Use the lab during its open hours to do your computer homework. The computer lab will be free the following days and hours. This is a good time for you to work on your assignments:

Mondays: 3:00–6:00 P.M.
Tuesdays: 9:00–10:20 A.M.; 1:30–6:00 P.M.
Wednesdays: 3:00–6:00 P.M.

Friday: ALL DAY
Saturday: 9:00–11:15 A.M.

Grading System

Time line 15 points
Research paper 15 points
Museum trip assignment 10 points
Computer assignment 15 points
Computer assignment 15 points
Computer assignment 15 points
5 map assignments (@ 3 points each) 15 points

Policy Regarding Incompletes

To request a grade of Incomplete: You must submit to me, in writing, no later than May 14, a list of all the exams/assignments that you have completed and that you intend to complete for your final grade. You must have completed at least half of all the written assignments. Unless there are extenuating circumstances, you will not get an Incomplete if you have more than four (4) absences. I will deny an Incomplete if any of the above information is missing.

Policy Regarding Rewrites

A note on papers: If you receive a grade of C+ or below, you have two weeks to rewrite the paper. You must see me first and go over the problems in the paper. The highest grade for a rewritten paper is an A-.

All Students Are to Get a Manila File Folder

Put all corrected assignments in your manila folder. On the last day that papers are due, hand in your file folder with all your evaluated work.

Due Dates for Written Assignments

- First map assignment February 19
- First written/computer assignment March 5
- Second map assignment March 10

- Second written/computer assignment March 26
- Third map assignment April 2
- Time line April 14
- Fourth map assignment April 16
- Museum trip assignment April 28
- Third written/computer assignment April 30
- Fifth map assignment May 14
- Research Part I April 28
- Research Part II May 5
- Research Part III May 12
- Research paper due May 21

Assignments

February Is Black History Month

Module I. The Native Americans—the European Settlements

Week 1. February 5. Introduction to the course. Purchase the hard density 3.5–inch formatted disk. Readings: **On reserve in the library,** "Africans and Americans: Inter-Continental Contacts Across the Atlantic, to 1500," in *Africans and Native Americans: The Language of Race and the Evolution of Red/Black Peoples,* by Jack D. Forbes, pp. 6–25.

Week 2. February 10. No class. *February 12.* Introduction to the world of CD-ROMs. Read all the material in *The American Pageant,* chapters 1 & 2; this includes the text, time line, maps, archival sources, points to consider. Read handout, "A Strange New World: The Europeans' First Contacts with American Indians." Go to the Museum of the American Indian on February 12 or during that week.

The Museum of the American Indian is at One Bowling Green, NYC 10004. Phone: 212-825-6700, FAX: 212-825-8180. The museum is open daily seven days a week, except Christmas. 10:00 A.M.–5:00 P.M. Admission is free. Travel information: 4 & 5 IRT Bowling Green; 1 & 9, South Ferry; M, J, Z Broad Street, N & R. Whitehall Street, South Ferry, 2 & 3, change at Chambers Street for 1 & 9.

Week 3. February 17. No class. Class meets February 19. **In class map quiz:** Be able to identify on a map of the United States: the Atlantic Ocean, Pacific

Ocean, the Gulf of Mexico, Mexico, Canada; the names of the Great Lakes, the Mississippi/Missouri, Columbia, Ohio; James and Hudson Rivers; identify and locate ten Indian tribes in North America prior to 1492; locate Plymouth, Jamestown, Saint Augustine, Quebec, and Santa Fe.

Week 4. February 24–26. Readings, chapters 3, 4, 5 of *The American Pageant.* **There will be a CD-ROM quiz February 24.** This will be a quiz that will measure your ability to navigate a CD-ROM. The quiz will not be graded, but you must pass the quiz. You will be tested on both your ability to access and to understand the CD-ROM assignment.
February 26. Outside speaker: Professor David Jaffe, City College/CUNY will make a presentation about using the Internet and the Web.

First draft of first paper due February 26.

First paper assignment: Using all the assignments, readings, CD-ROM, map work, visit to the American Indian museum, and media, write a three-page, double-spaced paper explaining how the Europeans created an identity for the American Indian. Then, using the materials you have read in class, discuss whether or not that identity created by the Europeans corresponded with the reality of the Indians you have studied. This paper must be word-processed. Use grammar checking and spell checking. You must use an example from your map work, from your readings, from the museum, and from the CD-ROM. If you do not include such citations and references, you will have to redo the paper. This paper will be corrected and handed back for final revisions on Thursday, February 27. **The final paper is due March 5.**

March Is Women's History Month

Module II. Africans in the Americas

Week 5. March 3–5. The American Pageant, chapter 6. **First paper due March 5.**

Week 6. March 10–12. Readings: *The American Pageant,* chapters 7, 8, 9, 10. Second map quiz, March 10. Be able to identify the thirteen English colonies; identify areas where people of African descent lived; describe the Triangle Trade; identify which states abolished slavery before 1800; identify the slave states and the free states before 1861; identify the areas where cotton production was greatest.

Museum trip assignment: Seneca Village, due April 28. Go to the Seneca Village Exhibition (see Black and Women's History Month handout). Write a three-page, double-spaced paper about the exhibit. In particular, I want you to focus on the similarities and differences between the African-Americans and the Irish-Americans who lived in and were later evicted from Seneca Village.

Week 7. March 17–19. Readings: *Celia,* Deborah Grey White, "Reflections on the Community of Slaves in the Ante Bellum South"; *The American Pageant,* chapters 11, 12, 13, 14, 15, 16.

Week 8. March 24–26. Readings: Finish *Celia; The American Pageant,* chapters 17, 18, 19, 20, 21, 22, 23; *Who Built America (WBA),* "The South Shall Rise Again."

Second paper due: Internet written assignment based on *Celia* and *The Valley of the Shadow.*

Module III. The West

Week 9. March 31–April 2. Readings: *The American Pageant,* chapters 24 & 28; *WBA* "How the West Was Lost." **Third map quiz April 2.** Identify on a U.S. map areas where there are Indian reservations; identify the state of Oklahoma; explain the significance of Oklahoma in terms of Native Americans; look at map "The Opening of the West" and write a paragraph, *based solely on this map,* "How the West was opened." By the way, look back at map entitled, "The Indian Tribes of North American Before 1492." Who really "opened" the West?

Module IV. Immigration and Migration

Week 10. April 7–9. Readings: *The American Pageant,* chapters 26–27, *WBA,* "Community and Culture." Media: The Mississippi Triangle.

Week 11. April 14–16. **Time line due April 14. Fourth map quiz April 16. This is a written assignment due in class.** Looking at the maps, indicate the nationality or ethnicity of those who immigrated to North America from 1609 to 1840; from 1840 to 1880; from 1880 to

1924. Where did most European immigrants settle? Where did Asian immigrants settle? What important immigrant groups have been left out of these maps on immigration? A hint—it's not Europe, Africa, or Asia. What do you think is the relationship between industrialization and immigration, based upon the maps and your readings?

No classes April 21–23—spring break! This is a good time to do the museum assignment, finish the third computer assignment, and begin work on the research paper.

Module V. Gender and U.S. History

Week 12. April 28–30. Readings, *The American Pageant,* Chapters 17 & 28, WBA Part IV. **Museum paper due April 28. Third computer assignment due April 30. Part I of research paper (see attached sheet).** For your third computer assignment: You are to prepare a three-page double-spaced, typed paper showing how you used *Who Built America?* and *The American Pageant* to research gender issues, for example, women of color, African-American women, Asian-American women, Native-American women, Latinas, women's suffrage, women and labor (sharecroppers, domestic workers, factory workers, teachers), women and immigration, women and education, women and temperance, women and reform, women and the KKK (yes!). In this paper, give the references from the two CD-ROMs. **Extra credit for this assignment will be given for finding Web sites.**

Week 13. May 5–7. **Part II of the research assignment due.** Readings, *WBA* part IV.

Module VI. Imperialism

Week 14. May 12–14. Readings: *The American Pageant,* Chapters 30, 31; *WBA,* "The Search for Markets." Media: *The Overthrow of Hawaii.* **Part III of the research assignment is due. Fifth map quiz, May 14. This is a written assignment due in class.** Based upon the maps, when did the United States begin acquiring lands outside the continental United States (after 1861)? How did the United States acquire territories? What were/are the territories? Have any become states? If so, which ones? According to the maps, how many times has the U.S. invaded or been involved in warfare in the Caribbean?

May 21. **Research paper is due in my office by noon. Late papers will not be accepted.** Your folder with all your assignments is also due.

Appendix B

HIST 200.004
Growth and Development of the United States
First Computer CD-ROM Assignment, October 23, 1996
Due in class Monday October 28.

Please work on this assignment in class. You may use the lab to finish this paper. Your paper must be word-processed, double-spaced. The paper is due in class on October 28. Late (and I mean even late after class) papers will not be accepted.

Use the *Who Built America?* CD-ROM.

Click on the chapter "The South Will Rise Again." Read the text, search the sources, listen to the audio portions, and look at the pictures.

Choose from one of the following topics:

- You are a white, racist, southern employer. How would you make sure your labor force is divided by race and gender? Write this paper as if you are writing a letter to a fellow employer. In your letter, make certain you let the reader know what kind of a firm/manufacturing establishment you own and run, where it is, how many people you employ. Let us know why it is important to keep your work force divided. Do you as an employer need and ask for outside help? In other words, tell the reader a bit about yourself and the community in which you live.

Two double-spaced, typewritten pages. On a separate sheet of paper, include all the references from the CD-ROM.

- You have been asked to give oral history testimony about your family, who were sharecroppers. Write an oral history of your family. How? Why? When? Where did they become sharecroppers?

Two double-spaced, typewritten pages. On a separate sheet of paper, include all the references from the CD-ROM.

Appendix C

HIST 200.001
Ungraded computer quiz.
Write on this piece of paper.

You have thirty minutes to complete this quiz. The purpose of this quiz is to test your ability to get around the CD-ROM, *The American Pageant.*

The Emphasis of This Quiz Is on How and Where
You Got Your Answers

Using the CD-ROM *American Pageant,* Chapters 1–4:

1. Find **both** maps of the West Indies and the Caribbean colonies (you have to find two maps). Name one Spanish, one French, one English, and one Dutch colony. How did you find these maps?
2. Identify **two** original documents which deal with the African slave trade. How and where did you find these documents?
3. Who was Yarrow Mamout? How did you find him?

Appendix D

HIST 200
Growth and Development of the United States
In-class computer exercise
This is not a graded exercise

Immigration to the United States: Visual Literacy

Use the CD-ROM, *The American Pageant.* **Click** on chapter 26, "American Moves to the City," **click on** New Immigration, move the text until you see on your left-hand side a picture called "sweatshop conditions." Click to enlarge the picture.

Look at the picture. Look at it again. Write down everything you see in this picture.

After you have described this picture, write down what you think this pictures tells us about work, working conditions, class and gender relations.

Appendix E

HIST 200.003
Growth and Development of the United States
Second written computer assignment

This Assignment Is Based on Celia and the WEB Site,
The Valley of the Shadow

The story of Celia takes place in Missouri, which during the Civil War was a border state, that is, a slave state which stayed in the Union. Augusta and Franklin counties are counties that are, respectively, in the northernmost corner of slave state Virginia and (nominally, that is, Frederick Douglass) free state Pennsylvania. Reading *Celia,* and going through the material in the *Valley of the Shadow,* we can glimpse into lives of people during the 1850s.

You have been given a handout which gives additional information about *The Valley of the Shadow.*

Write a three to five (3–5) page paper, typed, double-spaced. Write a paper comparing and contrasting the lives of slaves in Montgomery county, Missouri *(Celia)* with those in Augusta and Franklin counties. See if you can find information regarding the social lives of African-Americans, such as residential patterns, occupations in newspapers, place of birth, economic status, slave or free; also see if you can find information about political events (i.e., Missouri Compromise, Compromise of 1850, Kansas-Nebraska, the Republican Party, Bleeding Kansas, John's Brown's raid, slave revolts, the Underground railroad, differences between slaves and free African-Americans). Is there anything you can *generalize* about the lives of African-Americans based on your research?

Remember your paper must be well organized. Begin with an introduction which states your thesis. Every paragraph is about your thesis. Remember your paper must end with a conclusion, which shows how you proved or argued your thesis. Watch for spelling, grammar, punctuation and don't forget to **proofread.**

Appendix F

HIST 200
Growth and Development of the United States
In-Class Computer Assignment
November 13, 1996

The Triangle Shirtwaist Factory Fire

For this assignment, your are to choose a partner and work on this in class.

Use the CD-ROM, *Who Built America.* Click on the excursion "Why Did 146 Have to Die?," p. 298. Read text pages 1–7; read all of the press accounts and examine the photos.

Make sure you are all aware of the following:

- When did this tragedy occur?
- How was it possible?

- Why was it possible?
- What were the responses to this tragedy?
- Why did these responses occur at this particular time?
- What factors contributed to these responses?

Choose one of the following and write a newspaper account of this tragedy:

- You are the owner of the Triangle factory.
- You are a survivor of the fire.
- You are a male trade union organizer.
- You are a female political organizer.

Notes

1. Thanks to Steve Brier, Marisol Carpio, Brett Eynon, Donna Thompson, and K.C. Wiggins for all their help.

❖

II. Seeing the Bigger Picture: A Graduate Student/Assistant's Thoughts on Technology and Presentation in the Classroom
Kacy D. Wiggins

When Professor David Nasaw, executive officer of the Graduate Center's history department, approached me about working with professor Winslow, he had my rather unique background in mind. In a profession that often seems devoted to a neo-Luddite stance, I stand out. Since the age of twelve, I have owned and programmed computers. As a matter of fact, I first majored in computer science at the University of Cincinnati for two years. I guess I could say I luckily lacked the dedication at the time and performed poorly in many of my classes, earning a "vacation" from the university. When I returned a couple of years later, I chose history as my major. Computers, however, remained a side concern, a hobby of sorts. With such a background, I am always surprised by the rather low level of computer literacy held by many, but not all, of my colleagues.

My experience with computers does not stop there. For more than two years, I have worked for *Utne Magazine* as an on-line conference host. This position is not technical, per se. In fact, many of those who work with me have little or no technical background beyond day-to-day word processing and the occasional chat room visit. But I think this experience gives me a little insight into the Internet as a tool and as a possible means to develop a community. I also had the unique opportunity to work briefly as an research assistant for the American Social History Project on their second CD-ROM based on their *Who Built America* textbook.

Of course, this is just one side of my background. I am now a doctoral student in United States history fast approaching candidacy. I accepted this position as professor Winslow's technical and graduate assistant, not just because I have an interest in and experience with computers, but because I also wanted to move out of the seminar room and into the classroom. My goal as a historian is to bring history to the undergraduate in an interesting way, in addition to the usual research. So this is my background, a vital part of this story. On one level, it places me somewhere between professor and student. On another, I stand somewhere between computer novice and expert. And it is from this position that I make my observations.

When I accepted my current position, the idea of being involved in the first-time meeting of CD-ROM technology and a basic history survey class at Medgar Evers College excited me. I was optimistic, but guardedly so. I suspected that many students in a community college might not share my interest in history. More likely, most students probably dislike history and see it as a necessary evil, but this technology, I thought, might be the sugar that made the bitter pill a little more palatable.

But the background that made me a perfect candidate for this job influenced my assumptions. Growing up immersed in personal computer technology, I assumed that computer literacy would be widespread. I grew up hearing from teachers and reading in computer magazines that by the time I was an adult everything would be metric and computerized. I had little idea of the computer literacy levels of college students. In part, because of my unfamiliarity with working in the classroom, I assumed that a class of young adults would know their way around a computer, a CD-ROM, and the Internet. When I actually stepped into the classroom, a wide range of faces of varying ages greeted me, not just the young faces

I expected. In addition, many of the students, young and old, had not even sat in front of a computer before. Others knew computers nearly as well as, if not better than, I did. Naturally, I spent much more of my time with the former than I did the latter.

As we approached the end of the second semester, I saw that the effectiveness of computers in the classroom depended not simply on the technology itself but on the students' background. Having to teach computer basics detracts from a history class' main purpose, teaching history. For CD-ROMs like *Who Built America* to work successfully, computer literacy training must become a reality for all students. I would suppose that this sort of education should happen at the primary and secondary levels. But as we know all too well, public schools barely scrape by right now. Similarly, few students have the opportunity to learn the basics at home. Computers, despite all of the utopian hopes of recent years, have not found a place in the homes of all Americans, but however we overcome this barrier, once the students have the capability to use them, computers may very well have the ability to transform history in the classroom. I will now turn my attention to the software used in this class and make a few observations.

The American Pageant was a successful, albeit flawed, textbook, long before the CD-ROM. And I think 'digital textbook' best describes its new incarnation. Sure, the student has the benefit of searching the text for a particular word or topic and can even take notes on the computer, but it differs little from the textbook. The level of interaction remains the same. The student is a somewhat passive audience, but the addition of primary sources, graphs, and differing historical opinions takes advantage of some of the space available on the digital medium.

On the other hand, the *Who Built America* CD-ROM steps beyond the textbook, at least more so than the *American Pageant*. It transcends the digital textbook format. The many excursions often incorporate video and sound. It even has a game or two, all of this is in addition to the narrative text. Students respond well to hearing the words and seeing the faces of many historical figures and agents.

The mere use of the audio clips and visual images does not use the technology to its full advantage, however. And this generation of historians and those who follow must rethink the ways that we present history. As I speak the new digital video disc technology (DVD) will soon increase the potential of the computer. Yet we still have not used the present computer technology to its full potential. I think one of the more creative examples of how computer technology can be used to make history more lively is found on the World Wide Web.

The Valley of the Shadows goes beyond the additional excursions seen in digital translations of textbooks. It lacks the speed and the flashiness available on CD-ROM. The Web site, however, gives the students a look into the historian's craft, perhaps making up for the lack of bells and whistles. The student, if he or she chooses, looks behind the narrative to see the documents of differing types that support it and shape it. It is more than just a textbook in new form. Let us hope that software authors will take note and join the speed and flashiness of the CD-ROM with a similar format, but this is just one possibility.

I don't mean to sound so pessimistic about the available technology or to ignore what lies behind the technology. The material is just one-half of the bigger picture—the teacher is the other. We can change our teaching method much more easily than we can change the technology. Professor Winslow and I often sit down together to plan in-class assignments. Because of the technology at our fingertips, we have maps, charts, narrative and, most importantly, primary sources. The software cannot take the place of the teacher yet, so we must provide the thread that ties all of these things together. For the most part, the assignments served two functions. First, they helped the student learn to use the software (a vital function when they lack computer skills). Second, it allowed them to learn about the period under study much in the same way that reading a textbook would. In addition to in-class assignments, Professor Winslow took advantage of the resources in the software with small research papers. The students had to use the primary sources provided on the disks and give us clear indications of how they found the information.

As I mentioned earlier, many barriers stand in the way of using the technology effectively. Too many students and too few computers comes to mind, and even the flashiest of software cannot inspire interest in history. I have learned from this experiment that computer technology does not necessarily make our jobs easier. It challenges us to think of history and teaching in a different way. It gives us a new way to reach our students much more powerfully than the video cassette recorder did not too long ago. I think that professor Winslow, and numerous other pioneers, have taken that first important step.

For reasons not necessarily in any of our direct control, my pessimism has not faded completely, however. We live in a time when politicians and parents cry out for quick and cheap solutions to our educational problems at all levels. We make a serious mistake if we believe, as some might, that these CD-ROMs or any other technology are panaceas, especially when access remains limited and the technology as of yet hardly qualifies as cheap.

Finally, I must briefly answer the question that I have had in the back of my mind since the beginning of this project: how will this technology change they way we present history in the classroom? My first impulse is to say, "I am a historian, not a futurist." But I believe, in the hands of the prepared student and teacher, it allows us to appeal to our audience on their own terms. The student no longer finds herself locked in the linear progression of the textbook. She can piece together the narrative in a way that makes much more sense to her, thus, hopefully, making history interesting. Ideally, the teacher, too, escapes the confines of the pages of the textbook. But I place emphasis on the word "ideally."

III. Computers in the Classroom: A Non-History Major's Point of View
Marisol Carpio

This past fall semester (my senior year at Medgar Evers College/CUNY), I faced my first college history class. As a biology major, I had postponed this requirement because I felt it was unimportant to my future as a physician. I had also heard many stories from my peers about the absurdity of the course requirements, and these combined with my already negative feelings. Completely unaware of what the class I had registered for entailed, I entered the first day surprised to find out that it would be different from a "normal" history class. Instead of the required reading materials that are usually associated with such a class, CD-ROMs were being utilized. Using computers to teach history was such an unconventional idea that I did not think it would work. The professor herself was so unfamiliar with the software that she had a technician on hand to assist students.

The first couple of sessions with the machinery were a nightmare. I found it quite frustrating to spend a class session getting familiar with a computer, since I have a decent amount of computer knowledge and even already had my own e-mail account, although I only e-mailed the professor once. Also, there were several problems with installing the software. The *Who Built America* CD-ROM worked best with sound equipment, but this equipment was not attached to the computers. Although the technicians did show students how to access the software, many students, during the earlier sessions, were still unable to do so and therefore about ten minutes of each computer session was wasted getting everyone linked. After all these problems were worked out, the computer sessions ran more smoothly.

Using the CD-ROMs in class gave me a very different perspective on history. Instead of being told what happened and how it affected people, I could see and read about it in one medium. Unlike other media, with computers there is a sense of getting involved with what you read. You decide what picture or story to click on and then can get enormous amounts of information in minutes. I found it to be an important tool, to be able to get information so quickly on a topic that I was interested in. I recall reading the account of the Triangle Shirtwaist Factory fire; it was very descriptive, and the pictures that were available really drew me emotionally into the event. Then we were given the task to write our own accounts of the tragedy and how we survived it.

There was a great deal of freedom in this writing assignment, and, therefore, I became very involved in it. Generally, I hate to write anything, but I actually enjoyed the process of developing the story. I found out the next day that I was not the only one. It seems that everyone was also taken aback by the pictures and the text and, therefore, were moved to write the paper. This was not an isolated incident, either. We were more enthusiastic with most of the computer assignments versus the traditional work.

Two different CD-ROMs were used, *Who Built America* and *The American Pageant.* The first was much more useful than the latter. It had more visual attachments to the software and also seemed easier to access. I am aware that the other CD-ROM was a textbook-style software package, and that did have some impact on my use of it. With this type of CD-ROM, it would probably be more beneficial to have the actual textbook, instead of the disk. It is difficult to access the information and read long documents on a computer screen. It was quite useful, however, to many students when we had traditional assignments like our time lines and our research papers. The CD-ROM also provided a primary resource to get more information from the library and other sources.

Although the traditional sessions provided the foundation of our historical knowledge, the computer session sparked a greater interest in what we discussed. It is such a different experience from the traditional classroom set-up, and I received a great deal more from the course than I would have thought. My participation was probably greater in this type of atmosphere than in the traditional because the environment that was created allowed students to become generally more active. I recall a particular session in which we were analyzing a set of pictures. With the use of computers each student had a clear, color photo and could zoom in or out to examine it better. I still do not enjoy writing, but I am more aware now of its importance in all aspects of life and my career goals. Even though history does not have a direct impact on my life, it does affect how I look at situations and how I interact with other individuals in society. I guess that is what history is all about, developing people's minds to realize that our actions affect society as a whole. I would definitely recommend this course. I learned American history from a different angle than I was accustomed to, and, as a result, there was greater interest on my part. And, I increased my computer knowledge too.

12

Teaching Tomorrow's Teachers

Computing Technology, Social Studies Methods Instruction, and the Preservice Teacher

Frank E. Johnson

This paper originated in a syllabus request. As the new social studies education coordinator at my university, I was asked to redesign the methods course in my content area. In particular, I was charged with "updating" the course. I not only needed to bring a greater sense of cohesion to the class and the accompanying field experience, but also to consider the role and place of technology in teaching secondary social studies. The division chairman who solicited the syllabus simply smiled and bid me a good day. Seldom have I worked on a more inauspicious project, however. How could such a benign request prove to have been so ill-timed or somehow disadvantaged? In short, despite numerous textbooks for methods courses, scores of articles, and bibliographies on related topics, little attention has been given to teaching technology in the preservice arena.

Having devolved into a product of necessity for my own teaching, this essay claims a very limited objective. At issue here is not the role of computing technology in applying various educational theories, or an analysis of the resource options available to educators desiring to incorporate the multimedia technologies into their classroom. Instead, this paper follows a more modest course, that is, given the high profile of computing and multimedia developments, why is this topic given superficial treatment at best in methods textbooks? Secondly, and more to the point, when and how does the preservice teacher acquire the requisite skills to teach in the "wired" classroom? Quite simply, I have not found the answer I sought. Therefore this essay neither assumes a definitive tone nor offers a decree. On the contrary, I would like to use this opportunity to address an issue which begs for clarification within the academy—an issue both obvious and of vital significance to the continued success of social studies education.

This essay includes a review of current literature relating to the presence of computing technology in middle and secondary social studies methods textbooks. It then proposes several tentative corrections to the imbalance highlighted in the literature review: namely, that preservice teachers must master the rudiments of several software applications—including multimedia authoring and e-mail list management. Finally, this paper posits that while every student learns at a unique pace, all can, and must, attain "expert novice" proficiency in each medium. The net result for the preservice teacher reaches well beyond enhanced marketability; multimedia proficiency will assist him/her in engaging students in the learning process.

Methods Texts and Computing Technology:
A Brief Survey

Methods textbooks are the obvious and necessary point of entry for a reflective survey such as this. The foundation of this essay is a review of fifteen texts representing the last two decades of thought and practice regarding social studies methods instruction (see Figure 12.1). It is not the purpose of this essay to critically review each volume, but rather to investigate whether or not computing technology issues are addressed in the given texts, and if so, in what detail. Furthermore, this essay considers whether these texts successfully equip preservice teachers to incorporate computing technology into their classrooms. In short, with one exception (and a qualified one at that), the answer is no.

In 1985, John Michaelis was the first to incorporate computers into a methods text.[1] His popular *Social Studies for Children* identified "electronic learning" as one of several instructional mediums (essentially a variation on an audiovisual theme). According to Michaelis, not only were computers valuable resources, which facilitate diversification in lesson format/presentation, they promised the novelty of interactive instruction.[2]

Unfortunately, Michaelis stops short of exploring the many issues relating to incorporating computing in the classroom. For example, how

Figure 12.1. **Social Studies Methods Texts, 1977–1997** (in reverse chronological order)

Peter H. Martorella, *Teaching Social Studies In Middle and Secondary Schools,* 2nd ed. (Englewood Cliffs, NJ: Prentice-Hall, 1996).

Mary Burke-Hengen and Tim Gillespie, *Building Community: Social Studies in the Middle School Years* (Portsmouth, NH: Heinemann, 1995).

Michael G. Allen and Robert L. Stevens, *Middle Grade Social Studies: Teaching and Learning for Active and Responsible Citizenship* (Boston: Allyn & Bacon, 1994).

Jack Zevin, *Social Studies for the Twenty-first Century: Methods and Materials for Teaching in Middle and Secondary Schools* (New York: Longman, 1992).

Wayne Mahood, Linda Biemer, and William T. Lowe, *Teaching Social Studies in Middle and Senior High Schools: Decisions! Decisions!* (New York: Macmillan, 1991).

James L. Barth, *Elementary and Junior High/Middle School Social Studies Curriculum, Activities, and Materials,* 3rd ed. (Lanham, MD: University Press of America, 1991).

James L. Barth, *Methods of Instruction in Social Studies Education,* 3rd ed. (Lanham, MD: University Press of America, 1990).

David T. Naylor and Richard A. Diem, *Elementary and Middle School Social Studies* (New York: Random House, 1987).

John U. Michaelis, *Social Studies for Children: A Guide to Basic Instruction,* 8th ed. (Englewood Cliffs, NJ: Prentice-Hall, 1985).

James L. Barth, *Secondary Social Studies Curriculum, Activities, and Materials* (Lanham, MD: University Press of America, 1984).

Leonard S. Kenworthy, *Social Studies for the Eighties in Elementary and Middle Schools,* 3rd ed. (New York: John Wiley, 1981).

David G. Armstrong, *Social Studies in Secondary Education* (New York: Macmillan,1980).

Jack L. Nelson and John U. Michaelis, *Secondary Social Studies: Instruction, Curriculum, Evaluation* (Englewood Cliffs, NJ: Prentice-Hall, 1980).

Richard E. Gross et al., *Social Studies for Our Times* (New York: John Wiley, 1978).

M. Eugene Gilliom et al., Practical Methods for the Social Studies (Belmont, CA: Wadsworth, 1977).

would incorporating computers into the classroom benefit students or teachers? What were the potential problems, limitations, of doing so—software/hardware concerns as well as the willingness/ability of students to utilize the same? What was the pedagogic value of "electronic learning," as opposed to traditional methods of instruction? To his credit, however, Michaelis does charge the preservice teacher with two important considerations: 1) that cultivating computer literacy is merely a means to an end, not the objective itself; and 2) that computer-related activities must not be isolated affairs, but purposeful encounters fully integrated into well-designed units of instruction. Just the same, one is left to ponder how the incorporation of the computer "is essential to the attainment of unit objectives, the meeting of individual differences, and the achievement of well-rounded learning."[3] Michaelis' approach to the topic, both in detail and application, seemingly became the model for subsequent methods authors.

David T. Naylor and Richard Diem's *Elementary and Middle School Social Studies* indicates how, within a mere two years, computing technology had flooded over the educational marketplace.[4] Whereas Michaelis identified computers as an emerging technology within a chapter on instructional media, Naylor and Diem anchor their comparable chapter to the topic ("Using Computers and Other Technology"). Despite the title, however, little differs from the earlier perspective.

Naylor and Diem articulate four ways in which computers can be incorporated in the social studies classroom:

> 1) learning facts and skills through drill and practice instruction; 2) providing additional remediation or enrichment through tutorial lessons; 3) developing concepts, generalizations, and thinking skills through the use of simulations; and 4) using the factual information in databases to develop concepts and generalizations and to promote thinking skills.[5]

Having set the stage for thoughtful analysis, what follows is a cursory overview of each possible application. For example, regarding tutorials, Naylor and Diem note that "individualized social studies instruction is an often professed goal but one that time and circumstances in the precomputer era combine to make difficult to accomplish. Computer assisted instruction makes it possible to move closer to that goal." Yet, in the absence of specific guidance, one must conjecture the best route to this eagerly desired end. In other words, despite an elevated profile, little had changed from Michaelis' perspective. In short, the methods texts were doing little to equip the preservice teacher to put fresh ideas or innovative technologies into practice—they were supplying information as opposed to instruction. Naylor and Diem contend that although "computer mastery is not yet a necessity to teach, familiarity is helpful, especially if you want to keep up with your students." This is an ironic position, to be sure. To be acquainted with the system of government in America is not satisfactory preparation to teach high school civics; neither would a general knowledge of battles and casualty figures enable one to teach the history of American wars. Should the same standard not apply to the use of computers in the social studies classroom? In other words, how does familiarity empower one to teach effectively?[6]

In *Methods of Instruction in Social Studies Education,* James L. Barth concurs that computers hold much promise for the social studies teacher. Barth merely identifies their basic "applications" within the classroom, although (for example, facilitating computer literacy, as a database resource, and enabling learning through computer-assisted instruction). Interestingly, Barth's *Elementary and Junior High/Middle School Social Studies Curriculum, Activities, and Materials* overlooks the applicability of the computer as indicated in his *Methods of Instruction.* In fact, in this latter volume Barth proposes a unit on technological dependence which relies exclusively on research in print materials and group reporting—the suggested activities fail to incorporate technology despite the subject matter.[7] Barth was not alone in his indecision, however.

Wayne Mahood, Linda Biemer, and William T. Lowe, *Teaching Social Studies in Middle and Senior High Schools* likewise breaks no new ground on this issue.[8] If anything, Mahood, Biemer, and Lowe accentuate the central weakness of the literature. They acknowledge that teacher education programs must include computer studies. Moreover, they strongly encourage teacher education students to take computer-related courses even when not required. Mahood, Beimer, and Lowe assert that the consequences for failing to do so are clear: "the students you will teach may know more about computer use than you do, and that may be an awkward situation for a new teacher." (From a 1997 vantage, this is an understatement of epic proportions.) What is not articulated, however, speaks just as loudly: a preservice teacher's computer illiteracy manifests itself in a diminished capacity to meet the needs of students.[9]

Apparently not all methods authors shared the computer literacy conviction. For example, despite the title, Jack Zevin's *Social Studies for the Twenty-First Century* makes no mention of computers. Michael G. Allen and Robert L. Stevens' *Middle Grade Social Studies* also is silent on the subject. Likewise, one is hard pressed to find computing issues addressed in Mary Burke-Hengen and Tim Gillespie, *Building Community: Social Studies in the Middle School Years.*[10] Without over-dramatizing the point, these "new" texts for teaching teacher-candidates were not proving terribly helpful as I attempted to rethink social studies methods at my university.

Peter H. Martorella's recent *Teaching Social Studies In Middle and Secondary Schools* has reinvigorated the field.[11] Martorella presents the most thorough treatment of the subject available. For the methods instructor, as well as the preservice teacher, this text could not be more timely. Like Naylor and Diem, Martorella devotes an entire chapter to the topic. "Using Technology to Enhance Social Studies Instruction" explores several vital issues such as "Infusing Microcomputer Applications in the Social Studies Curriculum," "Identifying and Evaluating Appropriate Social Studies Software," "Telecommunications and On-line Information," and "Multimedia in the Age of Emerging Computer Technologies."[12]

Martorella charges future social studies teachers to envision computers as "electronic allies." Moreover, he posits that the computer must be "an object of instruction," as much as a utilitarian device *for* instruction.[13] This bi-modality, for lack of a better term, is quite intriguing. In short, Martorella underscores the need to purposely teach with technology. He encourages practitioners to continually consider how a given technology-based activity serves these dual objectives.

Despite the seemingly comprehensive sweep, close inspection yields limited specific instruction in exactly how one can enhance social studies instruction with technology. For example, Martorella notes that "teachers must select software carefully, choosing only programs that address important curricular objectives, regardless of other merits." The 1983 National Council for the Social Studies Microcomputer Courseware Evaluation guidelines are reproduced to facilitate such review. While teachers can compare and contrast curricular objectives, how can they evaluate software without a solid grasp of both general technical requirements and how the same might bear on the ability of student users to engage the given application? In the absence of such skills, the potential teacher is dependent upon peer review in professional journals at best, or the descriptive information provided with the software package at worst. Martorella continues this skewed logic when addressing the applicability of databases to social studies. Familiarity with software is presumed. In fact, generally speaking, he contends that "interactive multimedia technologies show promise of aiding social studies teachers in motivating students and translating abstract ideas into more concrete examples." He continues with a cautious note: "The effective and full use of these electronic aids, however, will depend on how skilled social studies teachers become in their applications." In response, then, this essay poses a central question: when does the preservice teacher acquire such knowledge?[14]

A Call for Change: Incorporating Computer Instruction in the Content Area

It is important to state plainly that this essay in no way intimates pedagogical malfeasance or shoddy scholarship on the part of methods textbook authors. Many methods texts have much to commend them. For example, Zevin's *Social Studies for the Twenty-First Century* is very sophisticated and offers one of the most probing rationales for teaching social studies to be found in the literature. Just the same, the general lack both of clarity and consensus regarding computing technology is unmistakable. Having briefly reviewed the literature, this essay also seeks to identify several ways in which computing technology can be incorporated into social studies instruction generally and the methods course in particular.

Practical Methods for the Social Studies, now twenty years old, is a model methods text. Although long forgotten (not referenced once in any source consulted for this essay), M. Eugene Gilliom and collaborators (hereafter Gilliom) took seriously the task of providing specific examples to support their approach to the social studies.[15] Ironically, Gilliom even includes a brief section addressing the newest technology of that period— the computer. Both the basic mechanics of the computer and the potential of simulations within social studies classroom are surveyed. While the material on computers is limited to be sure, the next methods text to venture even this far came eight years later.

Despite the dated material, each *Practical Methods for the Social Studies* insight and strategy can be applied to current as well as future technologies. A key reason for Gilliom's applicability to the present is his guiding principle that technology must be purpose- as opposed to product-driven. He posited that each media-related instructional device "should be selected to motivate students to ask questions and pursue solutions to problems." To this end, Gilliom provides specific instructions on how to construct media-based projects. The sections on incorporating "slides, filmstrips, and photographs" and "artifacts and material remains" are outstanding. Here one finds concrete instruction on how to use the technology, commentary on which commercial products have proven "teacher friendly," and selected samples of finished projects. Gilliom's objective is twofold: to equip the teacher and thereby empower the students.[16]

Using Gilliom as a reference point, how can computing technology be better incorporated into the social studies methods course? What is an acceptable range of skills? What constitutes mastery? For the methods instructor, an obvious point of entry is the course syllabus. Here these issues not only are introduced, but the standard is set for the entire course. In my methods course (see Figure 12.2), students come to understand that computing technology is part of an ongoing development within the field. They must realize that linking content area expertise with innovative instructional technologies is a never-ending process. At a minimum, preservice teachers should be competent in at least one presentation software application. (I use PowerPoint.) Moreover, they should understand the rudiments of, and be able to navigate, the Internet—both e-mail and the World Wide Web. In fact, activities can be designed in which preservice teachers dialog with their field-experience cooperating teacher over issues raised on the Internet. (I subscribe each student to a discussion group for this purpose.) Engaging in these activities would constitute a significant—and conscious—step toward computer literacy.

To reach this objective requires a significant investment of time for both student and professor, however. Dividing large classes into small groups is imperative; one-on-one instruction is preferable. Once the student begins to master the details, however, an increasing inertia and excitement propels most students ahead unaided. Finally, and what has served as a signal spur to action, students can collect their various projects into a portfolio (on-line or print version) which showcases their innovative use of the various media and ideally enhances their prospects for full-time employment.

Skill acquisition is not sufficient, however. The preservice teacher

Figure 12.2. **Methods of Teaching Secondary Social Studies**

SocSc 422

Dr. Frank E. Johnson
Class Meetings: TBA
Office: 111 Smith Hall
Phone: 782–3750, ext. 136
E-Mail: fjohnson@mnu.edu
Office Hours: as posted and by appointment

[Please note that concurrent enrollment in Ed 411 and Ed 441 is required.]

Course Objectives

As one of the last hurdles prior to student teaching, the "methods" course is a critical capstone to an undergraduate's professional formation. Here the cognate major(s), numerous practicums, and foundational theory courses converge in a hands-on dialogue/encounter of the techniques for preparation, presentation, and assessment. After successfully completing SocSc 422, students should be able to:

1. Trace the organizational and philosophical development of the social studies from 1890 to the present.
2. Formulate lesson and unit plans for U.S. history, World history, Political Science, Sociology/Anthropology, Economics, and Geography which utilize diverse instructional techniques.
3. Articulate a rationale and implementation strategy for assessing student learning (incorporating both objective and subjective measures).
4. Demonstrate a variety of computing technology skills cultivated in the course, as well as define the applicability of the Internet and presentation software to social studies curriculum development (i.e., strengths and weaknesses).
5. Synthesize and evaluate supplemental multimedia resources for preparation and presentation of lesson/unit plans.

Core Text

Peter H. Martorella, *Teaching Social Studies in Middle and Secondary Schools*, 2nd ed. (Englewood Cliffs, NJ: 1996). ISBN: 0–13–442070–5

Grading and Assignments

Please be advised that, while there are no formal exams in this course, the pace and intellectual rigor are demanding. This course is reading and writing intensive, requires the preparation and presentation of several course projects, and presumes regular and thoughtful participation in class discussions.

Figure 12.2 *(continued)*

"Research" Paper	35%	70 pts
Proposal	5%	10 pts
2nd Draft	10%	20 pts
Paper	20%	40 pts
Course Projects	65%	130 pts
PowerPoint Presentation	25%	50 pts
PowerPoint Resource		
Folder	10%	20 pts
Web Page	15%	30 pts
E-List Participation	15%	30 pts
	100%	200 pts

Research Project

Use this "research" opportunity to explore and develop a teaching ratio-nale/strategy which will be utilized when preparing course projects. Your paper must conform to the general topic of "intellectual engagement within the instructional process" (i.e., how can and to what end do teachers facilitate "thinking"?). The final version of this paper should be approximately fifteen pages in length and draw from a minimum of ten scholarly sources—four of which must come from the "core bibliography" listed below and may include no more than three Internet sources. A proposal identifying your approach to the topic and sources is due by the end of week three. Additional, specific, information regarding matters of style, citation, and remaining due dates will be distributed in class.

Research Paper Core Bibliography:

Alan Bloom, *Closing of the American Mind* (New York: Simon and Schuster, 1987).

Barry K. Beyer, *Critical Thinking* (Bloomington, IN: Phi Delta Kappa Educational Foundation, 1995).

Lynn Chenney, *American Memory: A Report on the Humanities in the Nation's Public Schools* (Washington, DC: National Endowment for the Humanities, 1987).

John Dewey, *How We Think* (Chicago: Henry Regnery, 1933).

Paul D. Eggen and Donald P. Kauchak, *Strategies for Teachers: Teaching Content and Thinking Skills,* 3rd ed. (Boston: Allyn & Bacon, 1996).

Joseph P. Hester, *Teaching for Thinking* (Durham, NC: Carolina Academic Press, 1994).

Fred M. Newmann, *Higher Order Thinking in High School Social Studies* (Madison, WI: National Center for Effective Secondary Schools, 1988).

Gary D. Phye, ed., *Handbook of Academic Learning: Construction of Knowledge* (San Diego: Academic Press, 1996).

Vincent R. Ruggiero, *Thinking Across the Curriculum* (New York: Harper and Row, 1988).

Figure 12.2 *(continued)*

PowerPoint Presentation and Resource Folder

Each student will prepare a forty minute lesson using presentation software. Specific details concerning this assignment will be announced in class; Prof. Johnson will work one-on-one with students to assist in the selection and loading of materials into presentation format. Each student will present their "loaded" lesson to the SocSc 422 class. The resource folder will contain data for two additional lessons via PowerPoint; combined, the three lessons must draw from separate social science disciplines.

Web Page

As a second component of multimedia authoring, each student will design (and publish?) a web page using HTML (don't panic—we will use an "editor"). Specific details concerning this assignment will be announced in class. Prof. Johnson will help here as well.

E-List Participation

With the professor's sponsorship, each student will be subscribed to an electronic discussion network relating to teaching: H-Teach (teaching issues in general, geared toward college-level instruction) or H-High-S (teaching high school history, some social studies). Students will monitor exchanges between teachers but will not post to their respective list without professor's permission. Observing these electronic discussion networks not only allows students to politely eavesdrop on conversations in break rooms and classrooms around the country, but also will serve to stimulate dialogue between the student and cooperating teacher. A two-page, single-spaced, "recap and reflection" is due every other Friday. These brief papers will *summarize* key points of discussion during the week (page one) as well as probe the strengths/weaknesses of same (page two).

The following scale will be used to calculate grades:

Raw Scores		Final Grades	
A+	.97–	A+	193 –
A	.94–.96	A	187 – 192
A–	.90 – .93	A–	179 – 186
B+	.87 – .89	B+	173 – 178
B	.84 – .86	B	167
B–	.80 – .83	B–	159 – 166
C+	.77 – .79	C+	153 – 158
C	.74 – .76	C	147 – 152
C–	.70 – .73	C–	139 – 146
D+	.67 – .69	D+	133 – 138
D	.64 – .66	D	127 – 132
D–	.60 – .63	D–	119 – 126
F	Below .60	F	Below 118

must be able to construct class activities and assignments using computing technology. Again, the point must be emphasized: the preservice teacher cannot teach what he or she has not learned. Obviously, no one emerges from a teacher education program having learned everything. On the other hand, the ability to transfer skills and or knowledge from one venue to the next is essential (and a reasonable expectation). For example, research and writing are fundamental social studies skills. Yet can the preservice teacher utilize those skills when designing class activities which incorporate the WWW? Do different mediums dictate different approaches and/or strategies? Would a student search for information in the same manner on the Internet as in their local library? These are the types of questions preservice teachers must explore and be able to answer.

Let me provide a more specific example. I have designed an exercise where my methods students must construct a series of activities using e-mail (see Figures 12.3 and 12.4). It is imperative that the instructor begin at the beginning—explaining the basic technical properties before expecting students to incorporate this medium in their lesson plans. To that end, I teach folder management, command structure, security issues, and so on. Once this context is established, the class then moves forward to application. Many e-messages, such as the one by John Avelis, Jr. reprinted in Figure 12.3, lend themselves to class activities.[17]

For one such e-mail exercise, each methods student must create a minimum of three distribution lists which, when combined, include each member of their hypothetical class. Each of these groups is to be assigned a question to consider or a problem to research based on an e-mail message from a listserv discussion network (Figure 12.4). Students are given a set period of time to complete the exercise: in this case the activity is announced on Monday, "collected" on Wednesday, and discussed on Friday. All responses would serve in turn as the basis of in-class discussion or activity. This particular exercise is a useful supplement to multi-session activities such as videos, readings, and the like. The preservice teacher might design an assignment such as represented in Figure 12.4 based on Ken Burns' recent *Thomas Jefferson* and various electronic discussion regarding it.[18]

Exercises such as this help forge and reinforce necessary computing technology skills, while simultaneously cultivating content-specific social studies skills. For example, to complete this exercise, a student will demonstrate numerous skills including (in part):

- identify (and participate in) scholarly electronic discussion groups
- create and utilize distribution groups
- transfer e-mail to word processor for editing and then to presentation software
- use the Internet to locate ancillary materials related to specific activity/exercise.

It is imperative to recognize that the goal for the preservice teacher is to master skills, *not* software. Internet browsers, e-mail clients, and presentation applications abound. However, each competing commercial product shares a basic repertoire of commands and functions. Empowering the preservice teacher to mine these products for their pedagogic value is paramount.[19]

Future computing-related instruction must be neither technology dependent nor technology driven; after all, such mechanical devices simply facilitate teaching. In fact, teachers must co-opt the intrinsic appeal of technology. Richard Gross concluded quite some time ago that students measured classroom activities in terms of entertainment value, always relative to what they experienced through television. "The teacher, of course, cannot compete as an entertainer, thus, he or she must be highly skillful in truly involving students in the learning process." For Gross, the immediate solution was "intense self-preparation." But, as Martorella notes, this logic is predicated on the ability of teachers to determine (both in terms of evaluation and incorporation) whether or not any given technology "can serve an important instructional purpose and advance students' thinking." True to form, Gilliom speaks directly to the issue. He offers the following cautionary note: "Do not pick a medium and then create a lesson around it; rather, design the lesson plan and then select the medium that will best complement that plan and its objectives." Having done so, "teachers who work side by side with students to design instructional materials will find that the number of students reached by instruction increases, that individuals and groups become self-directed and autonomous, and that the teaching-learning process becomes more enjoyable."[20]

Some might argue that the future will correct itself; that no real change is necessary. The concern for preservice computer instruction evidenced in this paper is largely unfounded if the beginning professional teacher is provided at least one "state of the art" PC which is pre-loaded with all necessary software (including help files) and guaranteed ready and reli-

Figure 12.3. **Transcript of John Avelis, Jr.'s Post**

Date: Sat. 22 Feb 1997 21:18:27 -0500
From: "Rev. Louis T. Garaventa, S.J." <garavaen@gort.canisius.edu>
Reply-To: Am H-Net List for Teaching Social Studies in Secondary Schools
<H-HIGH-S@MSU.EDU>
To: Multiple recipients of list H-HIGH-S <H-HIGH-S@MSU.EDU>
Subject: Re: Ken Burn's Jefferson on PBS

Date: Sat. 22 Feb 1997 15:38:11 -0600
From: John Avelis, Jr. <javelis@ms.k12.il.us>

I viewed the entire first episode, and more than half of the second. From what I saw, the production was up to Burn's usual quality for documentary film making. I think it treats the facets of Jefferson's life and character fairly, although there will of course be those whose responses vary from dissatisfaction to outrage, and toward the direction of the "right-wing" of those who worship at the altar of the Founding Fathers and those (many, no doubt, hopeful of having new fields to till for Ph.D.'s) who will decry the film for failing to decontruct Thomas Jefferson thoroughly enough to suit the tastes of the '90s.

I felt that the film's greatest strength lay in portraying what one of the commentators referred to when he alluded to Jefferson as our "sphinx." The essential mystery of a man who espoused the natural equality of men in society, democracy as a civil religion, and republicanism in government, who was also a slave holder and who, although I have no doubt about his views of the institution, could never part company with it.

The big mistakes (and I believe this mistake can be perceived even among some of the commentators Burns used in the film) one can make in trying to pursue the character of an 18th-century man in the 20th century is to believe that there is some final decision that can be reached about Jefferson: that we can ultimately decide that he was a "good man" or a "bad man" (see the latter in a particularly egregious and foolish essay by Conor Cruise O'Brien in the January *Atlantic*) or that his dust in a Virginia grave requires our approbation or forgiveness. What is fascinating is that in Jefferson we see reflected so much of *us*.

John Avelis, Jr. / Social Studies Dept.
Mahomet-Seymour H.S. / Mahomet, IL 61853
Transcript of John Avelis, Jr.'s Post

Figure 12.4. **Sample Questions for E-Mail Exercise Based on Figure 12.3 E-Message**

Group 1 [link to Avelis post: "up to Burns' usual quality"]
Provide a complete list of Burns' works (give as much information as possible: titles, when produced, awards, etc.). What questions does Burns seek to answer in these films? Can you identify any common themes?

Group 2 [link to Avelis post: pursuing eighteenth-century man in the twentieth century]
Do we reinvent historic figures? What is the difference between re-examining and recreating? How might historians (amateur or otherwise) distinguish between the two?

Group 3 [link to Avelis post:"sphinx" theme]
How does Burns characterize/evaluate his interpretation? Visit the PBS Web site for additional context <http://www.pbs.org/jefferson/>. Do not investigate Burns' thoughts on Jefferson, but those regarding himself. In other words, is Burns' *Jefferson* in fact an autobiography?

Post your response by 5:00 Wednesday. Be sure to read the other responses before class discussion on Friday. Finally, each group will briefly present their response to the class—to facilitate this, please provide an outline which can be viewed as a PowerPoint "slide."

able access to a building-level media resource consultant (a "techie"). If these conditions are met, then the newly christened teacher might be able to begin learning how to incorporate these elements into the classroom in the second or third year of full-time teaching. In the meantime, not having the skills has further burdened this teacher, however—knowing that a diverse range of activities is just out of reach, but clearly in sight. Students must acquire these skills prior to professional employment. A key objective of the social studies methods course is to provide application to content: to instill the principle that pedagogy is a performing art. By the methods course, preservice teachers have gained a functional knowledge of their subject areas, yet, typically, have limited practical experience with or understanding of the art of teaching such specific content. Therefore, the methods course must outfit the preservice teacher with new skills, which in turn empower that teacher to—most importantly—effectively convey/communicate and assess student performance.

Post-graduation inservices are not sufficient to cultivate computer literacy nor facilitate content-area application. In fact, Naylor and Diem write that skepticism and inadequate inservice training have slowed the momentum of acceptance and incorporation of computers in the social studies classroom. Here is another paradox relating to the subject. Methods texts are not written for the professional, but for the preservice teacher. Given the fact that preservice teachers constitute the sole audience, one would think that the methods text is a prime venue from which to advocate change.[21]

Conclusion

The prospective teacher unwilling or unable to navigate multiple electronic mediums is not at a disadvantage; he or she is an ill-prepared candidate on today's market—and will not be a candidate whatsoever in the near future. Granted, not being able to identify "html" as hypertext mark-up language need not necessarily disqualify an applicant from potential employment; on the other hand, however, first-hand knowledge of various multimedia applications, their pedagogic value, and a portfolio which showcases student-created on-line projects is a sure portent of success. The social studies methods course is a natural venue for such creative exploration, instruction, and development.

As one of the last hurdles prior to student teaching, the methods course is a critical capstone to an undergraduate's professional formation. Here the cognate major(s), numerous practicums, and theory courses converge in a hands-on dialogue/encounter of the techniques for preparation, presentation, and assessment. However, incorporating computing technology into social studies methods is more complicated than one would expect. Scholarly works trumpeting the benefits of multimedia are readily available; yet, ironically, articles and monographs designed to assist the preservice teacher (or methods instructor for that matter) in just how to identify, let alone master, the various media upon which success in the "real" classroom is predicated are scarce indeed.[22]

This essay does not purport to speak definitively. Much to the contrary, it purposely is incomplete in that it calls for consideration and reflection rather than boldly articulating prescriptive change; neither does it intimate the demise of traditional instructional methods. Teachers will continue to anchor their instruction to a text of one sort or another, assess performance with multiple choice and essay quizzes/tests, and so on. Instead, this essay seeks to highlight what appears to be a structural inconsistency within higher education—expecting preservice teachers to be computer literate and to deftly incorporate computing technology in the content area, while failing to (consistently) articulate exactly when or where, and what skills meet such an objective. In other words, this essay asks the academy to clearly articulate the requisite technological skills relating to preservice education, how the prospective teacher acquires them, and how the academy assesses them to ensure competence. Finally, this essay charges professional educators and teacher education professors to labor together toward a solution, reforging a collaborative spirit. Toward that end, this essay has identified several points of departure for this joint venture.

Notes

The author would like to express his thanks to several individuals at MidAmerica Nazarene University for their assistance with this project: Professor Paul A. Williams, Chair, Department of History, Mrs. Joyce Richter, Interlibrary Loan Coordinator, as well as Reference Librarians Robin Welch and Andrew Leonhart.

1. Of course one cannot fault methods authors for failing to address computing issues prior to this. Although Radio Shack's TRS-80 was on the market by 1977 and the Apple II was available by late 1980, the PC did not become a permanent fixture in American education until 1983. While it is an oversimplification of the advent of computing technologies in the classroom, 1983 was unquestionably a watershed: two signal highlights unveiled that year include the Apple IIe and Microsoft Word (1.0). Subsequent developments in hardware, applications, and peripherals have proven an seemingly endless stream. In fact, this change has been so profound that knowledge of the computer is now regarded a vital measure of "literacy." Students must demonstrate the ability to operate and incorporate a computer into their everyday lives. For a helpful overview, see Ken Polsson's "Chronology of Events in the History of Microcomputers," January 16, 1997, http://www.islandnet.com/kpolsson/comphist.htm (April 18, 1997), and James B.M. Schick, *Teaching History with a Computer: A Complete Guide for College Professors* (Chicago: Lyceum Books, 1990), 4–6.

2. John U. Michaelis, *Social Studies for Children: A Guide to Basic Instruction,* 8th ed. (Englewood Cliffs, NJ: Prentice-Hall, 1985), 61–67.

3. Michaelis, *Social Studies for Children,* 62.

4. David T. Naylor and Richard A. Diem, *Elementary and Middle School Social Studies* (New York: Random House, 1987).

5. Ibid., 397.

6. Ibid., 393, 399–400.

7. James L. Barth, *Methods of Instruction in Social Studies Education,* 3rd ed. (Lanham, MD: University Press of America, 1990), 152; Barth, *Elementary and Junior High/Middle School Social Studies Curriculum, Activities, and Materials,* 3rd ed. (Lanham, MD: University Press of America, 1991), 317–320.

8. Wayne Mahood, Linda Biemer, and William T. Lowe, *Teaching Social Studies in Middle and Senior High Schools: Decisions! Decisions!* (New York: Macmillan, 1991).

9. Ibid., 171.

10. Jack Zevin, *Social Studies for the Twenty-First Century: Methods and Materials for Teaching in Middle and Secondary Schools* (New York: Longman, 1992); Michael G. Allen and Robert L. Stevens, *Middle Grade Social Studies: Teaching and Learning for Active and Responsible Citizenship* (Boston: Allyn & Bacon, 1994); Mary Burke-Hengen and Tim Gillespie, *Building Community: Social Studies in the Middle School Years* (Portsmouth, NH: Heinemann, 1995).

11. Peter H. Martorella, *Teaching Social Studies in Middle and Secondary Schools,* 2nd ed. (Englewood Cliffs, NJ: Prentice-Hall, 1996).

12. Also addressed are "Using Traditional Media Effectively" and "Emerging Technologies and the Challenge of the Future."

13. Martorella, *Teaching Social Studies in Middle and Secondary Schools,* 326.

14. Ibid., 327, 332–333, 335–337, 343.

15. M. Eugene Gilliom, et al., *Practical Methods for the Social Studies* (Belmont, CA: Wadsworth, 1977).

16. Ibid., 229. For sections noted, see especially 230–236, 248–255.

17. E-mail does constitute intellectual property and one must take care not to violate copyright protections. Provided one does not republish that information in any form, teachers have free access to any e-message posted to a public listserv group such as the one reprinted in Figure 12.3. However, given the fact that this essay was to be published, I secured permission in advance to use this document. The author's sole restriction was that his post be published in its entirety.

18. PBS Home Video and Turner Home Entertainment, 1996.

19. As more stations become available in social studies classrooms the degree to which the Internet can be utilized as an instructional resource will be limited only by the teacher's ability to do so. Additional e-mail–related activities include distance learning wherein a class collaborates with another group of students elsewhere, establishing a tutorial resource/homework support center, sponsoring/hosting various community service projects, and so on.

20. Richard E. Gross, et al., *Social Studies for Our Times* (New York: John Wiley, 1978), 13; Martorella, *Teaching Social Studies In Middle and Secondary Schools,* 353; Gilliom, *Practical Methods for the Social Studies,* 229–230. Gilliom elaborated on the benefits of incorporating technology when concluding his "media" chapter:

> Student and teacher involvement in the production of inquiry-oriented audio-visual materials has a number of welcome effects. In particular, classroom climate undergoes positive changes. Students suggest high-interest topics, practice decision making, develop self-sufficiency, solve problems, and talk out problems without fear. "Hands-on" experiences help to create the learning atmosphere striven for by the inquiry teacher (270).

21. Naylor and Diem, *Elementary and Middle School Social Studies,* 405.

22. Some scholars might argue that computing-related matters are properly addressed in an instructional technology course. Ideally teacher education candidates would acquire technical knowledge and hands-on experience in this setting. However, content-specific application must be made of these skills. Again, the methods course is the natural arena for the latter.

Supplemental Bibliography of Related Readings

Books

Ahl, David H., ed. *Computers in Science and Social Studies.* Morris Plains, NJ: Creative Computing Press, 1983.

Braun, Joseph A. Jr. *Microcomputers and the Social Studies: A Resource Guide for the Middle and Secondary Grades.* New York: Garland, 1986.

Budin, Howard, Diane S. Kendall, and James Lengel. *Using Computers in the Social Studies.* New York: Teachers College Press, 1986.

The Current State of Social Studies: A Report of Project SPAN. Boulder, CO: Social Science Education Consortium, 1982.

Glenn, Allen, and Don Rawitsch. *Computing in the Social Studies Classroom.* Eugene, OR: International Council for Computers in Education, 1984.

Gooden, Andrea R. *Computers in the Classroom: How Teachers and Students are Using Technology to Transform Learning.* San Francisco: Jossey-Bass and Apple Press, 1996.

Gross, Richard E., and Thomas L. Dynneson. *What Should We Be Teaching in the Social Studies?* Bloomington, IN: Phi Delta Kappa Educational Foundation, 1983.

Martorella, Peter H., ed. *Interactive Technologies and the Social Studies: Emerging Issues and Applications.* Albany: State University of New York Press, 1997.

Nowicki, Joseph John, and Kerry F. Meehan. *The Collaborative Social Studies Classroom: A Resource for Teachers, Grades 7–12.* Boston: Allyn & Bacon, 1996.

Roberts, Nancy, Susan Friel, and Thomas Ladenburg. *Computers and the Social Studies.* Menlo Park, CA: Addison-Wesley, 1988.

Rooze, Gene E., and Terry Northrup. *Computers, Thinking, and Social Studies.* Englewood, CO: Teacher Ideas Press, 1989.

Ryan, Frank L. *The Social Studies Source Book: Ideas for Teaching in the Elementary and Middle School.* Boston: Allyn & Bacon, 1980.

Shaver, James P., ed. *Handbook of Research on Social Studies Teaching and Learning.* New York: Macmillan, 1991.

Schick, James B.M. *Teaching History with a Computer: A Complete Guide for College Professors.* Chicago: Lyceum Books, 1990.

Articles

Adler, Susan A. "The Social Studies Methods Course Instructor: Practitioner Researcher." *International Journal of Social Education* 7 (Winter 1993): 39–47. ERIC, EJ476694.

Bailey, Steve. "Using the Computer in Middle School Social Studies." *Social Studies* 78 (January–February 1987): 23–25. ERIC, EJ353110.

Barr, Hugh. "Social Studies by Electronic Mail." *Social Studies* 85 (November–December 1994): 28184. ERIC, EJ498320.

Beauvois, Margaret Healy. "E-Talk: Attitudes and Motivation in Computer-Assisted Classroom Discussion." *Computers and the Humanities* 28 (1994–95): 177–90. ERIC, EJ512785.

Bennett, Jack A. "The Utilization of Instructional Media and Technology in the Teaching of U.S. History: A Research Report." Paper presented at the meeting of the National Social Science Association (November 1990). ERIC, ED334093.

Berg, Roger. "Resisting Change: What the Literature Says about Computers in the Social Studies Classroom." *Social Education* 47 (May 1983): 314–16. ERIC, EJ281960.

Boldt, David J., et al. "The Internet: A Curriculum Warehouse for Social Studies Teachers." *Social Studies* 86 (May–June 1995): 105–12. ERIC, EJ510826.

Bolt, Robert. "The Role of the Computer in the Teaching of Social Studies." [1986]. ERIC, ED282802.

Boyer, Barbara A. and Penelope Semrau. "A Constructivist Approach to Social Studies: Integrating Technology." *Social Studies and the Young Learner* 7 (January–February 1995): 14–16. ERIC, EJ500329.

Brady, H. Robert. "An Overview of Computer Integration into Social Studies Instruction." *Social Education* 58 (September 1994): 312–14. ERIC, EJ492071.

Brady, H. Robert, and James L. Barth. "Social Studies Standards That Effectively Integrate Technology." *Social Education* 56 (January 1992): 14–16. ERIC, EJ447831.

Brooks, Diane L. "Technology as Basic to History–Social Science: It's Long Overdue." *Educational Technology* 34 (September 1994): 19–20. ERIC, EJ489810.

Budin, Howard, and Diane Kendall. "Technology and the Social Studies: A Vision." *Social Studies Teacher* 9 (November–January 1987–88): 9. ERIC, EJ362877.

Budin, Howard, et al. "Computers and Social Studies: Trends and Directions." *Social Studies* 78 (January–February 1987): 7–12. ERIC, EJ353107.

Burton, Vernon. "Teaching Historians with Databases." *History Microcomputer Review* 9 (Spring 1993): 9–17. ERIC, EJ478516.

Burton, Orville Vernon. "Computers, History, and Historians: Converging Cultures?" *History Microcomputer Review* 7 (Fall 1991): 11–23. ERIC, EJ445212.

Burton, Orville Vernon, and Terrence Finnegan. "Teaching Historians to Use Technology: Databases and Computers." *International Journal of Social Education* 5 (Spring 1990): 23–35. ERIC, EJ414118.

Butler, Judy D., and R. Wilburn Clouse. "Educational Technology and the Teaching of History: Promise, Practice, and Possibilities." May 1994. ERIC, ED373005.

Chiodo, John J., and Mary L. Flaim, "The Link between Computer Simulations and Social Studies Learning: Debriefing." *Social Studies* 84 (May–June 1993): 119–21. ERIC, EJ473645.

Clark, Dave. "Effective Use of Computers in the Social Studies: A Review of the Literature with Implications for Educators." 1992. ERIC, ED370828.

Coviello, Robert. "Immigration Lessons through Technology." *New England Journal of History* 50 (Spring 1993): 16–21. ERIC, EJ476759.

Davis, James E., and John D. Haas. "Microcomputers in the Social Studies." Paper Presented at the Annual Meeting of the Social Science Education Consortium (Athens, GA, June 8–11, 1983). ERIC, ED231733.

Deluca, Nicholas M. "Social Studies Teachers and Computer Technology: An Administrator's Perspective." *Social Education* 47 (May 1983): 333–34. ERIC, EJ281966.

Diem, Richard A. "Technology and the Social Studies: Issues and Responsibilities." *Social Education* 47 (May 1983): 308–10, 313. ERIC, EJ281959.

Dockterman, David, and Tom Snyder. "How to Incorporate the Computer into the Social Studies Classroom." Tom Snyder Productions, Inc., Cambridge, MA, 1986. ERIC, ED271372.

Doughty, Susan Grimes. "Integrating Montessori Curriculum and Technology: A Computer Approach to Social Studies' 'Fundamental Needs.' " *Montessori Life* 8 (Winter 1996): 33–35. ERIC, EJ520501.

Dumas, Wayne, et al. "Preparation of Middle School Social Studies Teachers in Major State Research Universities." *Teacher Education and Practice* 11 (Spring–Summer 1995): 58–64. ERIC, EJ509260.

Ediger, Marlow. "Philosophy of Computer Use in the Social Studies." (March 1989). ERIC, ED307206.

Ediger, Marlow. "Computer Use and the Social Studies." (1987). ERIC, ED292694.

Ehman, Lee H., et al. "Using Computer Databases in Student Problem Solving: A Study of Eight Social Studies Teachers' Classrooms." *Theory and Research in Social Education* 20 (Spring 1992): 179–206. ERIC, EJ456512.

Ehrlich, Heyward. "An Interdisciplinary Bibliography for Computers and the Humanities Courses." *Computers and the Humanities* 25 (October 1991): 315–26. ERIC, EJ449348.

Evans, Ronald W. "Reconceptualizing Social Studies for a New Millennium." *Louisiana Social Studies Journal* 17 (Fall 1990): 26–31. ERIC, EJ433664.

Farnworth, George M. "The Natural Link between Teaching History and Computer

Skills." *Canadian Social Studies* 27 (Fall 1992): 24–27. ERIC, EJ461821.

Feichtl, Franz. "Bibliography to Computer and History Instruction." *History Microcomputer Review* 10 (Spring 1994): 30–31. ERIC, EJ493949.

Fernlund, Phyllis Maxey, and Susan Cooper-Shoup. "A Realistic View of Hypermedia in the Social Studies Classroom." *Social Studies Review* 30 (Spring 1991): 66–70. ERIC, EJ440280.

Foyle, Harvey C., and Bill Yates. "Using Databases in the Social Studies Classroom." *Teaching History: A Journal of Methods* 18 (Fall 1993): 73–79. ERIC, EJ493910.

Furlong, Mary. "Introducing Microcomputers into the Social Studies Classroom." *Social Studies Review* 22 (Winter 1983): 61–65. ERIC, EJ277294.

Glenn, Allen D., and Daniel L. Klassen. "Computer Technology and the Social Studies." *Educational Forum* 47 (Winter 1983): 209–16. ERIC, EJ275685.

Glenn, Allen D., and Gregory C. Sales. "Interactive Video Technology: Its Status and Future in the Social Sciences." *International Journal of Social Education* 5 (Spring 1990): 74–84. ERIC, EJ414122.

Glenn, Allen, and Don Rawitsch. "Where Can Social Studies Computing Materials Be Found?" *Social Studies Review* 25 (Spring 1986): 89–93. ERIC, EJ338268.

Gooler, Dennis D., ed. "Perspectives: Technology as Content in Social Studies Curricula for Young Learners." *Social Studies and the Young Learner* 7 (January–February 1995): 27–30. ERIC, EJ500335.

Harris, Susan B., and Craig Blurton. "Promote Positive Cognitive and Affective Outcomes for Students with Special Needs: Integrate Computers in the Social Studies Curriculum." *Journal of Reading, Writing, and Learning Disabilities International* 5 (1989): 85–102. ERIC, EJ397846.

Herman, Wayne L., Jr., and William D. Schafer. "Transfer of Training: From the Social Studies Methods Course to Student Teaching." Revision of a paper presented at the Annual Meeting of the National Council for the Social Studies (November 15–19, 1984). ERIC, ED310033.

Higgins, Kyle and Randall Boone. "Hypertext Computer Study Guides and the Social Studies Achievement of Students with Learning Disabilities, Remedial Students, and Regular Education Students." *Journal of Learning Disabilities* 23 (November 1990): 529–40. ERIC, EJ420080.

Hockey, Susan. "Some Perspectives on Teaching Computers and the Humanities." *Computers and the Humanities* 26 (August 1992): 261–66. ERIC, EJ478452.

Jennings, James M. "Comparative Analysis, Hypercard, and the Future of Social Studies Education." Paper presented at the Annual Meeting of the National Council for the Social Studies. November 1994. ERIC, ED381439.

Keller, Shelia F., and Gay K. Gentry. "Teaching Social Studies via Multimedia." *Media & Methods* 32 (March–April 1996): 8,10,12. ERIC, EJ520305.

Kendall, Diane S., and Howard Budin. "Computers in Social Studies." *Social Education* 51 (January 1987): 32–33. ERIC, EJ344575.

Klenow, Carol. "Electronic Social Studies. Teaching with Technology—Update." *Instructor* 102 (October 1992): 65–66. ERIC, EJ458478.

Lancy, David F. "Microcomputers and the Social Studies." *OCSS Review* 26 (Spring 1990): 30–37. ERIC, EJ414157.

Laskey, Sue. "The Carnegie H.A.T. Project—History and Technology." *Social Studies Review* 30 (Spring 1991): 45–50. ERIC, EJ440278.

Lengel, James G. "Thinking Skills, Social Studies, and Computers." *Social Studies* 78 (January–February 1987): 13–16. ERIC, EJ353108.

Levesque, Jeri A. "Using Computers to Motivate Learners." *Social Studies and the Young Learner* 2 (September–October 1989): 9–11. ERIC, EJ404478.

Little, Timothy H. "Computers in the Social Studies Classroom." *Social Studies Review* 30 (Spring 1991): 58–65. ERIC, EJ440279.

Little, Timothy. "Microcomputers in Social Studies Education." *Michigan Social Studies Journal* 3 (1988–89): 21–24. ERIC, EJ417439.

Lloyd-Jones, R., and M. J. Lewis. "What Can We Do with Historical Databases?: Applications in Teaching and Research." *History Microcomputer Review* 10 (Fall 1994): 42–54. ERIC, EJ502263.

Male, Mary. "Cooperative Learning and Computers in Social Studies Integrating Special Needs Students into General Education Classrooms." *Social Studies Review* 32 (Winter 1993): 56–62. ERIC, EJ467884.

Martorella, Peter H. "Harnessing New Technologies to the Social Studies Curriculum." *Social Education* 55 (January 1991): 55–57. ERIC, EJ426391.

Martorella, Peter H. "Developing Computer Literate Social Studies Teachers." Paper Presented at the Annual Meeting of the National Council for the Social Studies (November 15–19, 1984). ERIC, ED254434.

Massialas, Byron G., and George J. Papagiannis. "Toward a Critical Review of Computers in Education: Implications for Social Studies." *Social Studies* 78 (January–February 1987): 47–53. ERIC, EJ353116.

McCarthy, Michael J. "The Historian and Electronic Research: File Transfer Protocol (FTP)." *History Microcomputer Review* 9 (Fall 1993): 29–46. ERIC, EJ488722.

McCoy, Jan D. "Databases in the Social Studies: Not Why But How." *Social Studies and the Young Learner* 3 (November–December 1990): 13–15. ERIC, EJ426405.

McGeown, Casimir. "The King Edward Debating Society Adds Current Events to Elementary and Middle–School Social Studies." *Social Studies* 86 (July–August 1995): 183–86. ERIC, EJ514182.

McKinney-Browning, Mabel C., ed. "What's Ahead for Social Studies? Perspectives." *Social Studies and the Young Learner* 6 (January–February 1994): 29–32. ERIC, EJ487183.

Mead-Mezzetta, Shirley. "Technology and the Social Studies—Where We Were; Where We Are, Where We Are Going . . ." *Social Studies Review* 25 (Spring 1986): 2–5. ERIC, EJ338254.

Mitchell-Powell, Brenda, ed. "History and Multimedia Technology. Media Corner." *Social Studies and the Young Learner* 7 (Nov–Dec 1994): 27–29, 32. ERIC, EJ496956.

Morrissett, Irving. "Four Futures for Social Studies." Presented to Rethinking Social Education: A National Conference on Future Directions for Social Studies Education, Wingspread Conference Center (August 16, 1982). ERIC, ED221420.

Napier, John D. "Computer Literacy and Social Studies Teacher Education: Changes in Form and Content." Paper presented at the Annual Meeting of the Social Science Education Consortium (June 8–11, 1983). ERIC, ED231740.

Northrup, Terry, and Gene E. Rooze. "Are Social Studies Teachers Using Computers? A National Survey." *Social Education* 54 (April–May 1990): 212–14. ERIC, EJ412373.

Northrup, Terry. "Are Social Studies Teachers Using Computers?" Paper presented at the Annual Meeting of the Texas Computer Education Association (March 1990). ERIC, ED342719.

O'Reilly, Kevin. "Making Students Decide: The Vietnam Computer Simulation." *Southern Social Studies Journal* 19 (Spring 1994): 20–32. ERIC, EJ502281.

Passe, Jeff. "Early Field Experiences in Elementary and Secondary Social Studies Methods Courses." *Social Studies* 85 (May–June 1994): 130–33. ERIC, EJ487229.

Penn, Irma. "A Social Studies Computer Simulation: Alternative Treatments with Grade Five Students." *History and Social Science Teacher* 24 (Fall 1988): 35–38. ERIC, EJ383088.

Puk, Tom. "Epistemological Implications for Training Social Studies Teachers. Just Who Was Christopher Columbus?" *Social Studies* 85 (September–October 1994): 228–33. ERIC, EJ492079.

Raben, Joseph. "Humanities Computing 25 Years Later." *Computers and the Humanities* 25 (December 1991): 341–50. ERIC, EJ452248.

Ramos, Donald, and Wheeler, Robert, A. "Integrating Microcomputers into the History Curriculum." *History Teacher* 22 (February 1989): 177–88. ERIC, EJ403150.

Reynolds, John F. "Multitudinous Multimedia: The American Memory Project." *History Microcomputer Review* 10 (Spring 1994): 22–26. ERIC, EJ493947.

Riegler, Edward R. "Laptops—An Exciting Addition to the Social Science Classroom" *Visions for Learning* 10 (September–October 1992): 38–39. ERIC, EJ454310.

Risinger, C. Frederick. "Webbing the Social Studies." *Social Education* 60 (February 1996): 111–12. ERIC, EJ526705.

Rocca, Al M. "Teacher Education Experiences in History/Social Science." *Social Studies Review* 33 (Spring 1994): 4–5. ERIC, EJ490121.

Roedding, Gary R. "Using Computer Assisted Instruction To Improve Student's Performance Skills in Social Studies." M.S. Practicum, Nova University, 1990. ERIC, ED332950.

Rooze, Gene E. "Integrating Computer Software into Social Studies Instruction." Paper Presented at the Convention of the National Council for the Social Studies (November 23, 1983). ERIC, ED239586.

Rooze, Gene E., and Terry Northrup. "Uses for the Computer in Implementing the Essential Elements of Social Studies." *Southwestern Journal of Social Education* 15 (Spring–Summer 1985): 9–14. ERIC, EJ336762.

Rosenzweig, Laura. "Teaming Up Social Studies and Computer Teachers." *Electronic Learning* 4 (Apr 1985): 16, 21. ERIC, EJ315716.

Rosenzweig, Roy. "'So, What's Next for Clio?' CD-ROM and Historians." *Journal of American History* 81 (March 1995): 1621–40. ERIC, EJ507493.

Ross, E. Wayne. "Microcomputer Use in Secondary Social Studies Classrooms." *Journal of Educational Research* 85 (September–October 1991): 39–46. ERIC, EJ440342.

Ross, E. Wayne. "Survey of Microcomputer Use in Secondary Social Studies Classrooms." Paper presented at the Annual Meeting of the National Council for the Social Studies (November 14–18, 1988). ERIC, ED306169.

Ross, E. Wayne. "Becoming a Social Studies Teacher: Teacher Education and the Development of Preservice Teacher Perspectives." Paper presented at the College and University Faculty Assembly of the Annual Meeting of the National Council for the Social Studies (November, 1986). ERIC, ED276674.

Ruef, Seth H., and Thomas N. Layne. "A Study of the Effects of Computer-Assisted Instruction in the Social Studies." *Social Studies* 81 (March–April 1990): 73–76. ERIC, EJ413994.

Sartor, Ron. "Computers in Social Studies Yesterday and Today." *Michigan Social Studies Journal* 1 (Fall 1986): 43–44. ERIC, EJ343057.

Schick, James B. M.' "HMR' Forum: Facing Old Problems and Looking in New Directions." *History Microcomputer Review* 9 (Fall 1993): 15–28. ERIC, EJ488721.

Schick, James B. M. "Constructing an Interactive Tutorial: 'Boston Massacre.'" *History Microcomputer Review 8* (Spring 1992): 9–22. ERIC, EJ453684.

Schick, James B. M. "Historical Computing: Looking Forward to 2001 from 1989." *Teaching History: A Journal of Methods* 14 (Fall 1989): 70–77. ERIC, EJ401595.

Schug, Mark C. "What Do Social Studies Teachers Say about Using Computers?" *Social Studies* 79 (May–June 1988): 112–15. ERIC, EJ376933.

Schwartz, Donald. "A Remedy for Student Boredom: Stimulation through Simulation." *Social Studies Review* 29 (Winter 1990): 79–85. ERIC, EJ414083.

Searles, John E. "Information Technology and the Social Studies." *Social Education* 47 (May 1983): 335–37. ERIC, EJ281967.

Semonche, John E. "Time Traveling: Historians and Computers." *History Microcomputer Review* 11 (Fall 1995): 9–14. ERIC, EJ523697.

Sesow, F. William, and Roy Stricker. "Computer Literacy: A Responsibility of the Social Studies." Paper Presented at the Annual Meeting of the National Council for the Social Studies (November 1982). ERIC, ED225894.

Shermis, S. Samuel. "The Past, Present, and Future of the Social Studies." *Louisiana Social Studies Journal* 17 (Fall 1990): 10–14. ERIC, EJ433661.

Stevens, Lawrence. "A Social Studies Computer Lab." *Social Education* 57 (January 1993): 8–10. ERIC, EJ464763.

Stolworthy, Reed L. "The Application of Academic Content to Practice by Preservice Secondary School History and Social Studies Teachers." (June 1992). ERIC, ED350255.

Sunal, Cynthia Szymanski, et al. "Introducing the Use of Communication Technology into an Elementary School Social Studies Curriculum." *International Journal of Social Education* 10 (Fall–Winter 1995–96): 106–23. ERIC, EJ528584.

Teague, Maryanne, and Gerald Teague. "Planning with Computers—a Social Studies Simulation." *Learning and Leading with Technology* 23 (September 1995): 20, 22. ERIC, EJ512172.

Vlahakis, Robert. "The Computer-Infused Social Studies Classroom." *Classroom Computer Learning* 9 (November–December 1988): 58–61. ERIC, EJ386139.

Vockell, Edward L. "Computers and Social Studies Skills." *Social Education* 56 (November–December 1992): 366–69. ERIC, EJ463237.

Wegner, Gregory. "The NCSS Curriculum Standards." *Social Education* 60 (February 1996): 83–86. ERIC, EJ526699.

Weiner, Howard. "Enhancing Student Performance in the Social Studies through the Use of Multimedia Instructional Technology. A Practicum Report." June 1994. ERIC, ED383598.

White, Cameron. "Relevant Social Studies Education: Technology and Constructivism." *Journal of Technology and Teacher Education* 4 (1996): 69–76. ERIC, EJ524827.

White, Cameron. " 'Remaking' Social Studies: The Importance of Integrating Technology into Social Studies." *Southern Social Studies Journal* 20 (Summer 1995): 44–53. ERIC, EJ520799.

White, Charles. "Two CD-ROM Products for Social Studies Classrooms." *Social Education* 59 (April–May 1995): 203–07. ERIC, EJ502251.

White, Charles S. "Information Technology in the Preservice Social Studies Methods Course." *Computers in the Schools* 8 (1991): 159–61. ERIC, EJ428871.

White, Charles S. "Access to and Use of Databases in the Social Studies." *International Journal of Social Education* 5 (Spring 1990): 61–73. ERIC, EJ414121.

White, Charles. "Using Computers in the Social Studies Classroom." *OAH Magazine of History* 1 (Winter–Spring 1986): 10. ERIC, EJ335116.

Willis, Elizabeth M. "Where In the World? Technology in Social Studies Learning." *Learning and Leading with Technology* 23 (February 1996): 7–9. ERIC, EJ518505.

Wilson, Elizabeth K., and George E. Marsh, II. "Social Studies and the Internet Revolution." *Social Education* 59 (April–May 1995): 198–202. ERIC, EJ502250.

Wilson, Elizabeth K., et al. "Preservice Teachers in Secondary Social Studies: Examining Conceptions and Practices." *Theory and Research in Social Education* 22 (Summer 1994): 364–79. ERIC, EJ495589.

Wolf, Alvin. "Preparing Secondary Social Studies Teachers for the 1980s: A Realistic Program." *Social Studies Review* 23 (Spring 1984): 74–80. ERIC, EJ300527.

Yeager, Elizabeth Anne, and James W. Morris, III. "History and Computers: The Views from Selected Social Studies Journals." *Social Studies* 86 (November–December 1995): 277–82. ERIC, EJ523806.

Part IV

Computers and Historical Research

13

Historical Research On-Line
A New Ball Game

Ryan Johnson

The study of history is a multifaceted, uneasily defined discipline. At the most extreme, history can be defined as the study of everything that has ever happened. A hundred years ago, history could be more easily capsulized. It was primarily the study of the actions of nations and significant individuals, or, more simply, "Great Man" history. The subjects that historians legitimately examine have increased enormously over the last fifty years. Everything from labor to women, from ethnic groups to sports, has become a separate field within the historical profession.

As the kinds of questions and issues historians address have increased, so too have the kind of sources they use. No longer do historians use only the letters and writings of individuals to explain history. Art, statistics, architecture, literature, and physical artifacts are all used to explain what has happened and why. However, until very recently, the only place to do this research was in a library or some other specialized repository. This is no longer the case. Just as the kinds of questions historians ask have changed, and the kinds of materials they use to discover the answers to those questions have changed, so too have the means of accessing information changed. As the Internet has developed, the ability to find historical information from remote sites has increased as well. The first databases to be made generally available on-line were library catalogs. For many researchers this alone was helpful because by knowing what books and other materials a library held, they could better plan research trips. Once libraries, archives, and other institutions began putting copies of their holdings on-line, research became even easier for some.

The Internet can be described in a variety of ways: a network of networks, an electronic Library of Congress without a cataloging system, anarchy. All three seem to apply. One thing about the Internet is that no one really knows how big it is or precisely what it contains. People have even less idea what it will become in the future.[1] The amount of historical information available on the Internet is growing at an extraordinary rate. This is true of historical information on the Internet as well.

Historical information appears on the World Wide Web (WWW) in a wide variety of formats. Photos, letters, government and other official documents, speech transcripts, and news articles, as well as the secondary writings of historians in on-line journals and on other Web sites are becoming more and more common every day. There is, however, no efficient means of locating just historical information or material on any other given topic in the miasma that is the WWW. There are some sites that try to locate and list information on a particular subject to aid users. For example, the Asian Studies WWW Virtual Library [http://coombs.anu.edu.au/ WWWVL-AsianStudies.html] provides access by means of hypertext links to sites around the world that deal with Asian and Pacific topics. This site is constantly changing, with more information added almost daily. This is just one of many "virtual libraries" available on the Internet. These are all accessible at [http://www.w3.org/vl]. Sites such as this, however, are rare. Most sites are either very specialized or very general; for example, the Argus Clearinghouse [http://www.clear-inghouse.com] and Infomine [http://lib-www.ucr.edu] index and provide hypertext links to information on a large variety of topics of interest to scholars and casual users alike.

To do research effectively on the Internet, one must be patient, diligent, and disciplined. Just as for research in traditionally published sources, a researcher on the Internet must begin with guides, directories, and finding aids. However, many of these are not as readily available as the traditional published reference materials; and before you can use them, you have to find them. In addition to the Internet, there is a wide variety of source materials available electronically from commercial publishers and other information providers. Many of the traditional periodical indexes are now available electronically, some on CD-ROMs, others on-line, and some in both formats. These indexes contain periodical citations, normally abstracts, and occasionally full-article texts. Some of these are very subject-specific, such as: *America: History and Life* or *ERIC,* while others are very broad in subject, including: *Periodical Abstracts, Expanded Academic Index,* or *Article First.*

Periodical indexes are just the tip of the electronic iceberg; however, they are the most visible and most easily used of the electronic sources. They are controlled databases with clearly understood rules governing both content and organization. The Internet, on the other hand, contains an enormous amount of information from a staggering variety of sources. It is conceivably possible to find something on almost anything on the Internet. Unfortunately, in order to find the one single item desired, you have to wade through the morass of personal and business Web pages, the plethora of entertainment information, and the static of a wide-open forum in which all are welcome to put forward their ideas on any and all subjects.

In a television commercial, America On-Line likens the Internet to a cross between the ultimate library and a one-stop warehouse wholesaler. Both images have some basis in reality, but neither image is completely accurate. Business on the Internet, or rather on the World Wide Web (WWW), is a nebulous and infant enterprise still lacking focus and any sustained level of profits. The library image is the most relevant to this paper. It is even more unrealistic than the business image put forward in the commercial. The WWW is not a library. It lacks a catalog describing its contents. In fact, no one knows exactly what is available on the WWW, and with the rapid rate of change and growth, it is conceivable that no one ever will. Not only does the Internet not have a catalog, there is not even a standard system of classification with which to describe the materials found there. Besides lacking a catalog, the WWW also lacks one of a library's most invaluable resources—librarians. There is no one to help researchers select the appropriate source for their searches or to assist them in the use of those sources. When working on the Internet or the WWW a researcher must truly be self-reliant.[2] A user of the WWW must also be disciplined. In order to use the WWW, you must control your searches through the effective use of search operators and the careful selection of keywords. Simply "surfing the Web" can result in wonderful discoveries; however, it takes far too much time to be a useful research method.

In addition to using periodical databases and active Internet searching, a third means of finding information on a wide variety of topics on the WWW is from other people. It is in the facilitation of communication between individuals that the Internet excels. It allows for rapid discussion among individuals with similar interests from around the world through listservs and the Usenet. Both are based in e-mail and contain virtual discussions. Listservs tend to be more controlled and are often edited and moderated for content, while the Usenet groups are more freewheeling and allow for much more diversity of opinion but often bog down in personal attacks called "flames." Both can be effective if used judiciously and with care. One of the best uses for these forums is the gathering of sources on a subject, or, if you are unfamiliar with the topic, getting some guidance on the best reference to use in gathering background information. Of course, one must take care when entering a forum for the first time to see if there are established rules of conduct or guidelines for postings, and be sure to follow them. As with any source, one must be cautious in the use of information gathered through listservs or news groups. These forums often contain a wide variety of individuals with a broad spectrum of experiences and qualifications. On the other hand, since you are the one asking for assistance, politeness or "netiquette" always goes a long way when dealing with others.[3] The sheer scope of the Internet means that it is highly unlikely that any one person would be able to find everything on a given topic there. Therefore, another great way to locate useful sites is to stay in contact with others researching topics similar to yours and to share the location of these sites as you find them.

In order to simplify the process of locating information among the variety of electronic sources, you must ask yourself some simple questions before you begin the search process. These questions will help you conduct your research in an efficient and successful manner. This personal evaluation should include questions such as "What do I need?" "How much material do I need?" "How comprehensive should it be?" And "How up to date does it need to be?" These questions often make up what librarians refer to as a reference interview, which they conduct each time a library patron comes to them with a question. This process will help you to narrow and refine your topic in order to maximize your effort. For example, if you only need general information on a topic, specialized periodical indexes are not the most efficient place to look. A more general monograph or reference work would be more likely to provide the needed information. The other questions posed in the personal reference interview also help refine a search, both in location and in structure. The answers to each of these questions will suggest the type of index or other kind of finding aid to use and will help formulate the search within each finding aid.

When research was conducted solely in printed indexes such as *His-*

torical Abstracts, the number of entries in each volume was limited to a single year, which allowed much simpler browsing than electronic databases allow for. The electronic databases often contain citations for twenty or more years and must be more carefully searched than an annual. Electronic finding aids also make the serendipitous discovery more unlikely than before. A computer will only give you what you tell it to. It is important to remember, however, that a computer will also give you *everything* you tell it to. Therefore, it is incredibly important that the terms used to search an electronic database be carefully selected and organized.

Selecting the appropriate keywords to use is a skill that grows through use.[4] There are some places to look for help. Many databases contain a thesaurus or a word list that you can use to find that database's descriptors or subject headings. Frequently, however, first impressions are the best. Once you have a results set, there are a number of ways to refine it. Replace one term with a synonym to find the term that the database constructors used to describe a given subject, or simply add additional terms to the search, thereby limiting the number of records found. Using results to help you find more records that relate to your topic is another way to find good keywords. Most databases (although this is less true of the Internet search engines) include a list of subjects or descriptors in each record that give the categories the database manufacturers used to describe the citation in question. By using the descriptors from good records, you can control your search results more effectively. These descriptors are not always the terms you would think of first. For example, in *Periodical Abstracts* if you want to search for articles on gun control, the database descriptor is firearms–legislation. If your first attempt does not produce the needed information, start with general terms and a large results set and then gradually reduce the results by adding additional keywords and by using the various limiting options which the database you are searching gives you.

In addition to the number of terms you use in a search, the organization of the terms can also help in limiting a search to a reasonable size. Boolean operators can be used to both narrow and broaden a search in order to find the information you need. Boolean operators are "AND," "OR," and "NOT." "AND" is used to limit a search by combining two or more terms and only finding those records that contain both or all of the terms. For example, if I was looking for information on Japanese security policies, I might attempt a search with the terms "Japan AND security." This would produce a results set with all records containing both terms without any relation to context. "OR" broadens a search by finding all records with either of the terms in addition to those with both. The same terms (Japan and security) used with "OR" creates a much larger results set because it would contain all records with either term. "NOT" eliminates terms from a search. "Japan NOT security" would create a set containing any record with the term Japan as long as it did not contain the term security. By eliminating all records that contain a given term, any records with both will also be eliminated; therefore, "NOT" should be used with caution.

In addition to using Boolean operators, most databases will allow you to limit a search by controlling the proximity of your keywords to each other in each record found. This is usually done with the commands of "WITH" and/or "NEAR." While all databases use "AND," "OR," and "NOT" fairly universally, the same is not true of "WITH" and "NEAR." Every producer of databases or search engines uses this option in a different way. Therefore, in order to use this function effectively, you must read the directions for the product you intend to use. By setting a proximity limit, you establish the number of words apart your keywords must be for the record to be included in the results set. The search "Japan AND security" resulted in all records with both terms, no matter how those terms were used. A search of "Japan within four words of security" (this is usually, but not always, denoted by the command w/4) will produce a set with records in which the term "security" is one of the four words following the term "Japan." The *near* command (n/# usually) would eliminate the designated order and find any record with both terms as long as they are within the designated distance from each other. This option is especially useful when using databases that allow you to search the full text of articles, because it limits your results to records in which the terms have some relevance to one another.

You can also further refine a search by using truncation. This will allow you to insert a wildcard character into a word to allow for alternative spellings or plurals. By using this you can search for both woman and women by simply inserting the wildcard character, often the question mark (?), instead of typing out both words. Truncation will also allow you to search for alternative endings of a word by using the stem and a symbol. For example, theat# (if the # is the command for stemming) would find the terms theater, theatre, theatrical, and so on. The symbols used differ from database to database; therefore, be sure to read the help or instructions before using this option in your research.

In order to effectively search any database, you must understand the particulars of that database. Whether you are searching *America: History and Life, Lexis/Nexis,* or using a search engine such as *Alta Vista* to find material on the WWW, you need to be familiar with the individual idiosyncrasies of each. There is no single format or standard for database searching, and in order to differentiate themselves from their competition, all the producers of electronic databases or Internet search engines make their product just a little bit different from any other system. This makes for additional work for researchers who need to use a variety of databases or search engines. However, once you know the ins and outs of a database, they can be used very effectively to cut down on research time over the long term.

When searching for information, there are also some fundamental mistakes that should be avoided if at all possible. In 1989, Reva Basch put forward the original Seven Deadly Sins of On-line Searching, which can be modified into a set of general guidelines for electronic research.[5] While there are no hard and fast rules to guide a researcher through the growing plethora of information sources, by avoiding common mistakes a researcher can save researchers time, effort, and money.

The Seven Deadly Sins of Electronic Research

1. Pride—assuming you need not read the manual.
2. Haste—rushing into a search before thinking through your search goals.
3. Avarice—trying to find more than you need.
4. Apathy—not thinking creatively about what sources would best cover the subject.
5. Sloth—using the same old databases/Web sites for every search.
6. Narrow-mindedness—trying only one formulation of the search.
7. Ignorance—not knowing the system's tricks and tools.

Pride

Sometimes it is fun to just jump into a new database or search engine and start searching. Unfortunately, it can lead to difficulties. Many databases are limited in the periodicals they cover, both in breadth (the number of titles) as well as depth (the years covered), and many are subject-specific. Search engine and database creators often index and organize information in a unique manner in order to set themselves apart from their competition.

If you are unaware of these limitations, you can waste considerable time and effort with little possibility of finding the desired information. In order to use any sources efficiently, either paper or electronic, you must first know what the source contains, how it is arranged, the cost, if any, and the format of the information.

Haste

Before any search is begun, you should ask yourself the basic questions discussed earlier: What type of information? How much? How comprehensive? How up to date? The answers to these questions help you select the best database or search engine to use, narrow the choice of search terms, and make it easier to scan retrieved records in order to recognize the material that will be most helpful.

Avarice

Before beginning a search decide how much information and what type of information you need. If you only need background information, or a few general articles on a subject, look for those and get them. Do not waste time, effort, and money (especially if you are using a source you have to pay for) finding the definitive works on a subject or a complete bibliography unless you really need them.

Apathy

Give a few minutes of thought to who might care about what you are looking for. For information on the growth of Asian trade in the 1980s, a site dealing with business and economics located in Hong Kong or Australia would probably be of more use than one dealing with the Cold War located in Washington. Similarly, a business database such as *ABI Inform* or *Lexis/Nexis* would almost certainly offer more and better results than *Historical Abstracts*.

Sloth

Most people want to do things with the least possible effort and tend to prefer that which is familiar. Unfortunately, the current question usually determines where you must search for the answer, not a previous one. Be sure, before you begin a search, that the database or Web site that you intend to use is likely to contain the answer or is the easiest or cheapest way to find the answer. Similarly, if dealing with more contemporary topics, restricting one's search to historical databases or Web sites can be self-defeating, because they are very exclusionary in their content.

Narrow-mindedness

One of the most common mistake researchers make is believing in the One True Search and blindly accepting the results as all there is on the subject. Rather than starting with a complex Boolean search (A OR B) AND (C OR D) NOT E, try a more general search, A OR B, and then limit the results as necessary. Scan some of the results of your wide search, and see what kind of records are included. See if a synonym for one of your terms appears regularly and add it to the search to see what effect that has on the search. Also examine the records to see what descriptors the creators of the database used and try to augment your search by replacing one of the original keywords with the descriptor. For example, in the database *Periodical Abstracts,* the term "firearms" is used instead of the term "gun." By replacing "gun" with "firearm" in your search terms, a more comprehensive results set can be created. Do not ignore non-electronic sources. Often it is easier to get information from a print source than from an electronic one. Never limit yourself to one source or search. Be creative about your research.

Ignorance

Before using a database, on-line system or search engine that you are not completely familiar with, be sure to know the essentials. How does it display results? How are the results arranged? Chronologically or by significance, and if by significance, how is that determined? How do you truncate search terms? How do you search for terms as they relate to one another? What kind of help is available and how is it accessed? If you are on a system that charges for access, how are those charges assessed? What kind of defaults are built into the search engine? For example, *America History and Life* uses AND as a default and treats a space between two words as an AND, but several of the Internet search engines use OR as the default, which can rapidly increase the size of the results set.

In addition to the Seven Deadly Sins, the other malady which can often infect Internet searchers is the "Ooh! That looks neat!" syndrome or OTLN. This is especially common among college undergraduates. Internet searching requires a great deal of discipline, not only in the selection of the proper search engine and search terms, but also in developing the ability to avoid the distractions of interesting and yet inherently irrelevant information.

There is no control over what kind of information is put on the Internet or over who puts it there. The amount of quality information is astounding, but so too is the amount of utter garbage. As a means for people to communicate with each other and to express themselves freely, the open nature of the Internet is a boon for free speech. However, this makes research on the Internet that much more difficult, because you have to sort through the polemics of precocious fourteen-year-olds and the often radical statements of the uninformed to find the quality, verifiable information that can be used. This means that to use the Internet as a research tool, you must be extraordinarily critical of the information there and be sure of its authenticity or accuracy.

Nevertheless, electronic databases and the Internet are a great boon for researchers of all stripes, including historians. As more and more information is put on the WWW, the problems of distance and time that historians have had to struggle with for generations are gradually being reduced—not eliminated, but reduced. The need to travel to wherever the information is housed and to accept the time schedule of the repository no longer exists once it is available on a gopher or WWW page. It can be accessed from anywhere in the world, any time of day. By making more and more information available, computers have increased the ability of researchers to use a wide variety of previously unfamiliar or generally unavailable information; however, unless you can effectively use the computer's searching abilities to find the quality information amongst the vast quantity available, you will be lost in the forest, unable to find the trees.

Notes

1. Mary Ellen Bates, *The On-Line Deskbook: On-Line Magazine's Essential Desk Reference for On-Line and Internet Searchers* (Wilton, CT: Pemberton Press, 1996), 207–209.

2. "The Internet for Researchers: What It Is, and What It Is Not," The History Computerization Project, On-line (http://www.history.la.ca.us/history/hdadvice. htm#Internet), April 2, 1997.

3. Reva Basch, *Secrets of the Super Net Searchers: The Reflections, Revelations, and Hard-won Wisdom of Thirty-Five of the World's Top Internet Researchers* (Wilton, CT: Pemberton Press, 1996), 13, 55, 61–62.

4. My thanks to Laura Davidson, Chair, Information Services Department, Zach S. Henderson Library, Georgia Southern University for her assistance and patience in helping me to begin to develop the skills described in this section of the article.

5. Reva Basch, "The Seven Deadly Sins of Full Text Searching," *Database* 12, no. 4 (August 1989): 15–23. These were later modified in Mary Ellen Bates, *The On-line Deskbook,* 207–209.

14

Historical Research and Electronic Evidence

Problems and Promises

Jeffrey G. Barlow

Introduction

It has become commonplace to argue that the changes which we ultimately will experience in the dissemination of ideas as a consequence of
the development of the Internet may well be comparable to those introduced by the printing press itself. The possibility that such a revolution
could be in process probably produces more apprehension than anticipation in most of us. Nevertheless, by many standards, this assertion is, I
believe, correct; we are in the midst of a revolution.[1] In this paper, I
propose to identify and discuss some basic problems and advantages
which this revolution presents to history.

Historians, by virtue of our work, have seen—or at least have visual-
ized in our mind's eye—quite a lot. Some might say that as a profession
we have seen everything come and, sometimes with great relief on our
part, go, and many of us hope that this may be the case with the digital
revolution as well. It is true that if our standard is solely the corpus of
materials produced, the Gutenbergian revolution will for some time be
greater than the digital one. The Library of Congress, it is estimated,
contains about twenty million volumes or, expressed in its electronic
equivalent, about twenty terabytes[2] of typed text. In April of 1997, the
World Wide Web, that popular portion of the Internet which can carry
both text and graphics, consisted of perhaps two terabytes of data, no
more than about 10 percent of the information contained in the Library
of Congress. In December of 1996, however, the Web contained but one
terabyte of data; it doubled in less than three months.[3] Nicholas

Negroponte estimated way back in January of 1996—the digital equivalent of the eighteenth century—that a new Web page, the basic frame for information on the World Wide Web, was coming into being every four seconds.[4] At this level of growth the Web would be the size of the Library of Congress by 1998.

However, the argument that the development of the Internet is as significant a change as the development of the printing press rests on far more than the corpus of data published. The economics of the Web make it possible for even many American children to publish information which, in theory at least, can be seen by millions. Almost any university student can now disseminate his or her thoughts to a potentially world-wide audience, whether those thoughts represent disorganized ramblings about incomprehensible pop-cultural topics or well-researched and creative responses to important problems in his or her chosen field. For a historian, it is as though we have suddenly achieved Carl Becker's goal of "everyman his own historian."[5] But this revolution extends beyond a simple increase in product and in producers. Electronic information differs significantly from that in the "old media." The Internet is going to change all our lives and our professions in radical if as of yet unforeseen ways.

In this paper I discuss the impact of the Internet on a key aspect of history: evidence. The handling of evidence has been central to every change in the ways historians have studied history during the long period that it has been written. If we understand the impact of the Internet upon the historian's use of evidence, then we have gone far toward comprehending its impact on history in general.

In analyzing this topic, I first review the manner in which successive generations of historians have thought about evidence and its uses. Then I examine how it is that some of the commonly held indictments of the Internet relate to the use of evidence. Next I discuss some of the positive aspects of the Internet for historians. I conclude by weighing advantages against disadvantages and suggest solutions for some of the problems.

Evidence Is Essential to History

In this discussion, by "essential to history" we mean essential to historians and to students of history.[6] Theodore Mommsen (1817–1903), one of the greatest of nineteenth-century historians, a group whose basic assumptions are discussed below, briefly defined history in his Rectorial Address to the University of Berlin in 1874:

History, after all, is nothing but the distinct knowledge of actual happenings, consisting on the one hand of the discovery and examination of the available testimony, and on the other of the weaving of a testimony into a narrative in accordance with one's understanding of the men who shaped the events and the conditions that prevailed. The former we call the critical study of historical sources and the latter, the pragmatic writing of history.[7]

R.G. Collingwood, in his important work *The Idea of History,* defines history as a field of study rather more closely. But central to that definition is his answer to the key question "How does history proceed?" His answer:

History proceeds by the interpretation of evidence: where evidence is a collective name for things which singly are called documents, and a document is a thing existing here and now, of such a kind that the historian by thinking about it, can get answers to the questions he asks about past events. Here again there are plenty of difficult questions to ask as to what the characteristics of evidence are and how it is interpreted. . . . However they are answered, historians will agree that historical procedure, or method, consists essentially of interpreting evidence.[8]

Evidence and its interpretation are then the *sine qua non* of historical studies. This is so for a number of reasons. Many human sciences can study that which is right before them or, in many cases, produce the object of their study in laboratories for their own purposes. Historians must work at a remove; that which we study is irretrievably gone, and we can attempt to understand it only through the traces it leaves, artifacts of bone or stone, coins, the foundations of buildings, eyewitness accounts, letters, and government documents; all of these and many other sorts of remnants, which we may term "evidence" if they pertain to the question which we are investigating.

Not only can we know our subject only through remaining evidentiary traces, but the interpretation of that evidence remains key to our history work even after it is done. Another philosopher of history, David Hackett Fischer, stated in *Historians' Fallacies:* "A historian must not only tell truths but must demonstrate their truthfulness as well."[9] This demonstration usually proceeds by laying out the evidence around which one has constructed a particular assertion, leaving it for others to agree or disagree that it is true based upon that evidence.

This interpretation and reinterpretation of evidence constitutes the collective work of historians over time. Historical studies are a sort of dialogue with other historians, usually conducted via the process of publication. Thus the process of writing history proceeds, generation by generation, but only if the evidence is continually available for analysis.

Evidence must continually be available for another reason: to prevent fraud, whether motivated by economic, emotional, or political gain. There are many famous frauds in historical studies. In my field, Chinese studies, one of the most interesting was the forging, apparently by Sir Edmund Backhouse (1873–1944) or a confederate, of a diary said to have been written (c. 1900) by a key figure at the Manchu court of late Imperial China. Backhouse very nearly parlayed the forgery, and other apparently spurious documents, into a Chair in Chinese Studies at Oxford, then the pinnacle of academic standing in that field. Circumstances kept the hoax from succeeding, and later analysis of the putative diary proved it a forgery.[10] More recently we had an attempt to forge the diaries of Adolph Hitler for financial gain, another hoax unmasked by an analysis of the artifacts themselves.

In addition to fraud, there is also the continual threat of confusion or error if standards for evidence are not strictly maintained. A recent incident, interesting because it pertains directly to the Internet, has been the recurrent surfacing of "evidence" that T.W.A. Flight 800 was hit by a U.S. Navy missile, which was the cause of its crash in July of 1996.[11] The ultimate source of this claim was an unsubstantiated speculation on the Internet, which continually circulated until traced back to its origins.

How Has the Reading of Evidence Changed?

As Collingwood suggested (above), though all historians agree upon the centrality of evidence, many important questions remain with regard to its interpretation and other issues. Here I present my understanding of key points in the development of the field of history, which both concern the use of evidence and are relevant to the issues raised by the Internet. In so doing, I also attempt to establish some concepts key to the subsequent development of my position.

Although we credit Herodotus (c. 484–425 B.C.E.) with being the Father of History, this is true only in a very narrow Western sense.[12] For Herodotus, there was only one sort of evidence—eyewitness accounts— and he gave remarkably little attention to a consideration of the strengths and weaknesses of this approach. Thucydides (c. 471–379 B.C.E.), unlike

Herodotus, thought explicitly about evidence and so carried the doing of history forward.[13]

Historians have always been greatly affected by the institutional context in which they work. In both the West and Asia the growth of the bureaucratic state stimulated the systematic collecting and archiving of documents. The Chinese Han-era historian Ssu-ma Ch'ien (c. 145–90 B.C.E.) then used these materials in writing a history of the Chinese state. His near contemporary, Livy (Titus Livius B.C.E. 59–C.E. 17), did much the same for Rome. There would, of course, be many later developments in the writing of history, but by the end of the Roman era in Europe and the end of the Han in China, these two great cultures had set their essential approaches to history as a study: it would be a critical analysis done for the needs of living men, based upon the evidence which had survived from the period under scrutiny.

In the following centuries many great historians lived and produced influential works but the essentials of the historian's craft changed little, so we pass quickly over them. Just as historians were affected by their institutional milieux, so were they affected by their intellectual ones. Major historical schools directly reflected the intellectual movements of their time and hence can usually be subsumed within broader cultural labels. One very important such label is "Modernism." The successor to Renaissance Humanism, Modernism is widely agreed to begin with Descartes (1596–1650). From the Modernist perspective, history can be said to be uniform, chronological, and teleological in that it tends toward progress.[14] Early Modernist historians such as Voltaire (1694–1778) put a renewed emphasis upon the reading of evidence.[15]

Within the broader construct of Modernism, we must also recognize counter-currents, such as the Romanticism of the early nineteenth century. Fritz Stern argues that the dominant characteristic of Romanticism was a devotion to the unique, the particular, and the local, a commitment whose human embodiment was Sir Walter Scott.[16] Scott greatly influenced the writing of history, and this would not be the last tie between literature and history.

A key question for Modernist historians was whether or not history was itself part of the wave of scientific studies that was, intellectually, pushing all before it. Dray argues that it was then that a true philosophy of history can be said to have developed; if history was a science, then no independent philosophy of history was necessary; it was subsumed within the philosophy of science. But if history was in some sense not a science, then a philosophy of history was possible.[17] The Modernist group that developed in the nineteenth century, confident that history was indeed a science, is often referred to as the "Positivists."

Positivist historians held additional beliefs. They believed that facts derived from evidence were capable of speaking for themselves and that scientific detachment on the part of the historian would permit them to do so. They did not interpret evidence then, so much as they discovered and announced it. They believed that the evidence was, in effect, itself the history; the history they wrote was the one true history, insofar as their evidence was complete.[18] Moreover, some Positivists, like Thomas Buckle (1821–1862), believed that objective facts enabled historians to discover general laws of historical development: a true science of history.[19] Karl Popper has labeled this wing of Positivists, the most influential of whom is certainly Karl Marx, the "Historicists."[20]

In the nineteenth century, history underwent another important change in its institutional base: it became an academic discipline, after having been the preserve of professional bureaucrats or largely upper-class amateurs in both the East and the West. This occurred in part because of the support of the modern nation-state for education in general.

At the same time, there was another important development in history as a field. Historical journals, growing in part out of the scholarly practice of serially circulating correspondence among intellectuals,[21] were created in the major states to further the study of history and to disseminate those studies. This development made standards for the use and interpretation of evidence increasingly subject to peer agreement. This material, taken from the preface of one such journal, the *Revue Historique,* founded in France in 1876, is broadly representative of similar journals in Germany, England, and in the United States. Note the Positivist and nationalist agendas:

> The *Review* will accept only original contributions, based upon original sources, which will enrich science either with their basic research or with the results of their conclusions; but while we demand from our contributors strictly scientific methods of exposition, with each assertion accompanied by proof, by source references and quotations, while we severely exclude vague generalities and rhetoric, we shall preserve in the *Revue Historique* that literary quality which historians as well as French readers justly value so highly.[22]

With these journals, historical writings acquired a recognizably modern form and a content.

These two changes, the shift to an increasingly academic base, and the development of journals, were of course interrelated. The development of the graduate school model of education at Johns Hopkins University in 1876 spread to other established institutions. Then, following the 1890 extension of the Morril act, state universities multiplied rapidly.[23] Great universities demanded presses for the publication of the research of their noted scholars. This, too, would be an important institutional shift, though its full impact would not be felt until much later.

As the universities were multiplying, the Positivist position was reaching its end. It was based upon an underlying Modernist assumption that mankind was steadily progressing, but the bloodshed and widely recognized dehumanization of World War I vitiated this Positivist premise. The rise of fascism and World War II largely finished it off.

For historians, Positivism was not succeeded by any clear "ism" but was replaced by a welter of uncertainty appropriate to late Modernism.[24] In its late form, Modernism accepted several additional underlying credos: the loss of community; material art becoming less important than the theory behind it; the consciousness of isolation superseding all other certainties.[25]

In historical studies, the use of evidence (and its meaning) was again central to these changes. One important school was Relativism, here represented by Carl Becker (though Charles A. Beard would do as well), who wrote:

> To establish the facts is always in order, and is indeed the first duty of the historian; but to assume that the facts, once established in all their fullness, will "Speak for themselves" is an illusion. . . . Left to themselves, the facts do not speak; left to themselves they do not exist, not really, since for all practical purposes there is no fact until someone affirms it.[26]

From Modernism to Postmodernism was but a short step. The Relativists had rebelled against Positivist surety, but had tried to pause half-way in the process, at that point where history became relative to the needs and assumptions of each generation of historians and their audiences, and evidence could be interpreted and reinterpreted accordingly; the Postmodernists careened full-tilt into indeterminacy. Their intellectual context had, of course, notably failed to improve from that of the late

Modernists. Hitler's death camps had been bad enough, but now to many the contingencies of the Atomic Age, when "good" and "bad" became as ambiguous as "winner" and "loser," superseded all else.

Postmodernism, represented by writers such as Derrida, Lacan, Kristeva, Foucault, Lyotard, and Baudrillard, now proclaimed that life was more than indeterminate, it had lost its meaningfulness, at least insofar as our ability to communicate effectively about it was concerned. Postmodernist discourse, taking a cue from linguistics, as cultural studies have often done in periods of intellectual confusion, attacked the very possibility of language as a shared system of communications. This, of course, materially affected the interpretation of evidence. As Abrams states:

> In recent developments in linguistic and literary theory, there is an effort to subvert the foundations of language itself, so as to show that its seeming meaningfulness dissipates, for an unillusioned inquirer, into a play of unresolvable though conflicting indeterminacies.[27]

Evidence now became a matter for negotiation and was necessarily relative to the context in which it was read; the context in which it had been produced was felt to be irretrievable.

There is another factor important to the development of both Modernism and Postmodernism, the consequence of which cannot be overemphasized, though it is difficult to assess. The multiplication of both "other" voices and the channels through which they could be communicated eroded the unity of previous intellectual positions. So far as academic studies are concerned, this multiplication is nicely represented by the growth in scholarly presses and their output. In 1948, there had been thirty-five members of the Association of University Presses; by 1968, there were sixty, with an additional twenty to thirty minor ones. Monographic publications had increased from 727 titles to 2,300.[28] In the past, scholarly dialogues were conducted at a relatively glacial pace and in a "gentlemanly" (a term deliberately chosen here) manner. Now a hundred schools began to contend. What had been academic fields presided over in a magisterial manner by monolithic scholarly societies, a few journals, and major presses were now inundated by polemical factions, many new periodicals, and a flood of scholarly monographs. Formerly national dialogues now became international ones; the boundaries between high and popular culture blurred. It is no wonder that indeterminacy increasingly became a characteristic of these schools of thought.

With Postmodernism we finally arrive in the present. There remain important elements in Postmodernism which merit a brief and highly tentative sorting out because they are particularly relevant to historical studies, but it is understood that no uncontested discussion of these elements is currently possible. Many intellectuals in many fields are struggling to understand precisely where they have bobbed up in the Postmodernist tide.

A characteristic of the current period is the continuing fragmentation of both the larger intellectual scene and of individual fields. For example, although Structuralism can be said to be part of the Modernist period, it has subdivided to the point where important voices cannot agree as to where to situate their field. There might be said to be four or five Structuralisms, each in some senses continuous from Modernism while simultaneously having important Postmodernist elements.[29]

There is a group within Postmodernism which is increasingly focused on the importance of electronic media and is hence particularly important to this inquiry. Often labeled "Co-opted" or "Commercial" Postmodernism, it argues that contemporary culture must be understood as an artifact of multinational capitalism and its associated technologies. Ann E. Kaplan assigns causality to these technologies: "The break that modernism initiated is at once fulfilled with the development of recent sophisticated electronic technologies and, at the same time, drastically altered in the process so as to become 'postmodern.' "[30]

Many writers in the social sciences and the humanities have taken readily to the vocabulary of the various Postmodernist schools, in part, I believe, because it is a highly figurative one in which formerly literal meanings shift and change. This has meant the possibility of creating useful new analytical terms and also the development of a language largely unintelligible to the non-initiate. Just as the traditional Chinese scholar utilized elliptical Confucian references as a polite means of testing social standing, so do Postmodernist tropes construct the boundaries of a self-referential, status-seeking community. Though we may sometimes doubt their grounding in any generally shared definition of reality, there is no doubt as to the fertility of the Postmodern analyses. In studies of "other" cultures for example, Post-colonial theory has proven extremely productive.[31]

Postmodernism, as I understand it, attempts to untangle many intellectual dilemmas which face us, though it often does so in a radically disjunctive manner, which makes it both threatening to those steeped in earlier traditions and difficult to comprehend. Postmodernism, whether viewed as the successor to Modernism or its extension, presents a more profound break with previous paradigms than was the case in earlier periods of change. For historians at least, it is truly a turning point, an *epistèmè* in the Foucaultian sense.

The Postmodernist approach to text began in literary criticism and flowed naturally into history (Sir Walter Scott *redivivus*), as history itself is necessarily text-based. Therefore, within the Postmodernist analyses, history is particularly problematized. As Brenda K. Marshall puts it:

> Postmodernism is about history. But not the kind of "History" that lets us think we can know the past. History in the postmodern moment becomes histories and questions. It asks: Whose history gets told? In Whose name? For what purpose? Postmodernism is about histories not told, retold, untold. Histories forgotten, hidden, invisible, considered unimportant, changed, eradicated. It's about the refusal to see history as linear, as leading straight up to today in some recognizable pattern—all set for us to make sense of. . . the postmodern moment is not something that is to be defined chronologically; rather it is a rupture in our consciousness.[32]

The Postmodern schools have had a profound impact upon the notion of evidence. For example, Structuralism, as represented by literary critics and writers such as Roland Barthes, denies that texts—including most especially historical documentary evidence—have any reference to any reality existing beyond the text itself. The author and the reader are reduced to little more than the act of writing and of reading.[33] Meaning in evidence, then, is in no sense inherent or objective but totally "constructed."

A very influential post-Postmodernist school, Deconstructionism, sometimes also labeled Poststructuralism, carries indeterminacy a step further by denying that any text can represent any reality. Demonstrations of "truth" via reading of "evidence" is impossible. Meaning is "negotiated" by "communities of discourse" and are always relative to those communities. Any text is "open" to simultaneous contradictory readings,[34] and the meaning of any text depends upon all other texts that reference it or are referenced by it; meaning now depends on "intertextuality."

Michel Foucault, who now signifies the semioticized embodiment of Postmodernism whether he merits that fate or not, denied the possibility or even the desirability of a continuous historical consciousness.[35] This amounts to a fragmentation of the past itself. Separate pasts now exist for each community of discourse, even for each reader.

Clearly this is not a desirable state of affairs from a historian's perspective. Many literary analysts and historians are currently trying to understand historical study within a framework which is both recognizably historical and appropriately Postmodern. There is as of yet no identifiable school whose formulations we can use to approach these paradoxes, but one loosely defined group has been referred to as "the New Historicism." We must understand this use of the term "historicism" to be a figurative one, in that it does not reference the "Historicism" criticized by Popper as mentioned above.

The New Historicism is defined, somewhat unsympathetically, by Elizabeth Fox-Genovese as:

> A bastard child of a history that resembles anthropological "thick description" and of a literary theory in search of its own possible significance, this "new historicism" consists in a plethora of converging, but also conflicting, tendencies within cultural studies broadly construed.[36]

To the Postmodernist schools, though, historicism provides a possible egress from an otherwise highly circumscribed intellectual position. Having denied the possibility of a unitary past, the extreme Postmodernist finds himself or herself constrained from making useful and interesting general statements about the past, even of their own field of study. Unless some sort of history is possible, the debate literally self-deconstructs.

Many Postmodernists have lauded the work of Hayden White. I understand White to be grounding his historical perspective in a largely Postmodernist framework in that his most obvious intellectual debt is to literary theory, wherein history is reduced largely to text and the mind of the historian is best understood as a variant upon the mind of the poet.[37] Any historian must applaud White's work as a thoughtful and provocative consideration of nineteenth-century Western intellectual history. It seems to me, however, this approach works best as White has used it, as historiography; it tells us more about historians than about history. It makes a virtue of the Postmodernist impulse to treat history as discourse, but it does not show us a way through the obstacles Postmodernism places between the present and the past as a knowable, unitary, series of events.

I have dwelt upon Postmodernism here not only because it takes our analysis of the historian's use of evidence into the present, but also because it particularly speaks to the problems raised by the Internet. We have argued above that historians have always existed within institutional and intellectual contexts, which invariably affect them and their work, including even their use of evidence. In the late twentieth century, the Internet suddenly has become an important part of our context. The historical school whose context most comprehends the Internet is, of course, the one contemporary with it, Postmodernism. Whether one has caused the other in some sense is unimportant here; each exists in a relationship to the other.

Contemporary critiques of the Internet are similar in some ways to the Modernist response to Postmodernism; I think that, in some sense, that critique *is* the Modernist response to Postmodernism. The Modernist critique of Postmodernist work has often been to accuse it of acute relativism and a general erosion of standards.[38] Most contemporary historians were trained by Modernists; it is not surprising that many view the Internet as a somewhat threatening intrusion. Its pages are suffused with relativistic and problematic intellectual positions; it envalues popular culture far more than high culture. The problems of Postmodernism and of the Internet are strikingly similar; it is appropriate and inevitable that the language and analysis of Postmodernism seem to many to offer the best tools with which to understand the Internet.

Electronic Evidence

Given this background in historiography, we now turn to consider the possible consequences of the development of the Internet for the historian's use of evidence. We first consider the problems presented by electronic documents and their rapid proliferation, then turn to some of the advantages this situation presents.

I find that an emotional element, which I interpret as fear or anxiety, is often present in my discussions with colleagues regarding the Internet. Sometimes it is expressed as contempt, the conveyance of the feeling that there is nothing new under the sun, and I am wasting my time with attractive machines when I should be in the library like Thucydides and Ssu-ma Ch'ien; real historians don't read bytes. In addition to this fear of the unknown, however, I think there are some solid objections to the use of electronic evidence. I number them here, for I wish to refer to them later.

1) The Documents Found on the Internet Are Potentially Unreliable

This is obviously true. An electronic document is often found well outside its original provenance, and it is frequently difficult to assess its validity or even to determine its authorship. An example is the e-mail report of the downing of Flight 800 mentioned above. Yet an electronic document exists, and in the mind of many students of history that is the same as, or at least as good as, being "true." If we as professional historians are more cautious, this may still mean that the document is a mere artifact, not useful as evidence, for we cannot fully assess its worth.

2) Electronic Documents Lack Authority

The conventional source of documents for historians, and particularly for undergraduate students of history, is a library. The library, though it too has pitfalls for the untutored, is quite different from the Internet. Most of the works found in a library have been filtered by multiple levels of authority. Somebody thought them worth writing; others then thought them worth editing and publishing; then a professional librarian found them worth collecting and cataloguing; frequently a professor then thought them worth assigning. The student goes to them with considerable confidence, though perhaps unaware of the reasons for that confidence.

Students have also picked up clues as to how to recognize varying levels of authority in a library. As Umberto Eco puts it, "I can glance at the spine of a book and make a good guess at its content from a number of signs. If I see the words Harvard University Press, I know it's probably not going to be a cheap romance. I go onto the Net and I don't have those skills."[39] Not only do students currently lack those skills, but the documents found on the Internet are much less filtered—often the filter is little more than that a virtually anonymous person found them worth writing and posting to an electronic site where other people have posted pictures of their dogs.

3) Electronic Evidence Blurs Authorial Credentials

As Eco suggests above, if we encounter a work from Harvard University Press, we are justified in approaching it with some degree of confidence— its author is, if nothing else, published by the Harvard University Press.

The Web may not provide us with any hint of such authority. Indeed, the nature of the Web encourages informality and discourages declamations of one's credentials. For example, as part of my research here on Postmodernism I discovered a very informative Web page written by one Michael Fegan, who included no information at all about him- or herself.[40] This page was an excellent one, with succinct definitions of troublesome terms, what I take to be footnotes of a sort, and a brief bibliography. I have drawn from it above what I trust to be a direct quotation from Brenda K. Marshall.[41] But Michael Fegan may be, for all I know, an unusually creative sixth grader in Missouri.

Brown and Duguid, in a very useful electronic paper, refer very elegantly to this problem by stating that new document technologies have made the formerly rigid separation between producer and consumer of information "an option."[42] Fegan may be a consumer passing on his research gleanings unaltered, according to the best scholarly standards, or he may have added significantly to the material he received, perhaps without being aware of his role as a producer. If he is a producer, then we need to know his credentials in order to fully assess his contribution.

4) Electronic Documents Are Too Easy to Collect

Besides raising the perhaps unworthy feeling that an important part of historical research is the suffering necessary to collect evidence, the ease of securing electronic documents has other objections from the historian's point of view. First, as Popper argues, "there can be no history without a point of view. Like the natural sciences, history must be selective unless it is to be choked by a flood of poor and unrelated material."[43] The problem with research done by a would-be historian in the library has rarely been that the work lacks a point of view; usually the concern is that it is not the student's point of view. Now, every student of history is a potential encyclopaedist. The skillful Web surfer can assemble reams of information and drag it into a paper, with the common result that the organization and analysis, the point of view, the original context, is quite lost.

5) The Internet Magnifies Errors

Once again conventional publication acts as a sort of filter; for an author to discover another's error is properly the occasion for many self-congratulatory footnotes. But the collecting of information for Web pages is often an uncritical process, and an error may be almost endlessly repeated in similar pages. An initial supposition, frequently repeated, becomes fact. One shudders at the possible effect of endlessly multiplied and widely disseminated electronic versions of "The Protocols of the Elders of Zion," for example.

6) The Ease of Electronic Publication Erodes Standards

Natalie Zemon Davis recently asked in *Perspectives,* the newsletter of the American Historical Association, the very interesting question: "Who Owns History?" The mood of this article is a rather up-beat one, some-what akin to Carl Becker's in *Everyman His Own Historian,* referred to above. Davis states, "After all, there is no absolute difference between the ways of seeking evidence and revising and checking views about the past in and outside of academe."[44] My own experience is that this is not true. I teach, for example, the history of the Vietnam War. To many of my students a year's experience as a rifleman in Vietnam more than qualifies one as an expert upon the war. There is now an entire monthly magazine, *Vietnam,* largely devoted to just this point of view. Edited by Harry Summers, the author of an influential book on the war,[45] *Vietnam* is in its ninth year of publication. While there is much that is useful in the publication, its perspective is the popular revisionist one, that all veterans know truths about the war willfully ignored by policy makers and suppressed by the professoriate—usually labeled as former anti-war protesters. In a recent issue, for example, there was an interview with a "Crusader for Vietnam Vets," B.G. Burkett. The interviewer asked: "Today it seems everybody wants to be a Vietnam veteran. Why the change in attitude?" Burkett replies:

> During the war the anti-war movement was trying to paint us as the worst monsters they possibly could: We committed atrocities everyday, we took drugs all the time, or whatever. So when we came home, we didn't do the things that veterans from other wars had done. We didn't form groups, we didn't join groups and we didn't become a political power or a lobby. That's different than the World War I, World War II and Korea vets. What that did was leave a vacuum. The person who gets center stage in our society is the victim. So what happened is, that vacuum was slowly but surely filled by phonies. They would put on the garb and play. . . . They put on jungle fatigues, decked themselves out with medals, and played Vietnam veteran. Pretty soon

you have half a dozen of these guys in town forming some kind of veteran chapter, and when a reporter wants a comment on veterans' issues, he goes to them.[46]

This argument tars not only all anti-war protesters, but many veterans as well. Certainly veterans of my acquaintance from organizations like the Vietnam Veterans Against the War or the Northwest Veterans for Peace would differ with Mr. Burkett. Now the magazine has a Web site as well, and documents such as the above can be endlessly replicated.[47]

This issue is a very complex one. There is a vital difference—vital to a historian at least—between the *experience* of a subject and the historical *knowledge* of it.[48] The nation-wide conflict during 1995–1996 between many veterans and many historians over the proposed Smithsonian exhibit on the use of the atomic bombs on Japan is a good example of this confusion. So far as Congress, and most Americans, were concerned, the opinions of veterans on the necessity of dropping the bomb were far more authoritative than those of experts in the historical evidence bearing upon this question.

The Internet facilitates the posting of first-person stories about historical events. This can be a good thing, but it can also erode usual standards for evidence, emphasizing the experiential at the expense of the reasoned, thoughtful perspective.

7) Electronic Evidence Facilitates Dishonesty

This assertion is true *prima facie* for plagiarism. I first understood that I had to learn more about the new media when I received three papers on the Great Wall of China—each quite different from the others—in an introductory Asian history course. By coincidence I saw an advertisement for a CD-ROM on that very topic, which I ordered. It was, of course, the source of each of the three papers.

Even relatively narrow topics are now covered on the World Wide Web, sometimes in surprising depth. In researching this piece I had searched for material on Jean Baudrillard, a French Postmodernist with some interest in cyberspace. I found nothing in our library at Pacific University, nor a great deal in our linked catalogue, incorporating a number of academic libraries. A search on the Web search engine AltaVista, however, turned up three thousand sites where he was at least mentioned. Pity the professor who assigns a topic on Baudrillard without being somewhat familiar with at least the existence of these resources, many of which would be wonderful research materials but which could also be cut and pasted into quite a dazzling paper. The days when we could be reasonably confident of the honesty of our students because we were familiar with "our" sections of our institutional libraries have passed. The possibilities for dishonesty among our peers is also multiplied quite dramatically by the existence of such materials.

8) Electronic Materials Are Unprecedentedly Mutable

When working with published texts, usually we have little concern in this area. It may be that a major work will go through several important revisions, but even that is rare. Electronic materials, however, change constantly. Some sites with multiple servers do not even have identical versions of a given document up on each machine; two visits a few minutes apart may produce different editions of the same document. Also, many documents will be revised locally as a result of interaction with readers, while the original remains posted on another site.

9) Electronic Evidence Is Unprecedentedly Volatile[49]

Worse than simply changing, electronic evidence can disappear completely. The site it was posted on may well disappear as well, and a Web browser will return that maddening "404 not found" response to your frustrated banging upon the keyboard. The continual dialogue among historians very much depends on the continual availability of key evidence.

10) Electronic Evidence Disturbs the Economy of Cultural Production

One of the most problematic areas of the new information media is their economic effect. Put simply, a book published by the Oxford University Press has a relatively fixed value, in part because its number is fixed (ignoring those perpetually busy Chinese Xerox machines). An entire economy depends upon that fixity—not only the value of the book, but the value of the author's royalties, the university presses' return on their investments, even, at not too abstract a remove, the value of an associate professorship as compared to an assistant professorship.

Now all of us, in addition to our fair share of royalties, also want our fair share of readers or, in my case at least, even more than we deserve. We care about our ideas and want them to find homes in somebody else's footnotes. But if I genuinely want to have my ideas at least glanced at, I would do well to simply post them on the Web. I recently learned, for example, that a Web page on Japanese baseball done by some of my lower-division students receives an average of more than twenty visitors per day, literally from all over the world. This is perhaps the total number of readers my own published works receive in a good month.

If we eventually pledge our intellectual troth to the Internet, however, how will our previous mistresses, the university presses, fare? The November 1996 *Journal of Asian Studies,* the professional quarterly most relevant to my own field, reviewed in some detail ninety-nine works and noted that the editors had received sixty-six others. Somehow, somebody manages to fund this tremendous outpouring, primarily through the university presses. This is another economic issue raised by the advent of electronic publication.

11) Electronic Evidence Lacks Weight

This is in effect a summary of all the previous problems; because of all the above factors, we properly are reluctant to give much weight to electronic materials in historical studies.

12) The Production of Electronic Materials Does Not Contribute to Professional Standing

At present, though we may not be proud of the fact, we must acknowledge that the competition for professional standing in part drives the production of academic publications. If there were no tenure, or if everybody were automatically tenured, or even if an important new degree, such as the ABD (All But Dissertation), were established, it seems reasonable to assume that there would be a fall-off in the rate of publication.

One of the factors holding back publication on the Web is that its rewards are primarily personal. We see our ideas flung far and wide, and we can even tell how many people "hit" upon them. But deans, often parsimonious and reactionary souls, are unlikely to count an e-publication as evidence of professional standing. To give them their due, none of us know quite how to assess the value of such publications, either. Unlike conventional publications, e-publications are not usually refereed and are rarely reviewed.

The most enthusiastic supporter of the Internet must acknowledge that the above twelve problems much reduce its appeal to historians. Let us now turn to a happier topic, the advantages the Internet presents with regard to evidence.

The Advantages of Electronic Documents

1) Electronic Delivery Makes Many Primary Documents More Available

One factor which I will give short shrift to here, because it is incontrovertible, is the ease with which digitally published works can be collected and disseminated. Classical works which are no longer restricted by copyright are being digitized and posted to the Web as "Gutenberg texts" at an amazing rate.[50] Even in a field as rarefied as Chinese studies, there are now available Chinese language versions of the classical histories of the Chinese dynasties—hitherto found in only the largest libraries. Many unpublished documents, one-of-a-kind items from archives in virtually every field of history studies, are also increasingly posted on the Web. Also, most of these documents are electronically searchable; if one wishes to know what Confucius said about gender, a quick search on a few key terms will enable one to appreciate classical materials in an entirely new way.

2) Electronic Materials Make Research in Secondary Materials Far Easier

This is another incontrovertible area; the electronic catalogue search and the ability to purchase materials from Web-based bookstores such as Powell's City of Books or Amazon Books[51] makes the Web useful to the most technophobic among us.

3) Electronic Documents Facilitate Constructing a Community of Discourse

We have argued above that history is a sort of dialogue in which historians speak to each other. One of the most exciting developments in recent memory, particularly for those of us who work at smaller and more geographically isolated schools, has been the growth of such electronic discussion groups as H-Net, H-Asia, or whatever the equivalent may be in one's own field of interest. Professor Michael McFaul of Stanford, discussing one such list, that operated by David Johnson in Russian studies, observes, "It used to be that unless you were at institutions like Stanford or Columbia or Harvard, you couldn't get this stuff very easily. . . . It has really leveled the playing field in academia."[52] Such lists are becoming increasingly influential. Johnson's list, for example, is said to be "changing the nature of academic and political scrutiny of Russia."[53]

An undeniable aspect of the current state of historical writing is its increasingly fractionized identity. Very few journals can appeal to all, journals have multiplied greatly, and journal subscriptions have grown terribly expensive, for institutions as well as for individuals. While we in history have not yet taken even partial advantage of its capability, the Web enables us to create electronic journals as broad or as narrow in their audience and purpose as we wish—communities of discourse in the Postmodern sense. It is estimated that there are now more than 600 so-called "e-zines," electronic newsletters for special-interest groups, on the Net.[54]

The e-journal can bring together a very small group of interested scholars. There are few venues where a discussion on, say, the Sung era (979–1279), Chinese historian Ouyang Hsiu, or on many far more influential figures we might name, can be carried on at present; but, assuming a community as small as eight or ten, a provocative discussion (provocative at least to those of us interested in Ouyang Hsiu) can be carried on in a formal manner, utilizing all the usual tools of academe, fixed texts, footnotes, and bibliographic references. In the past such discussion could be carried on only in small panels at large conferences, via private letters, or in the footnotes of learned articles and book-length publications.

Postmodernists refer to a particular sort of dialogue, arguing that the very meaning of a document is constructed in the discourse of a community. In either sense, electronic materials facilitate discourse. They might also be said to facilitate Postmodernism itself in that they add yet more weight and centrality to discourse by so facilitating it.[55] The e-journal speaks to the issue of the theoretical place of the audience for "texts," meaning texts in the Poststructuralist sense. Poststructuralism argues—or at least some Poststructuralists argue—that texts become "texts" only as read by an "interpretive community."[56] As I understand this notion, it suggests, at the extreme, that the text means whatever the body of readers agrees that it means and nothing else. In my experience, such discussions soon become more "discourses" on method than on the putative subject. The Web, however, lets us come together as small interpretive communities for whatever limited purpose we wish. If others wish to deconstruct our narrative, well, let them start their own e-journal and link to ours.

4) Electronic Resources Facilitate a Discourse Within a Community of Meaning

This advantage is similar to the foregoing argument, but here I wish to emphasize the *process* of discourse as opposed to the creation of communities which engage in it. As stated above, perhaps the most noteworthy aspect of publication is that it is fundamentally a dialogue, a conversation with the great historians of the past and with the peers of our present. Through publication we carry on analysis and argumentation through generations. Brown and Duguid refer to this process as a "negotiation," a sort of continual creation of meaning involving many parties over time.[57]

This negotiation has been, however, by virtue of the medium in which it is largely embedded—paper—necessarily halting and episodic. Ouyang Hsiu writes upon the history which came before him; I write upon Ouyang's commentary; perhaps some third party will one day build upon my commentary, and so on, *ad seriatim*. It will take heroic research skills to assemble all of the components of this dialogue in a useful manner. However, with hypertext, I can reproduce a translation of Ouyang's words on the Web (with a link to the Chinese-language original posted at the Academia Sinica in Taiwan) and insert my commentary; anyone who reads the Web page may, with the proper software, insert their comment upon either my words or those of Ouyang in that same text, and a subsequent reader may, via hypertext links, go to other relevant sources and back to the original discourse. The potential for professional dialogues and discussion has obviously been much increased and will be far more accessible via e-journals.

5) Electronic Documents Make Available New Universes of Data

Electronic materials present us with new classes of materials. Perhaps the most interesting of these at present is e-mail itself. E-mail is clearly the information-carrying foot-soldier in the digital revolution. Much of the internal communication of many organizations is now carried on via e-mail. Such materials have become tantalizing troves to historians. For example, an e-mail document revealed that the National Security Council warned Vice President Gore that a fund-raising luncheon planned by a Buddhist temple in California should be approached with "great, great caution."[58] Gore attended, and the e-mail, released with other documents by the White House, then dragged these events into the discussions over the ethics of the administration's fund raising. In the past, such exchanges as this would probably have been oral ones and usually lost to history.

6) Electronic Processes Are a Democratizing Agent

The Internet makes it possible for virtually everyone who is interested in doing so to publish his or her work. Some of this work will be historical studies; much of it will have a historical perspective. This will not strike all of us as an advantage. Intellectuals are, as a corporate body, largely a meritocracy. We are far more interested in the "great" historians than we are in the run-of-the-library drones.

The Internet also has contributed to an explosion of dubious material, produced by all the groups we love to hate—name your own. Our students will sometimes take these rantings as evidentiary documents. We will have endless debate and litigation over the proper limits of such electronic speech. My own belief is that the Internet is an important democratizing agent, and that on balance this will prove to be a good thing.

Weighing Advantages and Disadvantages

We begin by reconsidering the disadvantages. Those listed above will not strike all historians as equally problematic; Postmodernists, for example, should see these disadvantages:

1. The documents found on the Internet are potentially unreliable.
2. Electronic documents lack authority.
3. Electronic evidence blurs authorial credentials.
5. The Internet magnifies errors.
8. Electronic materials are unprecedentedly mutable.
9. Electronic evidence is unprecedentedly volatile.

as simply characteristic of the Postmodern condition, inherent in any text, electronic or not.

It is also apparent that some of the advantages and disadvantages are trade-offs. For example, these disadvantages:

3. Electronic evidence blurs authorial credentials.
4. Electronic documents are too easy to collect.
6. The ease of electronic publication erodes standards.
10. Electronic evidence disturbs the economy of cultural production.

when seen from another perspective, create Advantage 6—they are democratizing agents. If we did not have those disadvantages, neither would we enjoy the advantage.

Other disadvantages follow only because of the presence of earlier ones. For example, if it were not that:

1. The documents found on the Internet are potentially unreliable.
2. Electronic documents lack authority.
3. Electronic evidence blurs authorial credentials.
4. Electronic documents are too easy to collect.
5. The Internet magnifies errors.
6. The ease of electronic publication erodes standards.
7. Electronic evidence facilitates dishonesty.
8. Electronic materials are unprecedentedly mutable.
9. Electronic evidence is unprecedentedly volatile.
10. Electronic evidence disturbs the economy of cultural production.

We should not have to worry that:

11. Electronic evidence lacks weight.
12. The production of electronic materials does not contribute to professional standing.

Even acknowledging these ameliorating conditions, if at this point we were to weigh the relative advantages and disadvantages, I fear the Internet would be the loser; however attractive many of the advantages may be, there are simply too many problems with research in electronic evidence as it now stands. The Internet might well be a safe arena for professional historians, but not for students of history who could blunder into bad data, use good data unwisely, use good data only to see it disappear, and experience the other problems raised above.

For the advantages, as attractive as they are, to outweigh the disadvantages, there must be some means of avoiding many of the present pitfalls. I believe that a more careful consideration of the disadvantages suggests that they can be neutralized. Let us divide the disadvantages into three groups and discuss them.

Group I:

1. The documents found on the Internet are potentially unreliable.
2. Electronic documents lack authority.
3. Electronic evidence blurs authorial credentials.
4. Electronic documents are too easy to collect.
5. The Internet magnifies errors.
6. The ease of electronic publication erodes standards.

As stated above, Postmodernists may not see 1, 2, 3, and 6 as avoidable in any text, but for those of us with lingering leanings toward Positivism or at least Relativism, it seems to me that Group I can be dealt with in large part via a healthy dose of the old-time religion, accompanied by some doctrinal reforms. We must exercise a more rigorous application of our traditional standards for evidence, and we must better communicate these to our students and to the public.

I think that many of us, certainly myself included, have dealt with the problems of evidence facing our students by restricting the universe of data: we tell our students which classes of documents, if not specifically which documents, they may use in their research. In this manner, we believe that we are teaching analysis of documents, but what we are doing, at least in part, is establishing narrow boundaries behind which our charges can neither go far astray, nor much extend their understanding of standards for research and analysis. In particular, we give them few tools with which to approach the buzzing confusion of the Internet.

It is not until graduate school that students (and most students do not, of course, go to graduate school) really learn to analyze evidence, and then they usually learn as much by osmosis as by precept. We must begin earlier and do the work more thoroughly than we have done it in the past; we cannot restrict our students to safe quadrants of the universe of data anymore. It has come to them in its totality. We will not keep our students from either reading or writing on the Internet, but we can make them far more skilled consumers and producers of electronic documents by doing well what we have always told ourselves we were doing: teaching good research and writing skills.

We must, however, bolster the historian's classical skills with some new ones as well; analyzing an electronic document is different in some regards than analyzing a conventional one. Fortunately, a great many scholars have begun to think about this problem, and there are now a variety of sources on the Internet where help can be found. I recommend Esther Grassian's Web page, "Thinking Critically About World Wide Web Resources," posted at UCLA[59] or Widener University's Wolfgram Memorial Library's page, "Teaching Critical Evaluation Skills for World Wide Web Resources"[60] as places to begin.

Just as we teach students to criticize historical documents in part by writing their own essays, so can we teach them skills necessary to negotiate the Internet by having them produce for it. The technical questions of how to encode or format a Web page are minor ones; the tongue of the World Wide Web, HyperText Markup Language, is the Pig Latin of computer languages in that it is very quickly learned, following several general principles. It is taught in many places on the Web, and good design is likewise handled in many sites.[61]

Let us now turn to the disadvantages listed in Group II, which present quite different problems.

Group II:

7. Electronic evidence facilitates dishonesty.
8. Electronic materials are unprecedentedly mutable.
9. Electronic evidence is unprecedentedly volatile.
10. Electronic evidence disturbs the economy of cultural production.

Historians are not the only ones who encounter this group; similar problems present difficulties for those who depend on the Web for commercial transactions. Chicanery and theft, like the problems with evidence listed here, can usefully be thought of as problems of "trust." The problems for commercial data are similar to those for evidence: how can we trust that provenance has not been tampered with, content remains fixed, and that there is a level of accountability which permits us to check dishonesty? What methods can raise our trust level as high as possible in any given electronic transaction, whether it be of data or stored monetary value? Clearly we want this level of trust to approach one hundred percent, though we realize that this ultimate level is not finally attainable in any transaction. The area of study which has proved most relevant in dealing with problems of trust in data transactions on the Internet has been cryptography.[62]

Cryptographers have worked out protocols for digital "signatures," for example, which are at least as trustworthy as traditional means of evaluating handwritten documents so we may be confident of authorship. Digital signatures can have the following properties: they are unforgeable, verifiably authentic, not reusable, and unalterable; the signed document itself cannot henceforth be altered; neither can the signature itself later be repudiated.[63] We can also include a time and date stamp with the signature—the time when the document is "signed" or fixed is now verifiable.

If we wish to place a document on the Internet, then, we can use a software protocol (such as digital "watermarking"), which can be so automated as to be transparent—it will not interfere with our writing or our reading—to fix that document so as to be permanent for all practical purposes. This may seem to be a great limitation—are we to work only with documents which have been so encoded? Because of the commercial concerns and fear of theft of intellectual properties, however, it is probable that a great portion of the traffic of the Internet will, sooner rather than later, be so encoded.

If we encounter unsigned or unstamped electronic documents and wish to work with them at length, other protocols may be useful. There are numerous cryptographically based means ("hash functions") of permitting us to clearly mark and freeze the copy we are working on so that it is always identifiable; we can even store that proof with a third-party server without revealing the document itself. Those of us who wish to crouch in solitude over evidence which only we possess until we are ready to reveal our conclusions to a waiting world can still do so.

It is probable that fully satisfactory solutions to the trust issue will have to be collective ones. What precisely they may one day look like, we cannot say. But the footnote and bibliographic citation are classical ways of improving trust, and we can create standards for electronic equivalents. The hypertext footnote is itself an important development, in that one can view text in a Web document together with a citation—which can in turn link to the original—providing additional verification.

Such standards might be very complex ones, to achieve a high degree of trust. It would be possible, for example, to have our citations linked by hypertext links to archives, where a digitally signed and time/date stamped version of the evidence to which we were referring could be downloaded if desired. This is, I hope, carrying the desire for trust too far. At present we need only refer to the source where the evidence can be found, requiring the querist to search out his or her own copy if desired. The electronic equivalent would be to store the evidence in a server where it could be accessed if desired, perhaps at some minor expense. Fortunately most documents are words alone, hence easy to compact and requiring little room on disk or tape. If several major universities simply dedicated servers to storing such documents and marking them with time and date stamps at the request of users, many potential problems would be solved.

There may soon be even more powerful tools at our disposal. Several computer scientists have suggested the bold—and for historians, totally appropriate—notion of archiving the entire World Wide Web. Brewster Kahle, founder of the Internet Archive in San Francisco, points out that the media now contained in an average video store could hold about one-third the current Library of Congress.[64] This, too, would probably have to be a collective initiative of the sort which created the Internet in the first place.

Disadvantage 10, *Electronic Evidence Disturbs the Economy of Cultural Production,* remains to be dealt with. It is impossible for us as historians to solve this alone, should we wish to do so, but it is virtually certain that this problem will be solved by others, given the enormous commercial interest in seeing the Web become a safe and profitable place to do business. Millions of dollars are currently exchanged on the Web in any given week, and the great interest in intellectual properties as a resource will secure a place for historians in the information economy. Co-opted Postmodernists would probably point out that if we as historians face all the pitfalls of the Postmodern condition, so, too, do we occasionally benefit from some Postmodern advantages. We should use them in meeting our problems.

The problem of the university presses is a more complex one. One partial solution would be for them to themselves engage in digital publication. They have not, after all, always had their present forms and functions.

We now have to consider the remaining issues in Group III.

Group III:

11. Electronic evidence lacks weight.
12. The production of electronic materials does not contribute to professional standing.

These two are primarily reflections of Disadvantages 1–10. If we can solve some of the problems of electronic evidence, its use will become less threatening and more common, and many issues will be worked out by creative minds in the process. This having been accomplished, more and more of us will turn to the Internet as a venue for publication; we will, accordingly, work out means of accomplishing the equivalent of today's processes of peer review.

In any event, these elements of our craft are changing whether we like it or not. Commercial considerations have intruded even on such sanctum sanctoria as to when we historians may use footnotes in our published works.[65] It is also clear that the marketplace for sales and the marketplace for ideas are approaching congruency. The need to find sizable audiences for even narrow scholarly works is challenging the university presses and the whole apparatus of tenure and promotion, which is closely tied to publication.[66]

Page Smith argues that the usual justification for scholarly publication lies in two distinct areas: First, that research should be available so as to increase the total of knowledge accessible to scholars in given fields; second, that scholarly scrutiny is necessary to improve the quality of that knowledge. However, there is also a third factor: publications have become "certification tools" used to judge promotion.[67] These have become the holy trinity of academic publication, a ritually confirmed but rarely examined article of faith. The Internet, in providing new means of meeting the first two goals, calls into question the third. If the Internet forces us to create a more defensible system for allocating academic rewards, that may well be a positive result of this revolution.

Conclusion

This discussion has, like many intellectual ones, taken place under rather ideal conditions. Throughout we have engaged in a sort of *Sic et Non* evaluation, as though we possess free will with regard to the Internet; but not only is it not going to go away if we decide its disadvantages outweigh its advantages, it has been apparent for some time that the status quo has not been working all that well for us.

In our teaching, we try to maintain our classical standards and methods in the face of mounting pressure that we be able to demonstrate through outcomes assessment the value-added element in the education which we impart. Our students may love that which we teach them, if we have been successful, but they also, not unreasonably, want to know what they are to do with it.

Our communities of discourse have become so ingrown and ferociously partisan that we have trouble communicating even among ourselves. As a community we have become so distant from the populace, which must voluntarily support those institutions upon which we depend, that it seems that every encounter with them is an adversarial one from which we slink back to our carrels, noses bloodied.

The revolution represented by the Internet presents many threats. But it also calls upon us—indeed, requires us—to reconsider many of the central issues and practices of our guild. It may require also, if we are to fully benefit from these changes, let alone survive them, that we learn new tools and new ways to employ old ones. We may also have to work together in unfamiliar ways, perhaps even ourselves create novel organizations and institutions to meet unprecedented needs.

Notes

I would like to express my gratitude to three of my colleagues: Chris Wilkes, who read successive drafts with close attention; Jeb Weisman, who gently guided me into cryptography; and Larry Lipin, who gave me useful suggestions regarding the bibliography in postmodernism.

1. Thomas Kuhn, *The Structure of Scientific Revolutions* (Chicago: University of Chicago Press, 1962), defines a scientific revolution: "Scientific revolutions are here taken to be those non-cumulative developmental episodes in which an older paradigm is replaced in whole or in part by an incompatible new one," 91.

2. A terabyte is a trillion bytes of data.

3. John Markoff, "When Big Brother is a Librarian," *New York Times* (March 9, 1997): E3.

4. Nicholas Negroponte, *Being Digital* (New York: Vintage Books, 1995), 233. Negroponte estimates that the size of the Web is doubling about every fifty days, which is quite close to the estimate of Brewster Kahle, cited in Markoff.

5. Carl L. Becker, *Everyman His Own Historian. Essays on History and Politics* (New York: Appleton-Century-Crofts, 1935). A shorter essay by that same title is found in the *American Historical Review* 38 (January 1932): 221–236. This work is also excerpted in Robin W. Winks, *The Historian as Detective: Essays on Evidence* (New York: Harper Colophon, 1968).

6. I recognize that postmodernist schools are in some cases an exception to some of the following generalizations, an issue dealt with at length below.

7. Fritz Stern, ed., *The Varieties of History* (New York: Meridian Books, 1956), 192.

8. R.G. Collingwood, *The Idea of History* (New York: Oxford University Press, 1956), 9–10.

9. David Hackett Fischer, *Historians' Fallacies: Toward a Logic of Historical Thought* (New York: Harper Torchbooks, 1970), 40.

10. See Hugh Trevor-Roper, *Hermit of Peking: The Hidden Life of Sir Edmund Backhouse* (New York: Alfred A. Knopf, 1977), 62–95.

11. Matthew Purdy, "Missile Theory Is Rebutted in T.W.A. Flight 800 Crash," *New York Times* (March 12, 1997): A17.

12. The Chinese, for example, believed that they had already had official state historians for almost a thousand years by the time Herodotus wrote. Burton Watson, *Records of the Historian: Chapters from the Shih Chi of Ssu-ma Ch'ien* (New York: Columbia University Press, 1958), 3.

13. Collingwood, 19.

14. Henry Giroux, "Postmodernism as Border Pedagogy: Redefining the Boundaries of Race and Ethnicity" in Joseph Natoli and Linda Hutcheon, eds., *A Postmodern Reader* (New York: State University of New York Press, 1993), 466.

15. Stern, 35.

16. Stern, 17.

17. William H. Dray, *Philosophy of History* (Englewood Cliffs, NJ: Prentice-Hall, 1964), 2.

18. See Becker's analysis of positivism at page 18 in Winks.

19. Stern, 120.

20. Karl R. Popper, *The Poverty of Historicism* (New York: Harper Torchbooks, 1961), 3.

21. John Seeley Brown and Paul Duguid, with an introduction by Esther Dyson, "The Social Life of Documents" http://www.firstmonday.dk. May 1996, 3.

22. Stern, 173.

23. Page Smith, *Killing the Spirit: Higher Education in American* (New York: Viking Penguin, 1990), 50–61.

24. For a very useful summary of this period, and of the "New History," which I have neglected here, see Brook Thomas, "The New Historicism and Other Old Fashioned Topics" in H. Aram Veeser, ed., *The New Historicism* (New York: Routledge, 1989), 194–195.

25. These are suggested by the treatment of Robert Phelps, *Twentieth Century Culture: The Breaking Up* (New York: George Brazziler, 1965), 16–20.

26. Becker, in Winks, 18–19.

27. M. H. Abrams, *A Glossary of Literary Terms* (Chicago: Holt Rinehart & Winston, 1985), 110.

28. Smith, 181.

29. My thanks to my colleague, Chris Wilkes, for making this particular point.

30. Ann E. Kaplan, *Postmodernism and its Discontents: Theories, Practices* (New York: Verson, 1988), 1, 4.

31. See the introduction in Patrick Williams and Laura Chrisman, *Colonial Discourse and Post-colonial Theory: A Reader* (New York: Columbia University Press, 1994).

32. Brenda K. Marshall, *Teaching the Postmodern* (New York: Routledge, 1992), 4–5. Cited in Michael Fegan, "Postmodernism" at http://at146.atl.msu.edu/atl/reh/ams/post.html.

33. For a numbing example of this approach, see Roland Barthes, *Empire of Signs* (New York: Hill and Wang, 1982).

34. The language here is from Abrams, 203.

35. John D. Schaffer, "The Use and Misuse of Giambattista Vico: Rhetoric, Orality, and Theories of Discourse" in Veeser, 90.

36. Elizabeth Fox-Genovese, "Literary Criticism and the Politics of the New Historicism," in Veeser, 213.

37. Hayden White, *Metahistory. The Historical Imagination in Nineteenth-Century Europe* (Baltimore: Johns Hopkins University Press), X.

38. Natoli and Hutcheon, 199.

39. Lee Marshall, "The World According to Eco" *Wired* (March 1997): 148.

40. http://at146.atl.msu.edu/atl/reh/ams/post.html.

41. B. Marshall, as cited in Fegan.

42. Brown and Duguid, "The Social Life of Documents."

43. Popper, 150.

44. Natalie Zemon Davis, "Who Owns History? History in the Profession," *Perspectives* 34, no. 8 (November 1996).

45. Harry G. Summers Jr., *On Strategy: A Critical Analysis of the Vietnam War* (New York: Dell, 1984).

46. B.G. Burkett, "Jug," "Telling it Like it Is," *Vietnam* (February 1997): 29.

47. http://www.thehistorynet.com.

48. Collingwood, 302.

49. I am indebted to Marti A. Hearst for this argument: "Research in Support of Digital Libraries at Xerox PARC," Part I: "The Changing Social Roles of Documents," *D-Lib Magazine,* May 1996. E-journal http://www.dlib.org/dlib/may96/05hearst.html.

50. For background on these projects, see Denise Hamilton, "Hart of the Gutenberg Galaxy," *Wired* (February 1997): 108.

51. http://www.powells.com/cgi-bin/track.pl/Welcome-80.html?id=860285323–5 6&; http://www.amazon.com/exec/obidos/subst/index2.html/8147–9510684–400798.

52. Sarah Koenig, "Academic Discourse, Internet Style," *New York Times* (March 17, 1997): C8

53. Koenig, C8.

54. Brown and Duguid, 3. These, too, are expanding exponentially, at about 20 percent per year.

55. Again, I am indebted to Chris Wilkes for this notion.

56. Brook Thomas, "The New Historicism and other Old-fashioned Topics" in Veeser, 184.

57. Brown and Duguid, 7.

58. Alison Mitchell, "Gore was Warned on '96 Buddhist Event," *New York Times* (February 15, 1997): 8.

59. Esther Grassian, "Thinking Critically About World Wide Web Resources," http://www.library.ucla.edu/libraries/college/instruct/critical.htm.

60. Widener University, Wolfgram Memorial Library, "Teaching Critical Evaluation Skills for World Wide Web Resources," http://www.science.widener.edu/withers/cklistlnk.htm.

61. My own students have found useful the site: "Web Pages That Suck: Learn Good Design by Looking at Bad Design," http://www.webpagesthatsuck.com/index3.html.

62. I am indebted to my colleague Jeb Wiesman for this suggestion.

63. Bruce Schneier, *Applied Cryptography: Protocols, Algorithms, and Source Code in C* (New York: John Wiley & Sons, 1994), 31. As Schneier points out, any system of

protection can be defeated, given enough computer time and motivation, but the necessary scale of such an effort itself is a protection against dishonesty.

64. Markoff, 3.

65. William H. Honan, "Footnotes Offering Fewer Insights," *New York Times* (August 14, 1996): A16.

66. Peter Applebome, "Publishers Squeeze Making Tenure Elusive," *New York Times* (November 19, 1996): 1.

67. Smith 180, 184.

15

Maps and Graphs, Past and Future
Using Technology-Based History
to Study the City

Etan Diamond, Cynthia Cunningham,
and Arthur E. Farnsley II

Introduction

For historians working in the late twentieth century, technology offers seemingly endless opportunities for research; opportunities that previous generations of historians could only dream about. Computers, databases, statistical analysis packages, geographic information systems, "multimedia," and, of course, the Internet are all technologies that scholars in past decades lacked. With these capabilities, historians can document, analyze, and communicate information faster and more thoroughly than ever before. Calculations that once required several days of painstaking labor can be done almost instantly, with far fewer chances for mistakes. Maps that once had to be drawn by hand with each location plotted individually can now be created at the push of a button. Global research that once took months to coordinate and complete can be organized and transmitted around the world in minutes, allowing for greater ranges of collaborative research than ever.

In addition to offering opportunities for better, more sophisticated research, these tools can also be harnessed for better, more sophisticated teaching. Students of all ages are themselves becoming familiar with new technologies, often knowing more about computers and multimedia than do their teachers. Teachers have a responsibility, then, to use technology to educate an increasingly sophisticated audience. The stereotypically dry history lesson can be made more relevant and more interesting to students when a variety of media and technologies are used.

Given the many options for technology-based history research and teaching, how should historians set about their task? Are there any existing models of such research and teaching that others can draw upon? This paper discusses one such model developed by The Polis Center, an urban research center located on the campus of Indiana University–Purdue University in Indianapolis. As this paper discusses, The Polis Center brings together technology and history in many different projects and for many different purposes—all of which funnel back to The Polis Center's central goal of using academic research as a basis for public teaching and for engaging in a public conversation.

Four examples from The Polis Center's projects demonstrate the variety of opportunities for technology-based history research and teaching. The first two examples come from the Project on Religion and Urban Culture, a broad project that studies the place of religion in the life of the community and the city. The third example focuses on a database of contemporary social service information, developed as a public resource for making policy decisions and program planning. The final example looks at the creation of digitized photograph archives. While each of these examples offers a different angle on the use of technology for historical research and teaching, they all draw upon the same types of technologies. Two technologies in particular—relational databases and geographical information systems—form the backbone of much of The Polis Center's research. To be sure, neither the storage of information in databases nor the mapping of information is a new idea. Yet, the value of research lies not in the collection of as much information in as many filing cabinets as possible. Rather, a research project's worth lies in its ability to track these data; to link them together, to interpret them, and to present them in a variety of media and formats. As this paper argues, The Polis Center's research projects do all this and more, using technology to store, manage, interpret, and present information that helps to advance the public's knowledge and understanding of past and present. Through a discussion of these projects, this paper can serve as a model of technology-based history, a model that historians and other researchers can apply to their own research topics and projects.

History of Religion in Indianapolis

The most obvious place to start in discussing the use of technology in historical research is the Project on Religion and Urban Culture (RUC).

Funded by a $2.25 million grant from the Lilly Endowment, the project's central research goal is to investigate the role of religion in the neighborhoods and communities of Indianapolis. Out of this research, which is rooted in historical and contemporary studies of Indianapolis urban and religious life, come many different products, including a documentary video on Indianapolis religion; a book of essays and photographs on the theme of *Spirit and Place;* a civic festival with national literary figures discussing religion and spirituality; religious and community resource directories for neighborhoods; and many different types of publications, discussion papers, and newsletters. Whomever the audience and whatever the medium, the RUC Project seeks to understand and explain religion's role in building community and strengthening local ties within the context of physically and socially dispersed metropolitan regions of the late twentieth century.

Two components of the RUC project draw heavily on technology-based history for public research and teaching. The first is the "History of Religion in Indianapolis" component. At its core, this component argues that the way to understand the history of religion in Indianapolis is to look at the broader history of the metropolitan context. After all, over the course of the twentieth century, Indianapolis has grown physically and demographically. What was once a small urban island in a rural county grew into a dispersed and diverse region with a thriving downtown, sprawling suburban subdivisions, and several "edge city" commercial centers. Issues of suburbanization, downtown decline and renewal, neighborhood decay and gentrification, and infrastructural development all radically reshaped Indianapolis's metropolitan landscape over the past several decades; Indianapolis simply looks different than it did eighty, fifty, or even twenty years ago. These urban changes affected all parts of metropolitan society, including religion. People who moved from one neighborhood to another often moved from one congregation to another. A declining neighborhood often led to declining churches. New subdivisions brought with them new congregations. Many of Indianapolis's highways plowed through neighborhoods with existing congregations and networks of religious communities. Starting with this hypothesis, that metropolitan change and religious change were part of the same process, the history component uses technology—databases and maps—to tell this story.

The core database in the History of Religion of Indianapolis component is a giant collection of biographical, institutional, programmatic, and demographic data about Indianapolis's religious history. Among the pieces of information captured in this database are names and addresses of congregations and congregational members; names, ages, and other biographical information about pastors; dates of congregational founding; denominational affiliation, racial mix, and gender distribution of congregations; and youth and other social service programs offered by congregations. Information for this database comes from membership lists, congregational histories and anniversary booklets, obituaries and other newspaper clippings, city directories, and interviews with pastors and lay leaders. Each individual and institution is assigned a unique identification number, and any additional information about that person or institution is linked through that number. These linked pieces of information enable researchers to trace individuals and institutions over time. How long did a particular individual belong to a congregation? How did that congregation change in the interim? For a pastor who served for a particularly long period of time, was his tenure marked by congregational growth or decline? Has the overrepresentation of women in religious institutions been a constant in Indianapolis churches? In addition to collecting and organizing data, we can map it as well, answering questions about where churches have moved over time or how suburbanization reshaped a congregation's membership distribution.

With this database feeding both graphical and tabular data inquiries, we return to our overall research question: What does this information tell us about the changing metropolis? For one thing, it is clear that congregational development and urban change are linked. Consider the following example: In 1920, almost all members of St. Patrick Catholic Church lived within a mile of the parish (Map 1). Seven decades later, the church membership had diffused considerably; many members had moved to outlying suburban neighborhoods (Map 2). But, as this membership map shows, the patterns of suburbanization were not random but followed the major north–south avenues in Indianapolis. In a similar analysis, a map of 1996 church locations shows a clearly linear pattern of church location, particularly along Brookville Road in the southeast, 10th Street to the west, and along Michigan Road to the northwest (Map 3). Using these maps to display historical and contemporary information helps The Polis Center to translate our research into a publicly accessible format.

Technology is crucial to another product of the RUC's History of Religion of Indianapolis component, the "Teaching Religion in Amer-

230

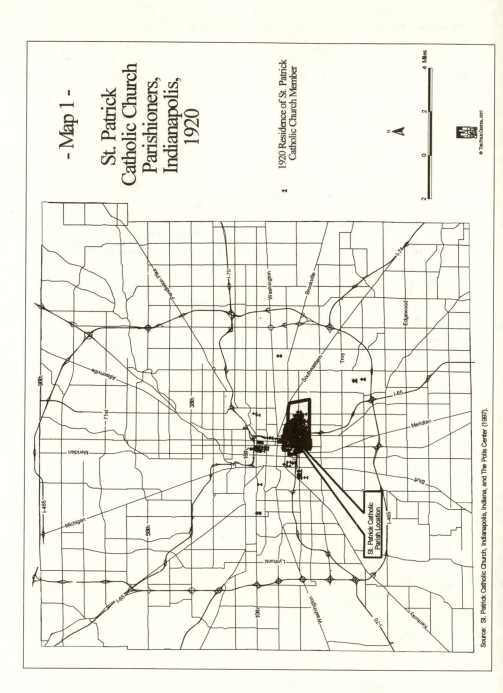

- Map 1 -

St. Patrick
Catholic Church
Parishioners,
Indianapolis,
1920

✝ 1920 Residence of St. Patrick
Catholic Church Member

© The Polis Center, 1997

4 Miles

Source: St. Patrick Catholic Church, Indianapolis, Indiana, and The Polis Center (1997).

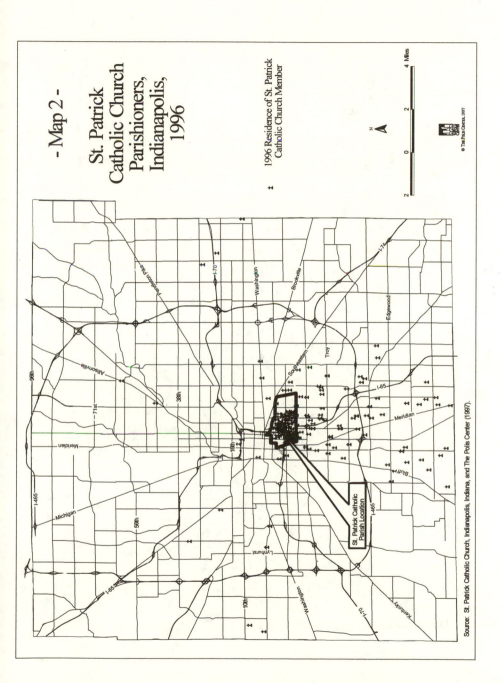

- Map 2 -

St. Patrick
Catholic Church
Parishioners,
Indianapolis,
1996

++ 1996 Residence of St. Patrick
Catholic Church Member

N

0   2   4 Miles

© The Polis Center, 1997

St. Patrick Catholic
Parish Location

Source: St. Patrick Catholic Church, Indianapolis, Indiana, and The Polis Center (1997).

232

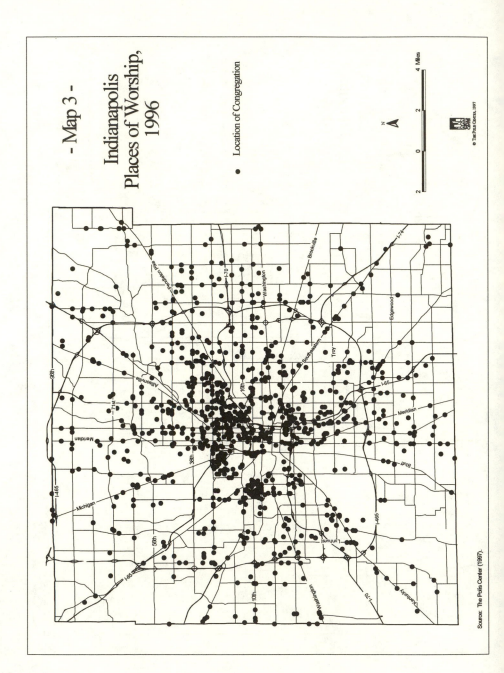

- Map 3 -
Indianapolis
Places of Worship,
1996

• Location of Congregation

Source: The Polis Center (1997).

ican History" curriculum. This project emerged out of concern expressed by historians, educators, and other humanists across Indiana about the absence of religion in the current secondary school curriculum and textbooks. Recognizing the public's sensitivity about discussing religious matters in public space, The Polis Center and the Indiana Humanities Council worked with historians and educators throughout the state to plan a historically and constitutionally sound project that identified key themes in national, state, and local history that emphasized religion's role in those respective arenas. These themes include religion's role in the creation of immigrant/ethnic neighborhoods, or religion's influence in various episodes of social reform, such as temperance, abolition, or civil rights. Seeing value in combining national historical events with local examples, the curriculum developers included primary source materials, such as documents, photographs, maps, and newspaper articles. Although this project was developed in paper form, it is becoming a truly public teaching tool through its presence on the Internet. By accessing a particular Web site, one can read the curriculum material and follow many multimedia links built into the system. For example, the text might mention a particular church; clicking on that link would bring up a photograph of that church and other information about it. Elsewhere, a reference to the religious life of Greek-Americans is linked to a sidebar essay on this ethnic group. This Web-based curriculum, then, is technology-based history in perhaps its purest form: a publicly accessible tool that allows students to teach themselves at their own pace using familiar technology.

Faith and Community

While the History of Religion in Indianapolis component is the primary area where technology-based historical research occurs at The Polis Center, other components of the Project on Religion and Urban Culture use history to support particular research activities. One of those components is Faith and Community (FAC), a sociologically driven study of the place of religion in contemporary neighborhood and community life. FAC researchers spend much of their time in neighborhoods, visiting churches and church services, attending meetings of non-profit and other community organizations, and talking with community leaders, clergy, and activists. This "ground-level" research provides a great deal of information on how religion and religious institutions function within a particular community.

As important as the primary field research is for FAC, however, it does not occur without an extensive technologically-based historical review of the neighborhood. These background studies are collected in a "briefing book" for neighborhood researchers to draw upon. The first part of the briefing book is a neighborhood history. Often written by a graduate student, the history provides an overview of the major events and institutions in the life of the neighborhood, information that puts the contemporary issues into an historical context for the researcher. The briefing book presents this history in two ways, as a narrative and as a timeline. Not only are these crucial tools for our field research, but they become teaching products for audiences in the neighborhoods.

In addition to the history, briefing books also contain historical census data for the neighborhoods. Among the census statistics that are used are key demographic information, such as age, sex, and rates of marriage, as well as other economic data such as housing values and occupations. The statistics for each neighborhood are compared with those for Indianapolis as a whole, to provide a degree of context. In addition, the statistics are presented in both tabular and chart form, and in some cases in map form. As with the neighborhood history and timeline, the multiple presentations are essential to communicating with as wide an audience as possible. The final pieces of information that the briefing book provides are a series of maps of the neighborhood, showing streets, non-profit organizations, schools, parks, community centers, and, of course, churches.

With the qualitative and quantitative historical information provided in the briefing book and the ethnographic field research, the FAC researchers have the ability to gain a unique perspective on the many types of metropolitan neighborhoods. More importantly, this perspective could not be achieved without using the range of technologies, most notably databases and maps. FAC does not exploit technology-based history just to make fancy maps or graphs that impress a public audience, however. Rather, it becomes an essential tool for telling the story of religion in the urban context—a tool without which the story could be told wrong.

Consider the following example, using a comparison between two of the original neighborhoods studied in the FAC component. On the north side of downtown are two neighborhoods—Mapleton–Fall Creek and Martindale–Brightwood—which, according to the 1990 census, appear almost demographically identical (Table 15.1). Both have a population that is roughly 90 percent African-American. Both have a poverty rate well above that of Indianapolis. Levels of educational attainment and of home ownership are similar and are well below the average for Indianapolis. Despite these similarities, the two neighborhoods have strikingly different religious ecologies. One neighborhood contains over eighty churches, most of which are small, storefront congregations with an average membership of about seventy-five people. The other neighborhood has fewer than twenty churches, most of which are large (over 500 members), tall-steeple-type churches. More striking, the large churches of this latter neighborhood have predominantly white congregations.

For someone looking at the contemporary situation in these two neighborhoods, the facts appear almost inscrutable. How can one explain the existence of two very similar neighborhoods with very different religious communities? This is where the ability to track and link historical variables enters the play. Until roughly thirty years ago, the neighborhood with the large white churches was *the* upper-middle-class neighborhood of choice in Indianapolis, occupying the city's main north–south corridor. In the 1960s, however, a radical demographic shift occurred. Within ten years, this middle-class and upper-middle-class population was replaced by a poorer African-American population. Yet, as the population began to shift, a group of these large, established churches consciously chose not to relocate out of the inner city. Instead, their members continued to drive down on Sunday mornings and maintain their church as an important institutional presence in the neighborhood, by forming ministerial alliances and providing social services. In contrast, the demographic transition in the other neighborhood was less disruptive. Although a white majority did leave the neighborhood in the 1960s, there had always been a sizable black population in the area so the transition to an all-black neighborhood was not as dramatic. Moreover, the area had always housed a small middle-class population; as a result, white flight did not have as large an economic impact as in the first neighborhood.

The ability to decipher differences between these neighborhoods follows directly from the ability to harness technology for historical and contemporary analysis. With the ability to trace the history of churches and neighborhoods alongside the history of other churches and neighborhoods, and the ability to link and display this information in a number of media such as graphs and maps, The Polis Center can reach and teach a wide audience.

Table 15.1

Mapleton—Fall Creek and Martindale—Brightwood Historical Statistics

Mapleton—Fall Creek	1930	1940	1950	1960	1970	1980	1990
Total Population	25,376	25,298	25,584	25,055	23,043	19,097	16,167
Percent Growth		−0.31	1.13	−2.07	−8.03	−17.12	−15.34
Racial Makeup (%)							
White	88.84	86.04	82.04	61.88	20.53	11.19	10.80
Black	11.14	13.95	17.82	37.89	79.23	88.28	88.23
Other	0.02	0.01	0.14	0.23	0.25	0.53	0.97
Foreign Born	4.00	3.89	3.59	3.06	1.45	1.25	1.88
Number Employed	—	—	12,698	11,397	10,523	7,227	6,480
Percent Employed	—	—	58.35	57.43	65.65	51.20	53.43
Median Household Income	—	—	$3,514	$4,894	$6,386	$10,588	$14,135
Percent of Indianapolis	—	—	112.42	95.40	70.10	61.27	48.73
Percent Below Poverty	—	—	Not Reported	Not Reported	15.20	21.90	33.48
Median Housing Value	Not Reported	$4,996 (1941)	$9,750	$11,976	$11,789	$20,952	$37,305
Number of Churches	9	7 (1941)	7 (1951)	8	—	—	16 (1995)

Martindale–Brightwood	1930	1940	1950	1960	1970	1980	1990
Total Population	21,869	22,947	25,418	25,702	18,928	15,366	11,289
Percent Growth		4.93	10.77	1.12	−26.36	−18.82	−26.53
Racial Makeup (%)							
White	58.18	57.49	50.33	44.68	22.90	5.06	4.10
Black	41.81	42.50	49.63	55.26	76.92	94.55	95.55
Other	0.00	0.00	0.04	0.07	0.18	0.40	0.35
Foreign Born	1.41	1.06	0.63	0.57	0.11	0.53	0.26
Number Employed	—	—	9,522	8,597	6,217	4,804	4,073
Percent Employed	—	—	52.49	51.62	54.10	46.60	49.46
Median Household Income	—	—	$2,608	$3,901	$6,318	$10,844	$14,975
Percent of Indianapolis	—	—	83.43	76.05	69.36	62.76	51.63
Percent Below Poverty	—	—	Not Reported	Not Reported	20.36	27.80	37.76
Median Housing Value	Not Reported	$2,007	$4,537	$6,924	$8,923	$16,058	$26,019
Number of Churches	44	47 (1941)	50 (1951)	65	—		80 (1995)

Sources: U.S. Bureau of the Census, *Census of Population and Housing* (1930–1990); *Polk's Indianapolis City Directory* (1930, 1941, 1951, 1960); and The Polis Center, Indiana University/Purdue University (Indianapolis) (1995).

History and technology come together in Faith and Community in a second, more intriguing, way that looks not backward but forward. The research on the contemporary city established a baseline of information that will be invaluable ten years from now as researchers assess how the city has changed. It may be even more valuable one hundred years from now when future historians look back on these efforts. When we *are* history, a repository of data and interpretative stories will remain to provide a thorough documentation of what Indianapolis was like at the close of this century—a luxury that present-day historians do not have in their work on earlier times.

Social Assets and Vulnerability Indicators

As much as the Faith and Community component uses technology to create a future historical repository of information, the Social Assets and Vulnerability Indicators project (SAVI) is another piece of The Polis Center that is creating a similar data repository. Created out of a joint venture between The Polis Center and the United Way, SAVI's purpose is to improve the effectiveness of human service and community planning in Central Indiana by increasing the accessibility of information. Through the use of databases and maps, SAVI contains a wealth of contemporary detail on the indicators of community and neighborhood welfare. Some of the data included in SAVI are: extracts from the 1990 census, police case reports; uniform crime reports, juvenile court records; welfare recipient information, vital statistics, public school student information, permit information; church locations, school locations, and district boundaries, library locations and catchment areas; community development corporation service areas, hospital and clinic locations, non-profit organization locations, and United Way agency locations.

For community-based planners and social service organizations, having this data obtainable in a central repository marks a major time savings in obtaining a variety of information about a single area of the city (Map 4). Prior to SAVI, a project planner for a social service agency would have to contact the police department to gather crime data, the health department to gather health information, the Community Service Council for census information, and a host of other agencies, which might or might not have the data actually available at the neighborhood level. With its consolidated database, SAVI now provides a single-source location that eliminates the time-consuming tasks of finding data and reduces the duplication of data collection efforts.

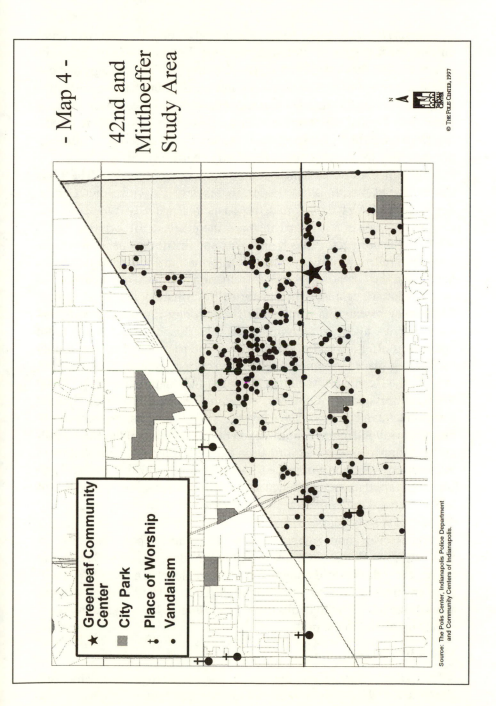

- Map 4 -

42nd and
Mitthoeffer
Study Area

N

© THE POLIS CENTER, 1997

Greenleaf Community Center ★

City Park ▪

Place of Worship ✝

Vandalism •

Source: The Polis Center, Indianapolis Police Department
and Community Centers of Indianapolis.

Because SAVI is designed for an external audience, it naturally relies on that most public of technologies—the Internet—to communicate information to the outside world. Through the SAVI Web page, one can obtain a variety of social service information stored in an executive database. Having this Internet presence allows SAVI to reach an audience wider than it could ever hope to in pre-technological days. More important from the public's perspective, outsiders can gain access to information that they would never have received in earlier years.

Although SAVI's audience is predominantly external to The Polis Center, the database is invaluable to researchers within the Center. Specifically, SAVI data forms the basis for many of the Faith and Community tables and maps that are included in the briefing book. Without this project to collect, organize, and distribute this information, FAC researchers would have far less information about their neighborhoods than they do now. SAVI's information also provides a contemporary benchmark against which historical information can be compared. The history research is continually finding long-forgotten reports that social service agencies commissioned in earlier decades. While these documents offer a wonderful insight into the past, they become doubly useful when placed in comparison with the current situation. For example, in 1957, the Health and Welfare Council of Indianapolis (today's United Way) commissioned a report on recreational facilities in Marion County. The result was a comprehensive inventory of all schools, parks, community centers, youth clubs, libraries, and other recreational facilities available to county residents—information that is, fortunately, quite similar to information contained within the SAVI database. When the historical and contemporary data are combined and mapped, one can see the degree to which the availability of recreational facilities has increased or declined over the past forty years.

Perhaps even more important than the value for past comparisons, SAVI offers an almost unlimited potential for future research. By creating this vast storehouse of demographic and social welfare data, SAVI will be an invaluable boon to historians of the future. They will know more about urban life in Indianapolis in the 1990s than today's historians know about any period in the past.

Visual Resources

A fourth area where technology and history come together is The Polis Center's Visual Resource collection. In many cases, photographs provide the only link to the urban landscape of the past. At the very least, they provide a level of detail and description that a text cannot; it is one thing to read about a particular place, but an entirely different experience to *see* it. Photographs also play an essential role in understanding the landscape that no longer exists. In Indianapolis, as in many cities, urban redevelopment in the postwar period destroyed hundreds of old buildings and obliterated dozens of neighborhoods. Interstate highways, university expansions, and downtown skyscrapers all removed people and houses from the map. For these places, photographs are all that remain.

Photographs, and particularly old photographs, do not always preserve well, however. Many people simply keep pictures in boxes or envelopes, with little protection from damage. Moreover, people often do not catalogue or index their photographs, relying instead on their memories. As a result, the identities of individuals in a picture, the location of the photograph, or the date when it was taken all go unrecorded and, unfortunately, can be lost forever when the owner of the photograph dies.

The Polis Center recognizes the value and necessity of preserving the images of and the information about historical photographs. It has developed, therefore, a process for digitally capturing images and recording their contents in a database. The centerpiece of this system is a digital camera. Unlike flatbed scanners, which can only record images that fit onto the scanner frame, a digital camera can focus on an object of almost any size. Like a regular camera, the digital camera snaps a photo of the image, and then records it in digital form, ready to be manipulated like any other digital information. The image is then linked to an entry in a database that records any information about the photograph, including photographer's name, date of photograph, and content of picture. If the picture is of a particular place in a particular neighborhood, that information is recorded as well.

With the images linked to the database, one can then search the database according to whatever fields are contained within. For example, if one wanted to see all the photographs of amusement parks, one would search on "amusement parks" to retrieve those photographs. Similarly, if one was researching a specific neighborhood or individual, one could search using the name of the place or person and find whatever photographs were available.

Not surprisingly, digitized images offer numerous advantages over original photographs. For one thing, they do not decay, rip, or disappear. Obviously, they must be backed up in multiple places, in case a computer crashes, but for all intents and purposes, the image is far more permanent. Moreover, the image can be used in a variety of formats. Researchers can transfer digitized images directly into a paper, obviating the need for copying an image onto a piece of paper and inserting it in the text. Digitized images also can be linked to public Internet Web sites, as with the Teaching Religion in American History curriculum discussed earlier in the paper.

Of course, digitized images present a danger that people will manipulate and distort the original information. For historians, such manipulation is particularly frightening, since one can easily imagine the problems of doctored historical photographs. As in Woody Allen's *Zelig* or Robert Zemeckis's *Forrest Gump,* digital image technology permits one to change the historical record. Teachers and researchers must educate students and the public about this technology and about their responsibility to use it correctly.

Conclusion

The many examples discussed in this paper should serve as a guide for other historians embarking on their task of using technology to study history. Obviously, no one historian can implement all of these ideas. No individual has the time, money, or interest to develop a Web-based curriculum, a comprehensive historical database of urban and religious information, an intensive neighborhood research project, a social service indicators database, and a digital imagery lab; but almost every individual historian or other social scientist has some interest in the past and its connection to the present. Anyone who teaches students, whether in elementary school, high school, college, or in non-academic settings, wants to be able to communicate their information as successfully as they can. Fortunately, the late twentieth century offers the technological capability of maximizing this communication. To be sure, not every technology is foolproof or appropriate; there will always be opportunities for misuse. The potential for abuse, however, should not deter an historian or any other researcher or teacher from experimenting and expanding the possibilities for using technology to study the past and to educate the public.

Glossary

ASCII (The American Standard Code for Information Interchange).
This is a way of formatting data so that it can be read by any program, whether DOS, Windows, or Mac.

BBS (Bulletin Board System). This term usually refers to small, dial-up systems that local users can call directly.

Bitmap. A type of graphic file. Bitmapped files contain a picture that is composed of a pattern of dots (bits).

Browser. A program used to access the World Wide Web. The most popular browsers—Netscape and Microsoft Internet Explorer—allow users to interact audiovisually with the World Wide Web.

Client. A synonym for Web browser or browser.

Domain Name System (DNS). The system that locates addresses on the World Wide Web. When a DNS error message is given by a browser, the address it is looking for cannot be found.

Document. On the World Wide Web a document can be either a file or a set of files that can be accessed with a Web browser.

Download. The process of getting a file or files from a remote computer (that is, a computer other than the one on your desk or local area network).

Electronic Mail (e-mail). Sending typed messages and attachments through an electronic mail network.

File. A file is a collection of data stored on a disk or other storage device under a certain name.

File Transfer Protocol (FTP). A tool for moving files from another computer site to your local service provider's computer, from which it can be downloaded.

GIF (Graphic Interchange Format). A set of standards for compressing graphic files so that they occupy less space in a computer's memory or on a storage device. GIF was developed by CompuServe and Unisys.

Gopher. An older method of navigating the Internet developed at the University of Minnesota (where the mascot is the Golden Gopher). It displays information and links to documents, but is not graphics based and is more difficult to use than the World Wide Web. Gopher is rapidly being replaced by the World Wide Web.

H-Net (The Humanities Network or Humanities On-Line Initiative). An organization dedicated to exploiting the potential of electronic media for history. It is supported by the National Endowment for the Humanities, the University of Illinois–Chicago, and Michigan State University. H-Net sponsors discussion lists, Web sites, book reviews, conferences, and other activities.

Hits. Internet slang for both the number of times a site is accessed by a user and for the number of sites found when using any Web search engine.

Home Page. The designated beginning point for accessing a World Wide Web site.

Hypermedia. Computer-generated displays that combine text, images, and sound.

Hypertext. Text that provides links to other text, allowing one to move from one resource to another.

HTML (Hypertext Markup Language). The computer language used to construct documents on the World Wide Web; most home pages are written in HTML.

HTTP (Hypertext Transfer Protocol). A method of coding information that enables different computers running different software to communicate information. It permits the transfer of text, sounds, images, and other data.

Icon. A graphic image that is used to represent (and usually activate) a file or program.

Internet. The worldwide network of computers that is linked together using the Internet Protocol, TCP/IP.

Java. A new programming language developed by Sun Microsystems that allows programmers to create interactive applications that can be run within Web browsers.

JPEG (Joint Photographic Experts Group). The standard format for compressing graphic files so that they occupy less space in a computer's memory or on a storage device.

Link. A connection point that might take you from one document to another or from one information provider to another.

Local Area Network (LAN). A group of computers connected together by cable or some other means so that they can share common resources.

Log In. The process of gaining access to a remote computer system or network by typing one's login name and password.

Listserv. A computer that serves a discussion group by processing, distributing, and storing messages and files for all members of the list.

Log-in Name. The name you use for security purposes to gain access to a network or computer system.

Macroinstruction (MACRO). A single instruction in a programming language that results in a series of instructions being performed. In many software applications macros can be created to allow simple keystrokes to activate a complex series of operations.

MPEG (Moving Pictures Expert Group). The standard for compressing video images so that they occupy less space in a computer's memory or on a storage device.

Multi-User Dungeon Object Oriented (MOO). A virtual reality simulation on the Internet in which individuals can interact in real time and can change their virtual environment as they act within it.

Netiquette. Etiquette for the Internet.

Netscape™. A popular World Wide Web browser developed by Netscape Communications Corporation.

Network. A group of interconnected computers.

Newsgroups. Internet discussion forums devoted to a topic or theme. Individuals who subscribe to a newsgroup can e-mail comments and questions to which the other subscribers can respond.

Optical Character Recognition (OCR). The process of using a scanner or other optical input device to capture and encode text. OCR software packages "recognize" the text on a scanned page and convert it into a usable text format.

Page. Page can refer to either a single screen of information on a Web site or it can refer to all of the information on a particular site.

Reflector Account. A type of listserv discussion group where the owner controls membership.

Service Provider. Any organization that provides connections to the Internet.

SLIP/PPP (Serial Line Internet Protocol/Point to Point Protocol). A connection that enables a home computer to receive TCP/IP addresses. To work with the World Wide Web from home, via a modem, a SLIP or PPP connection is necessary.

TCP/IP (Transfer Control Protocol/Internet Protocol). The most basic language on the Internet. The rules of TCP/IP govern the sending of packets of data between computers on the Internet, and they allow for the transmission of other protocols on the Internet, such as HTTP and FTP.

Telnet. An Internet protocol that enables you to log on to a remote computer.

UNIX. Like DOS or Windows, UNIX is an operating system run by most of the computers that provide access to the Internet.

URL (Uniform Resource Locator). The address for an Internet site.

USENET. A network of newsgroups dedicated to thousands of different topics.

Web Browser. A program used to access the World Wide Web. The most popular browsers—Netscape and Mosaic—allow users to interact audiovisually with the World Wide Web.

Winsock. A program that runs in the background on a Windows-based personal computer allowing one to make a SLIP/PPP connection to the Internet and to use the TCP/IP protocols.

World Wide Web (WWW). An Internet service that enables one to connect to all of the hypermedia documents on the Internet. The Web is a network within the Internet.

About the Editor and Contributors

Jeffrey G. Barlow is a professor of history and the Matsushita Chair of East Asian Studies at Pacific University in Forest Grove, Oregon. His academic field is modern Chinese history. He has written a number of books and articles, which have been published in the United States, China, Taiwan, India, and Vietnam. He is also the Webmaster for the Association of Asian Studies on the Pacific Coast. His personal WWW page can be found at: http://ssd1.cas.pacificu.edu/as/faculty/barlow.html.

Marisol Carpio received her B.S. in biology from Medgar Evers College in May 1997. She spent the summer of 1996 in Finland on a Minority Internship Research Training Program study of the amyloid beta proteins in amyloid accumulation, which leads to Alzheimer's Disease. She has since enrolled in medical school.

Cynthia Cunningham is an urban analyst with The Polis Center where she works on the identification, collection, documentation, and analysis of data relating to the Social Assets and Vulnerabilities Indicator Project (SAVI). Prior to her employment at The Polis Center, she was with the City of Indianapolis for seven years as a senior planner with both the neighborhood Planning and Information Resources and Policy Analysis sections.

Etan Diamond is research associate with The Polis Center's Project on Religion and Urban Culture. He received his Ph.D. in American social history from Carnegie Mellon University. Prior to joining The Polis Center, he conducted an extensive study of the history of Orthodox Jewish suburbanization in North America.

Larry J. Easley is an associate professor of history and a technology associate in the Center for Scholarship in Teaching and Learning at Southeast Missouri State University. He teaches courses dealing with Africa, American film, and Progressive America, and his interest and research in multimedia education dates back more than twenty years.

Arthur E. Farnsley II is the author of *Southern Baptist Politics* and the co-author of *Congregation and Community.* He holds a Ph.D. in religion and society from Emory University and an M.A.R. from Yale Divinity School. He is currently research director at The Polis Center in Indianapolis, where he leads the Faith and Community research project.

Leslie Gene Hunter received B.A., M.A., and Ph.D. degrees in history from the University of Arizona. He has been teaching at Texas A&M University–Kingsville since 1969. He is the "review editor" for *History Computer Review,* "book editor" for the *Journal of South Texas,* serves on the board of Directors of the South Texas Historical Association, and on the Editorial Board of the *Social Studies Texan* (the official publication of the Texas Council for the Social Studies). He was recently named a Minnie Stevens Piper Professor for 1997—a distinction awarded to only ten professors in Texas in recognition of distinguished teaching.

Frank E. Johnson is an assistant professor of history and social studies methods at MidAmerica Nazarene University (Olathe, Kansas). He has published in the field of United States religious history and is beginning a new project exploring the intersections of faith and technology. He also is a tireless advocate for incorporating computing technology into the classroom, manages a United States historic documents Web site, and moderates an on-line discussion network (Fjohnson@mnu.edu).

Ryan Johnson received an M.A. in history from Villanova University in 1991 and is completing a Ph.D. in United States foreign relations at Ohio University, where he was a member of the Contemporary History Institute. He is currently an information services librarian for Georgia Southern University.

James A. Jones graduated from the University of Delaware in 1995 after completing a dissertation on the impact of a French colonial railroad on the Middle Niger Valley. He is presently an associate professor of African history at West Chester University of Pennsylvania and the author of several articles on history and information technology, as well as a book on travel in West Africa. His work using computers to organize and analyze historical data explores new methods for studying the social history of the industrial age.

Scott A. Merriman is a doctoral candidate in modern American history at the University of Kentucky. He has previously taught history at the University of Cincinnati, Northern Kentucky University, and Thomas More College. He is the co-author of *The History Highway: A Guide to Internet Resources* and is an associate editor for *History Reviews On-Line*. He has contributed to the *Historical Encyclopedia of World Slavery, American National Biography,* and *Buckeye Hill Country*. (SamerrO@pop.uky.edu)

Ellen Meserow Sauer is a consultant for BlueWorld Communications and is the former manager of *Project Muse* for the Johns Hopkins University Press. She received her B.A. in English and art history from Fairfield University and has published numerous articles on the future of scholarly communication and publication in the computer age.

Timothy Messer-Kruse received his doctorate from the University of Wisconsin and is assistant professor of labor history at the University of Toledo. His articles have appeared in *Wisconsin Magazine of History, Labor History,* and the *Encyclopedia of the American Left*. His book, *The Yankee International: Marxism and the American Reform Tradition, 1848–1876,* will be published by the University of North Carolina Press in 1998. He is chair of the University of Toledo history department's computer committee and is the author of its Web page (www.history.utoledo.edu). He is director of "Toledo's Attic Virtual Museum Project," an on-line exhibit of the industrial, labor, and cultural history of Toledo, Ohio.

M. Daniel Price received his doctorate from the University of Chicago in modern intellectual history. He has taught at the University of Detroit, Xavier University, and for the past nine years at The Union Institute, where he is professor in the Center for Distance Learning. He has published on a variety of topics, including the influence of classical rhetoric on preaching in eighteenth-century France, the role of Aristotle in drafting Church decrees during the Renaissance, and the response of the French Church to the rise of fascism. He also has made a number of local and regional presentations about the new electronic delivery of education and has twice made presentations at the national gathering "Computers on Campus." (Dprice@tui.edu)

David B. Sicilia, assistant professor of history at the University of Maryland, specializes in business, economic, and technology history. He is co-author of three books (one forthcoming) and numerous articles. He regularly uses a variety of information technologies in the college classroom, including electronic listservs and reflectors, multimedia, digital projection in large classrooms, and interactive learning tools. Dr. Sicilia chairs the strategy and policy advisory committees on new technology for his department and for the College of Arts and Humanities. (Ds190@umail.umd.edu)

G. Mick Smith is a professor at Allegheny University of the Health Sciences, where he teaches the history of world medicine on the Internet. Dr. Smith earned a Ph.D. at UCLA, and more recently, a Distance Learning Administration Certificate from Texas A&M University. His publications include *The Reasoned Rhythm of Ritual* (University Press of America), and he has published widely on computers and history, including: "Computing Across the Curriculum: A Department Online," " 'Reach Out I'll (Who Will?) Be There,' " and "Back to the Future of Pre-Med Ed: Alternative Medicine & New Technologies."

David J. Staley is an assistant professor of history at Heidelberg College in Tiffin, Ohio, where he teaches European history, World Civilization, and Japanese Culture. He also teaches and writes on technology studies, historiography, pedagogy, globalization, and information/communication studies. He lives with his wife and son in Columbus.

John D. Thomas holds a B.A. and a B.Ed. from Queen's University, Kingston, an M.A. from Duke University, and a Ph.D. from York University. He has published in *The Canadian Historical Review,* the *Dictionary of Canadian Biography,* and the *Journal of Canadian Studies.* He is currently completing a monograph on the development of the Methodist Church in Canada. He teaches history and Canadian studies at Acadia University, Nova Scotia.

Dennis A. Trinkle is visiting assistant professor of history at DePauw University. He is the co-author of *The History Highway: A Guide to Internet Resources* and is the co-founder of *History Reviews On-Line,* the first on-line historical journal devoted to scholarly book reviews. He has published widely on the marriage of computers and history. (Dtrinkle @depauw.edu)

Kacy D. Wiggins is a doctoral student in history at the Graduate School and University Center/CUNY. He received his B.A. and M.A. at the University of Cincinnati. His research interests include late nineteenth-century African-American history, African-American education, social and grassroots movements, and gender relations in the United States.

Barbara Winslow is assistant professor of history at Medgar Evers College/CUNY. She received her Ph.D. in European–U.S. women's history from the University of Washington in Seattle. Her book, *Sylvia Pankhurst: Sexual Politics and Political Activism,* was published by St. Martin's Press in 1996. She is currently writing a book about the women's liberation movement in Seattle, Washington (1966–1972).

Index

255